D1446696

Lisbon to Shanghai
in Four Summers

A Memoir by
Tom Sweeney

Quotes by Alan Watts courtesy of the Alan Watts Foundation
Title: Coincidence of Opposites
Album: Tao of Philosophy
Source: **www.alanwatts.com**

Names and Places
With two exceptions, names are real. Place-name spellings are based on Google Maps.

Photos and Additional Information
Cover images, clockwise from top left: Consuegra, Spain; central Turkey; the Bund, Shanghai; near Sauran, Kazakhstan. More photos are available at **www.lisbontoshanghai.com.**

The views expressed in this work are solely those of the author, and do not represent any individuals, organizations, or institutions mentioned in the book.

Copyright © 2021 Tom Sweeney
All rights reserved.
ISBN: 979-8-7293-0241-3

Imprint: Independently published

To Kendra, for being with me every step of the way.

TABLE OF CONTENTS

ROUTE OVERVIEW

Measurements:
1 mile = 1.61 kilometers
1000 feet = 304.8 meters
40° Fahrenheit = 4.4° Celsius
90° Fahrenheit = 32.2° Celsius

Please visit **www.lisbontoshanghai.com** for additional photos and maps, as well as information about the summers past Shanghai.

PART I: 2014-2015

The existence, the physical universe, is basically playful.
There is no necessity for it whatsoever. It isn't going anywhere.
That is to say, it doesn't have some destination
that it ought to arrive at.

-Alan Watts

Tom Sweeney

PROLOGUE

"I want to ride my bicycle around the world!"

The moment the words left my lips, I felt like an idiot. How many middle-aged men had declared similarly ridiculous intentions, the kind that never became anything more than a nagging sense of lost opportunity years down the road? Yet there they were, out in the open, hanging in the chilly November air.

My wife stared at the fire, shimmering in a small dirt pit in our summertime garden, the descending evening darkness heavy around us. In the quiet moments that followed, I could see Kendra struggling to absorb my ludicrous declaration.

"When were you planning on telling me this?" she asked.

"Well, I, uh ..."

Kendra shook her head. "I wish you'd talked to me about it first."

I nodded. "I've been thinking about it for a while. I probably won't even do it."

The flames flickered. Kendra didn't look at me.

"So what do you think?"

"If it's something you need to do, then I guess you have to do it," she said.

That was a good start. We talked until nighttime engulfed our yard and there was nothing left to say.

In the ensuing silence, my mind drifted upward to the stars that surrounded our small corner of the universe. I thought back to the prior summer. We had planned to fly to

Europe and see a stage of the Tour de France before going to Geneva, where Kendra was planning to visit potential practicum sites for her graduate students while I cycled around the French countryside.

But we never went. Instead, our big vacation in the summer of 2014 was a trip to Park City, Utah, a mere six hours from our home in Fort Collins, Colorado. It was pleasant, but hardly the exotic holiday we'd envisioned.

After returning home, we quietly walked back into the routine of our everyday lives. I taught fifth grade at Sarah Milner Elementary School in Loveland, twelve miles south of our home. Kendra was the assistant director of a graduate program at Colorado State University.

We lived in a modest house in a safe neighborhood. We'd succeeded in not having the children we didn't want. We paid our mortgage and utilities every month, filed our taxes, owned two cars, and maintained a stable marriage.

We had officially attained whatever it is that adults are supposed to achieve, and in my modern Western mindset, fueled by a hyper-sentient, first-world anxiety that I might be living less than full, the notion that I was all grown up with nothing left to look forward to really bothered me.

Adulthood had not delivered the feelings of contentment and fulfillment I'd been led to believe it would. In fact, I wasn't feeling much of anything at all.

In my late teens and twenties, I drifted and sometimes raced from one life to the next, each new episode filled with excitement and hope. I was eighteen when I left my home in Michigan to start a new life as a freshman at Colorado State University. My parents were sad to see me go, and it pained me to leave them behind, but I took solace in the fact that my brother lived nearby, there to look after them.

In my dorm, I met people from across Colorado and around the country, bouncing from one group of friends to the next, hiking with some and cycling with others. It was fun and exciting, yet sometimes lonely and confusing as I struggled to find my niche.

Rather than figure anything out, I joined an exchange program my sophomore year and moved to Leicester, England. I traveled around Europe and befriended people from around the globe. It was a whirlwind adventure, both exhilarating and bewildering, and left me with an aching desire to go abroad again.

After returning to Fort Collins, I struggled even more to understand who I was and where I belonged. I loved to hang out with friends, but needed time to recuperate, alone, to battle inner demons that left me insecure and angry for no particular reason. I started working as a bicycle mechanic that fall at Lee's Cyclery, located across the street from the university. It was an ideal job for an amateur bike racer, and I found a fitting crew of friends there to while away my college days.

After graduating, I moved to Tucson, Arizona, on a whim, ready to experience somewhere new and escape myself for a while. I delivered pizzas, rode my bicycle through the desert, and made a few new friends. I left in April with scarcely a goodbye to any of them.

I was twenty-three when I hopped on a plane to Mongolia, to join the Peace Corps. I spent the first three months outside the capital city, Ulaanbaatar, training alongside forty-four other volunteers. Pulled from everything we ever knew, we quickly established close-knit friendships. Soon, however, we were called individually to talk to the Peace Corps staff about the type of site we envisioned for the remainder of our service.

Starry-eyed and ambitious, I told my advisor that I wanted a remote location, somewhere no other volunteer had been before. I still remember the smile on his face. To this day, I don't know if he was amused by my brashness or happy he'd found someone for a hard-to-fill site.

I was stationed in Khurmen Soum, a village of seven hundred people in the middle of Ömnögovi Aimag, the least densely populated province in the least densely populated country in the world. If I wanted to get in touch with another volunteer, I had to send a letter or go to the local telegraph office.

I lived in a Soviet-era apartment block with only the wind and the occasional camel outside my kitchen window to keep me company. Being in the small town, with the vast Gobi Desert just beyond my front door, left my stomach in knots and my head reeling with the immensity of it all. I could feel life itself arching from one side of the horizon to the other in an inconsequential haze.

If I'd envisioned myself becoming some kind of Buddha out there, enlightened and detached, that reality never emerged. Instead, I became an anxiety-ridden shell of myself, thinking constantly about everything other than where I was, wondering what my friends and family were doing at any given moment. My worst attributes rose to the surface and I couldn't escape the dark thoughts that encroached from all sides.

The basic foundations of life in Khurmen were no different than anywhere else. But on the desert steppe, the realities of existence were laid bare and there was nowhere for me to hide from them. To calm myself, I moved. I never sat still. Growing up in Michigan, I would accompany my dad on trips to Meijer to jolt myself out of my adolescent woes. In Khurmen, I walked or ran any chance I had. I never rode my bike during those two years. I didn't have one.

The only reprieve from the relentless unease came in the evenings. The colors evoked by the setting sun, those gentle blues, violets, and reds reflected in distant rounded mountains, calmed me to the point of near contentment. Once a day, the desert sunset lifted me out of my existential malaise. Over time, I came to appreciate the small stones scattered among the tiny plants lifting millimeters above the rock-hard Gobi soil.

In the twilight hours I took special note of the moon passing over my small community, a familiar sight in an unfamiliar land. I measured my remaining days of service by its celestial phases and pondered what I would do with the rest of my life.

When I wasn't musing on the nature of existence, I kept busy at my job. I had been assigned to teach English as a second language; that's what volunteers with history degrees do. I had never thought of myself as a teacher before, but there I was, fumbling from one lesson to the next in front of fifth and sixth graders.

Although our school lacked adequate heat in the winter, and the kids saw little point in learning English, I enjoyed being in the classroom. I loved to listen to my students chat as they lined up for their next class, even though I couldn't understand much of what they were saying. I was proud when they began putting together simple sentences in English.

If ever I had formative years, it was those I lived in the Gobi. To this day, I hoard peanut butter, because you never know when you might run out, and I have a hard time relaxing, because whatever melancholy consumed me there in Central Asia lingers in the background, ready to pounce if ever I have a moment to sit still.

After completing my Peace Corps service, I moved to Atlanta, Georgia, for a ten-month stint with EcoWatch AmeriCorps, working in nature preserves and teaching environmental education in local schools. In a span of three months, I moved from a village of seven hundred people in the middle of Asia to a city with a metropolitan population of four million.

In my new home, I was around people all day, people my age, people who spoke my language. I had internet access, my first cell phone, and a car. I could ride my bike again and even started doing a few weekend races.

I had every distraction imaginable, and no longer noticed the sun arching across the sky. After the previous two years, with their emotional ups and downs, I felt so gratifyingly calm the year I lived in Atlanta. I hoped it would never end.

But it did. The following summer I volunteered at a nature preserve in Guatemala for five weeks. I spent my days hacking new trails through the forest with a machete and socializing in the evenings with volunteers from innumerable countries.

My interest in environmental issues was sparked in Mongolia, where the vast expanse of steppe was unmarred by human hands and fences were nonexistent. Volunteering in Guatemala further fueled my desire to save the planet.

I was twenty-six when I returned to my home state to start a graduate program in environmental policy at the University of Michigan. I was near my parents again and only two hours from my brother and his family.

It was in Ann Arbor where I met Kendra, who was working on her master's degree in public health. The first time I saw her, standing on the stone-covered patio behind Dominick's bar, I was too scared to introduce myself.

There's no way she'd want to talk to you!

I had a negative side to my personality that spoke in accusatory tones and usually took the safe, easy way out of situations.

Fortunately, my rational side interjected in its usual inclusive way.

'She might find us interesting.'

I didn't move. For as forward-thinking as my sensible side could be, it sometimes lacked confidence.

Kendra was standing next to a picnic table. Hanging lights illuminated the scene. All the other faces around me ceased to exist.

"Tom, go talk to her."

Like my accusatory side, my resolute and confident self talked to me in the second person. It spoke up when it truly mattered, and it spoke out loud.

I looked to make sure no one had seen me talking to myself. Then I took a breath, walked to Kendra, and introduced myself.

We spent the better part of our graduate experience together. I was the dreamer, Kendra the realist. Her responses to new situations were measured and thoughtful, whereas I made quick decisions with only cursory consideration of the outcome. We balanced each other.

Kendra was with me when my mom was diagnosed with esophageal cancer. She helped whenever she could during my mom's treatment at the University of Michigan hospital, a mile down the road from my apartment. And she was with me when my mom passed away.

I was grateful to be close to my family when it mattered, but even the devastation of losing my mom, and seeing my dad cast adrift, couldn't compete with the inner yearning to keep moving. My hope in the future included going somewhere new, and I hadn't quite extinguished my dream of living in Colorado, again.

My father had my brother and my sister-in-law, I told myself, as well as their oldest daughter and the triplets, born a few months earlier. After graduation, I said goodbye to my dad in the driveway of my childhood home and piled into a U-Haul with Kendra, en route to Fort Collins.

Kendra found a job shortly after relocating, but I didn't have any practical experience in my field. I returned to my position as a bicycle mechanic at Lee's Cyclery, master's degree in hand, the same workplace where I'd created some of my best undergraduate memories.

It took me a long time to figure out that I wanted to be a teacher again, that educating young minds to think critically about the issues facing our planet was a worthy cause. It took me longer to make it happen, to complete my educator licensure program, and I found comfort in moving toward another goal.

In 2008, I started my first salaried job as a third-grade teacher at Lincoln Elementary School. I began riding my bicycle to work, nine miles each way, to reduce my carbon footprint. But commuting by bicycle became far more important.

At five feet, eight inches tall, with a weight of 175 pounds, I was indisputably overweight. In my mind, though, I was downright fat.

In elementary school, I was teased regularly about how fat I was. My friends would cast sideways glances my way at sleepovers when I shoved those extra slices of pizza into my mouth. My mom took me to a doctor once, to brainstorm ways to help me lose weight, but his suggestion to eat smaller portions didn't help. I hated being fat and fantasized daily about being able to peel away the layers of flab on my belly and reappear looking like all the other kids. That didn't help either.

As I grew older, I became more athletic, but although I loved to run and was born to ride a bike, I loved to eat and drink even more. The calories from eating and drinking outweighed anything I burned off exercising.

Adipocytes, or fat cells, expand and contract based on how much energy there is to store. The more excess calories a person consumes, the larger those cells become. If our caloric intake exceeds the amount of storage space in our existing adipocytes, new ones are created. You can reduce the amount of fat in them, but they'll always be there, clinging to your body.

It's funny how a word like adipocyte can have such a huge effect on how a person views themselves, on who they are. For me, adipocytes have literally shaped my life.

Riding my bicycle to Lincoln Elementary, I burned four hundred calories round trip. Yet I was eating leftover Halloween candy and nibbling on snacks in the teachers' lounge like I was riding a hundred miles a day. I couldn't understand why I was gaining weight despite all the pedaling. So I started doing the math. I started counting calories. And the results were terrifying.

On February 1st, 2009, I bought a heart rate monitor that calculated my caloric expenditure. I entered those totals and my caloric consumption into an Excel spreadsheet every single day. It became a big game to me, trying to hit my target numbers for the day, week, and month.

Although the odds were stacked against me ever losing weight, I found I was more addicted to numbers than I was to food. I lost thirty-five pounds in five hungry, miserable months.

That fall, I started a new job as a fifth-grade teacher at Sarah Milner Elementary School. In my new environment, everyone saw me as skinny and healthy. I didn't view it that way. I'd only been thin for six months and had spent the past thirty-some years of my life being overweight. I was fat and couldn't understand how anyone could perceive me otherwise.

I continued commuting to school by bicycle. A snowstorm might convince me to drive, but otherwise I rode. I had fat to burn and hated sitting idle in my car at stoplights. My new colleagues took my cycling as one more sign that I was a health fanatic.

If ever I found it hard to relax and take a breath before my dieting began, now it was impossible. I spent every waking moment exercising to burn calories. I was terrified of gaining the weight back. Over time, my fear of remission turned into habit. I didn't feel right if I wasn't working out three or four hours a day. Because of that obsession, my body became extremely efficient at turning pedals.

In the fall of 2014, I hit my nine hundredth day of cycling to Sarah Milner Elementary. At twenty-four miles per day, I had almost ridden far enough to travel around the planet. But I hadn't gone anywhere. It was an endless circle, south on

Shields in the morning, north on Taft Hill in the evening, a never-ending clockwise loop.

The monotony extended past my pedals. After five years, I had grown comfortable in my job. I wasn't meeting anyone new or doing anything new. I wasn't feeling anything new.

Now that I was done hopping from one life to the next, part of my identity was slipping away. I was no longer the American living abroad in England or Mongolia. I was no longer Team Leader Tom driving his EcoWatch volunteers around Atlanta, or the graduate student studying protected area management in Belize.

Certainly, being a teacher was an identity in itself, and I was the weird guy who rode his bike to work. But without a sense of moving forward, without the traveling or seeing new things or meeting new people, I was listing in the doldrums of adulthood, living the dream with nothing left to dream about.

That little trip to Park City, Utah, pushed the seeds of discontent just deep enough for them to take root and grow. I needed to find an epiphany, a sense of accomplishment and contentment, that my quotidian existence wasn't giving me. Something had to change.

I considered my options.

I was a teacher. I had summers off.

I was a cyclist and a mechanic. I had done a six-day loaded bicycle tour in the mountains of Colorado a few years earlier. While I deemed myself a novice, I had a good idea of what to pack.

I was OK being alone for long periods of time.

These thoughts drifted around my head for months before coalescing into the fantastic notion that I could solve my middle-age woes by riding my bicycle around the world.

Initially, I rejected the proposition on the grounds that it would never come to fruition. But the idea held firm. There was an opportunity in front of me, and I was getting too old not to take a chance.

Even as I resolved to give the asinine journey a go, I felt guilty for feeling conflicted at all. I had a good job, a comfortable home, and an amazing wife. Traveling abroad meant leaving Kendra in an empty house for weeks on end, there to take care of the chores while I gallivanted abroad.

Part of me wished I could be happy doing what normal people like to do: beach vacations in Mexico, watching football on the weekends, working in the garden, and maybe simply relaxing. My vision of what life should be was out of tune with everyone else's, and that caused me more distress. What I did know was that I was cycling to school and back in circles on some proverbial horizontal hamster wheel.

Making a commitment to do something, to embark on some grandiose quest, filled me with purpose, and that made me feel better. It was as though two different people would emerge from the decision, the Tom that went on the journey and the Tom that didn't.

I was pretty sure I didn't want to be the Tom that didn't try.

The only problem with finding my determination was that now I had to do something about it, and the prospect of riding my bicycle around the world seemed improbable at best. When I embarked on my Colorado tour, I'd packed up my gear and pedaled from my driveway. Now I was proposing loading everything on a plane and dealing with innumerable logistics.

And even if I went somewhere one summer, what were the chances that I'd have the willpower to pick up where I left off the summer after that, and the summer after that? It wasn't like this was going to be a two- or three-year commitment. I was looking at the next seven or eight summers, and desires and circumstances, indeed, life itself, can change a lot in that amount of time.

As fall turned to winter, and winter into spring, and I laid the groundwork for the first leg of my adventure, doubts nagged at me. My little proclamation over that November campfire was, after all, just a nonsensical comment spouted from the haze of middle age. I wasn't actually going to do any of it. People don't just hop on a plane to some foreign country, unbox their bicycle, and start pedaling around.

It couldn't possibly be that simple.

THE ROUTE: 2015

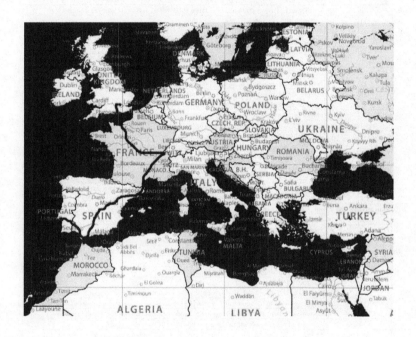

Daily Log

2015 June	Miles	Description
Thurs 4	68	Ride Lisbon International Airport to Melides campground.
5	105	Melides to Mértola, with getting lost, intense and hot.
6	80	Mértola, Portugal, to La Palma de Condado, Spain, mountains to rolling hills with sunflowers
7	101	La Palma de Condado to Arcos de la Frontera, Spain, flat and tiresome, headwind whole way
Mon 8	77	Arcos de La Frontera to Tangiers, Morocco, ride in evening Tangiers traffic, awesome!
9	75	Tangiers to Ceuta, Spain, lots of climbing, 47 miles...then Algeciras, Spain, to Jimena La Frontera
10	102	Jimenez de La Frontera, to outside of Jauja, 1000 meters in the first 30 miles, camped
11	101	Campsite outside Jauja to Fuencaliente.
12	127	Fuencaliente, to Herencia, via Consuegra. Tailwinds all day. Last 20 miles trying to find hotel
13	110	Herencia, flat with a tailwind, then hills, then semi-mountainous at the end, in Cuenca
14	70	Over two mountain passes today, Cuenca to Albarracin, 6+ hours, with climbs 10% at times
Mon 15	70	Albarracin to Ultrillas, easy as possible, stomach issues and rain
16	110	Utrillas to Falset, Catalonia, mod/fast at times, felt much better after stomach issues all night
17	117	Falset to Mataro, Catalonia, easy at first, but through Barcelona racing-mode activated
18	47	Easiest, shortest day yet, from Campground Barcelona to Platja de Aro campground.
19	65	Platja de Aro to Begund, Pals, Playa l'Escala, to Campground Riells, where I met the Belgians
20	37	Playa l'Escala to Macanet de Cabreny campground, 3 miles out of town; 6 miles from France
21	113	Camp at Macanet to La Pinede Campground, Lezignan-Corbrieres, France, headwind whole way
Mon 22	103	Lezignan to St. Martin de Londres, France, wrong round-about cost me two extra miles
23	89	St. Martin de Londres to Souz , headwind whole way, first flat at mile 1755
24	80	Suze le Rousse to Lus la Croix Haute, 8 + hours, legs are completely burnt out
25	92	Lus la Croix to La Piscine campground at base of L'Alpe d'Huez, raged up the climb in 1:20
26	77	La Piscine campground to Aix-les-Bains, easy as possible
27	47	Campground in Aix-les-Bains to Geneva, Switerland. Woman opened car door which I ran into
28		Ride around Geneva, easy-moderate; afternoon with Kendra!
June 29 - July 15		Road trip with Kendra!
16	105	Goodbye to Kendra; Geneva to campground 5km uphill from Vinay, France
17	85	Vinay to Aubenas, France,, over the Col de Escrinet, where the Tour will go in two days time
18		Easy ride unloaded, Aubenas to Jaucec, where I'll watch the Tour de France. Easy day
19	68	Aubenas to La Col de la Croix de Bauzon,watched Tour and then 40 miles to Loudes, France
Mon 20	104	Loudes to Accueil Campground, Pont de Menat
21	105	Pond de Menat France to Buzancais
22	133	Buzancais to Belleme. Lightning show at 3am
23	115	Belleme to the Atlantic coast of France, Port-en-Bessin, where I wandered the cliffs..
24	45	Highway 6 west to the American Cemetary @ Omaha Beach, then to Ouistreham/Caen, France
25	79	Portsmouth Harbor through Winchester to random hotel in Cholderton, near Stonehenge
26	56	56 miles, in the rain, but with a tailwind, Cholderton to Stroud, England
Mon 27	55	55 miles, sans gear, south and east of Stroud, aimless, cloudy, windy, sprinkles at times.
28	55	Stroud to Culham, just south of Oxford.
29	44	Culham to London, Heathrow, 44 miles easyish; walk 3 miles to Halford's to get a bike box too.
30		Ride Hounslow to Windsor, Castle, after riding around the airport perimeter once.
31		Ride Hounslow to the southwest, moderate, had a map so I made a loop.
Sat 8/1		Exerbike at+A1:C45 Hilton Garden Inn, before my flight home. Read a lot.

CHAPTER 1

On June 4th, 2015, as the first hints of sunlight crested the darkened horizon, United Airlines Flight 64 touched down at Lisbon International Airport. I stared out the clouded oval window, catching my first faint glimpses of Portugal.

Waiting to exit the plane, I feigned an outward calm that belied my inner impatience, watching as every single passenger extracted their luggage from the overhead bins and shuffled toward the door. Free in the terminal, I hastened to passport control where another line greeted me. I stood obediently, pushing from my mind the logistical challenges that awaited.

Twenty minutes later, a border agent stamped my passport, the familiar sound offering a moment of relief. I found a bathroom where I changed into my cycling gear, pulling on a pair of cargo shorts so I wasn't walking around in head-to-toe Lycra.

I paced for some time across the off-white tile floor of the baggage claim area. I used one of my panniers, the packs that attached to my bicycle, as a carry-on bag. The pannier was filled with snacks, toiletries, guidebooks, and electronics. The strap dug into my shoulder and my helmet, hanging off the waterproof bag, bounced against my leg with each step.

I listened to the hum of air vents and muffled voices while eyeing the luggage carousel and oversized baggage claim, waiting for my bag and bicycle to arrive.

The bike didn't make it!

My negative self panicked easily.

'Relax. It'll get here.'

The calm, rational side of my personality interjected frequently. Today, it wasn't helping. I pictured my bicycle, packed in its box, in the belly of a cargo jet on its way to the far reaches of the globe.

I continued to pace.

When the massive cardboard rectangle arrived, I grabbed it with trembling hands and inspected every corner. It appeared intact.

I dragged the box toward the luggage carousel. A few minutes later, my black duffle bag arrived. It contained three more panniers, which collectively held a mess of clothes for every type of weather, cycling shoes, eight spare tubes, two extra chains, a multitude of tools, my tent, sleeping bag, sleeping pad, and every other item I conceived I might need on my trip. Three jars of peanut butter and eight packs of gum were stashed somewhere inside.

Belongings in hand, I paused to consider my next move. I had dreaded this moment for months. Unpacking the bicycle was only one piece of the puzzle. It needed to be reassembled, the handlebars reattached, the seat repositioned, the pedals screwed on, the cables recalibrated. In my mind, the best place to do that was in the baggage claim area, safe from the uncertainties of the outside world.

The security guards will never let you put your bike together in the airport.

I looked around. Not far away, I noticed a trio of men pulling their own bikes out of boxes.

'If they can do it,' my rational side said, 'so can we.'

I dragged my belongings toward them. One of the men glanced at me. I smiled and gave a quick nod.

"Where are you going?" the man asked in accented English.

The question caught me off guard. My plans were not entirely clear.

"To Spain," I said. "And eventually Geneva."

All three men nodded in silent approval.

"And maybe Morocco," I said, feeling silly mentioning it. I was hoping to go to Tangiers and ride a short stretch of highway along Morocco's northern coast before returning to Spain and onward to Geneva.

I peeled the tape from the top of the cardboard and opened the lid. My Soma was tucked inside, its black steel frame covered in plastic and foam. I pulled it from the box.

"Where are you headed?" I asked the man closest to me.

"We flew from Amsterdam, for a tour of the wine regions," he said.

"Off to the Portuguese countryside," his friend added.

"Nice," I replied.

We continued putting our bikes together in silent camaraderie.

When the Soma was pieced together, I pulled out a small knife and tore into the bike box.

The third Dutchman widened his eyes in horror. "What are you doing?"

I looked at him, confused.

"Don't you need the box to take your bike home?"

"I'm not flying home from here," I responded. "I'm getting home from … somewhere else. Heathrow, I guess." I had a return ticket to Colorado from London in early August. "I won't be coming back to Lisbon."

The man gave a confused nod. "We're all returning here to the airport. We're going to hide the bike boxes in some bushes nearby and retrieve them when we come back. Hopefully they'll still be there!"

I envied their simple plan to fly in and out of the same airport. My summer would not be so straightforward.

I shoved the box and packing material next to a trash bin, leaving the duffel bag hanging out in case anyone could use it.

Bleary-eyed, I affixed the four panniers to their respective racks, two over each wheel, stood back, and inspected my bicycle, clean and ready to ride.

My Soma Double Cross, a steel cyclocross bike, had the symmetry and feel of a road racing bicycle, but was designed with a sturdier build for its original intention of racing on dirt. I worried that my 700 x 28c tires, not much wider than my usual racing tires, would be too narrow for loaded touring, but they were a nice compromise for the bicycle racer in me.

I said goodbye to my fellow cyclists and walked through customs into the hazy summer heat, a stark contrast to the stale climate-controlled atmosphere of the airport terminal. I heaved my bicycle past the taxi stands and stopped at a money-exchange kiosk, handing over US dollars and receiving euros in exchange. Cash in hand, I bought a few bottles of water and secured them under the top flaps of my panniers.

Having successfully negotiated the technicalities of the airport, I threw my right leg over the Soma and pushed away from the curb. The extra seventy pounds of gear registered immediately. Traffic was heavy, but fluid, and motorists swerved around me, unhampered by the mass of my four panniers.

I followed my intuitive sense of direction south, toward the Tagus River, which marks the southern boundary of Lisbon, weaving my way through the narrow streets. The paper maps I'd packed weren't much use at this scale; they showed only the major highways through Portugal. I discovered Google Maps didn't work on this side of the Atlantic either, at least not on my phone.

'No matter,' I thought. 'We just need to go south.'

And find somewhere to camp.

I sighed.

'Yes, I guess we need to camp.'

Whenever I told anyone I would be cycling in Europe this summer, they asked me if I planned to camp. The idea was carved into my head, something I was supposed to do, even if I wasn't crazy about camping.

Maybe you should have done a bit more research on campgrounds.

I swerved around a small Eurovan that had stopped in front of me.

'Maybe we should have researched a lot of things.'

But it was impossible to research lodging options when I didn't know what the roads in rural Portugal would be like or how hilly they would be. I also had no idea which direction the winds would blow from one day to the next, a minor technicality motorists can ignore but cyclists can't. Strong winds can change a six-hour ride into ten hours without warning.

To further complicate matters, I wasn't sure where I was headed. After finishing my Peace Corps service in 2001, I returned to the United States via a six-week detour through Europe. I had an itching desire to make it all the way to Morocco, to touch the African continent, simply to say I'd been there. But the closest I got that summer was Madrid.

Now, fourteen years later, the desire to go to Morocco was stronger than ever. But I needed to get to Geneva by June 28th to meet Kendra. Morocco was two hundred miles in the opposite direction.

Logistics meandered through my brain as I worked my way to the Tagus River, following the breeze I knew would come off a large body of water. I found a ferry station and walked my Soma into the belly of a small boat.

Though I hadn't slept much for the past forty-some hours, I couldn't help but grin as the vessel swayed through the water and the opposite shore came into focus. My grin was replaced by a moment of regret as I glanced back at the city. My first—and only—time visiting Lisbon lasted less than an hour.

I continued south along a flat, sandy stretch of western Portuguese coast. Storks lounged in expansive nests atop telephone poles, buildings, and any other structure they could find.

With the help of two police officers, I found a campground a few miles inland from the Atlantic Ocean. After setting up my tent and eating dinner, I rode to the beach and took a moment to ponder the vast expanse of water, visualizing the coast of the United States beyond the horizon.

From there, I walked uphill to a small café with an amazing view of the beach, the ocean, and the beginning of it all. I ordered a glass of port and sat and sipped contentedly while gazing at the Atlantic.

The sinking sun cast the scene into deep shades of blue and yellow. Twenty-four whirlwind hours earlier, I was in Colorado; now I was in Portugal. I pondered the journey ahead, visualizing a map of the Eurasian continent and contemplating where I'd get to this summer, and the next, a slight smile forming on my lips as I considered the miles of concrete in my future.

*****

By eight the next morning, it was blistering hot. In town after Portuguese town, I caught fleeting glimpses of whitewashed buildings and navigated narrow roads that danced away in every direction. I got lost in Alvalade and again in Ourique, places that faded from memory the moment I passed through them.

Under the midday sun, I found myself riding through groves of cork trees that lined winding country roads. The cork, embedded in the bark, had been removed from the trunks and was somewhere being prepped to seal the finest bottles of wine, whisky, and whiskey.

As I pedaled, the soft hum of rubber on pavement, the smooth grinding interface of chain and gears, and the flooding pressure of wind around my face were drowned out by the rhythms of base channeling through my headphones. The upbeat but slightly sad tempo of "Close Your Eyes," by The Chemical Brothers, took on new meaning as I cruised around countless bends in the road. Every tree, every field of grass, every solitary tractor, and even the scentless yellow dust of central Portugal seemed so novel and refreshing.

I almost stopped for the night in Castro Verde, a beautiful windswept town with a campground, but I couldn't give up the strong tailwind and the calming evening colors. I continued another thirty miles to the city of Mértola, which lacked a campsite but did have a twenty-eight-euro hotel room with a balcony overlooking the river.

I locked my bicycle in a storage room and lugged my panniers up a flight of stairs. I washed my clothes in the shower, plugged in all my power converters, and charged every device I had. Then I wandered the narrow, cobbled streets, illuminated by dim streetlamps, happy to have a moment to relax and call my wife.

"How's everything going?" asked Kendra.

"Good," I said. "I rode 105 miles today. That puts me close to Spain. I thought I'd be in Portugal longer, but I've had some amazing tailwinds. I can't give those up."

"I'm sure you can't," Kendra said with a slight note of sarcasm. "You'll make it to Geneva with no problems at that rate."

"None at all," I replied. On a map, a straight shot from Lisbon to Geneva was roughly twelve hundred miles.

Kendra sensed my hesitation. "Still thinking of going to Morocco?"

"Kind of."

"You can do what you want," she said, "so long as you meet me at the airport in Geneva." I could see her grinning on the other end of the line.

Our plans from the previous summer were coming to fruition. We would be in Geneva for four days while she scouted out potential practicum sites at the World Health

Organization. Then we planned to rent a car and explore a bit of Germany, Austria, and Slovenia. I only needed to arrive in Geneva before her flight touched down.

"I'll be there," I repeated.

Images of Morocco danced in my head. If all else failed, I knew I could take a train. Focused as I was on riding the whole way, I wasn't going to ruin my marriage over it.

Our conversation shifted to where I'd been and what I'd seen. I glanced at my phone several times as we spoke, amazed at the flawless connection across five thousand miles.

"Well …"—I wasn't sure how to end the call—"I should find something to eat." Delicious smells from nearby restaurants filled my nostrils. "It's nine here."

The reality of having to say goodbye hit me, much like it had at Denver International Airport two days earlier. "I'll talk to you tomorrow?"

"Yes," she said, trying to sound upbeat.

"OK. I …"

"You need to eat."

"Yes."

Silence.

"Love you."

"Love you too."

We both hung up. I gazed at the lonely, pale storefronts and dark cobblestones for a moment. Then I walked into a random restaurant, picked up a menu, pointed at a beer I didn't know and food that I didn't understand, and waited for my meal.

I woke up the next morning itching to move. Instead, I forced myself to visit the fortress towering over the city. The views from the medieval ramparts of the long-lost castle revealed distant rugged hillsides, steep and brown, and for a few minutes I was glad to be a normal tourist and soak in a bit of history.

It didn't take long for a growing unease to unfurl in my stomach. An invisible force that I couldn't ignore pulled my body back to my hotel and back to my bicycle.

You need to stay longer and soak this in.

My admonitions did nothing to placate the urge to move.

'There will be other things to see,' I replied.

I returned to my room, packed, and was soon cruising through rolling straw-colored hills, across a series of narrow backroads. I smiled when I spotted a big blue sign with the stars of the European Union and the words "Espanha: 1 km" written on it.

My brakes screeched as I made the mile-long descent toward a new country, my brief sojourn through Portugal already a happy blur of memories.

CHAPTER 2

I crossed a river into Spain without slowing down, all signs of a border crossing between the two European nations long since gone. The road climbed upward from the brown waterway, past a rugged landscape marked by rocks, dirt, and short brown trees. Sunscreen and sweat dripped down my arms onto my hands, making it difficult to grip my handlebars.

My route took me forty miles north of Palos de la Frontera, where the likes of Columbus set sail for the New World. I had been teaching my fifth graders about European exploration of the Americas for years, and as I ground my way up steep, long climbs, pondering those distant events proved a welcome distraction.

Late in the day, the hills turned to flat farmland. I spent the night west of Seville in the small enclave of La Palma del Condado, at the Pension Los Morenos, situated above a café-restaurant on a main road through the quiet town. I berated myself for not camping even as I savored the hot shower and sterile, cold air-conditioning of the spartan, clean room.

The next morning, I examined my map. To the south lay Tarifa, where I could catch a ferry to Tangiers. The fastest route to Geneva was in the opposite direction.

You're not actually going to Morocco, are you?

My doubtful self didn't like making things harder than they needed to be.

'We've been thinking about Morocco for years.'

I looked at the map again. My eyes fixated on the Moroccan coastline.

"It's time," I said out loud, "to see a bit of Africa."

The determined side of my personality ended the debate. I pointed my front wheel south and started pedaling.

My initial bravado waned by midafternoon when insidious headwinds developed, becoming so distressing at times that tears welled in my eyes. Views of roads winding through distant Spanish hillsides and fields of sunflowers offered some compensation for my troubles.

I crawled into the town of Arcos de la Frontera at six. Despite spotting several places to stay, I continued riding the hilly streets until my odometer measured an even hundred miles for the day.

I parked my bicycle at the entrance to a small, family-run *hostal*. I felt self-conscious walking inside wearing my sweaty cycling gear, but the receptionist gave no indication that she noticed. As she showed me to my room, I tried to discern the difference between my *pension* from the night before and this *hostal*. I couldn't figure it out.

After cleaning up, I walked downstairs to the attached restaurant. I attempted to talk to the waitress in my rudimentary Spanish. Her replies were too fast for me, so I pointed to a few random tapas on the menu. I also tapped on the word *caracoles*, wondering what snails would taste like.

I glanced at the well-dressed people around me, laughing and talking with friends and family. I admired the ease with which they all spoke, so engaged with one another and so seemingly happy. I thought about what I would be doing back in Fort Collins.

You'd be at home, by yourself, not out with a group of friends.

I sighed.

Dinner did not improve my mood. It was a bland assortment of bread covered with various toppings. Only the *caracoles* offered a saving grace. The tiny snails came to me in a glass cup full of broth, shells and all. I sucked out each rubbery critter, the novelty of it making me smile.

*****

Outside the *hostal* the next morning, I held my loaded bicycle firmly in both hands. The smooth black paint glistened in the morning sun and I glanced down at my Ultegra crankset. The teeth on the chainrings showed moderate wear, but the bike itself was in its prime, comfortable but responsive, all the glitches tuned and every component familiar to me.

The Soma itched to move.

I looked at the spectacular city on the frontier of southern Spain, its buildings glistening white against the brown hills in the predawn hours.

You need to check this place out. You need to practice your Spanish.

'We should look around a bit,' I admitted.

People are supposed to relax on vacation, aren't they? Why can't you?

The badgering voice continued as I wheeled my Soma to the highway and hopped on the saddle. The cleats on the bottom of my cycling shoes clicked into the steel pedals, ready for another day of riding. I cranked up Sia's "Chandelier" on my headphones and drowned out the bantering in my head.

The skies were hazy and merged with distant brown hills. I passed through several villages, most small clusters of white buildings. Others were more expansive and difficult to navigate, slowing my progress. The headwind from the day before continued, compounding my frustrations. I stopped only occasionally, sometimes at a gas station for water and snacks, other times on the side of the road to reapply sunscreen.

I wasn't sure what kept me pedaling other than the idea that I had to get somewhere. My efforts were rewarded when

I glimpsed the coast of Africa across the Strait of Gibraltar, a faint sliver of land rising above the deep blue water.

I followed the Spanish shoreline for ten miles, noticing numerous campgrounds along the way where I could relax on the beach or fly a kite. But I kept pedaling, straight to the ferry terminal in the city of Tarifa.

I was going to Africa, if only for a day.

Two hours later, I stood on the balcony of a large boat, listening to the hum of diesel engines push the craft away from the dock and away from Europe. During the hour-long passage, I met a Dutch couple who were familiar with Tangiers. They gave me directions to a campground near the pier. I was grateful to know where I'd be staying ahead of time, especially since Morocco was the first Muslim country I'd visited and I was burdened by a certain paranoia accumulated over one too many American newspaper articles.

My passport offered me easy access through border patrol. After exiting the customs house, I pedaled a mile south before taking a sharp left up a steep hill, like the Dutch couple had told me.

I found the campsite easily, and after setting up my tent and throwing my panniers into it, I rode toward the city center. My Soma felt fast and agile, and I weaved in and out of rush-hour traffic, dodging cars, mopeds and buses, forgetting that I was supposed to be afraid.

I envisioned criteriums from my previous lives, short-circuit bike races where hordes of cyclists careen through corners at mind-numbing speeds. I had raced a hundred of those hour-long competitions in my life and sometimes missed the exhilaration that pedaling solo couldn't give me.

I hopped off my bicycle in a pedestrian area high above the waterfront. No one noticed me, even as I walked through crowds of people, the only person wearing shorts for miles around. I stopped at a kebab shop where my nostrils filled with the smells of sizzling meat and French fries. I pointed at an image of a kebab on the menu and was soon sitting at an

outdoor table, filling my stomach with my first true meal of
the day. While I ate, I gazed in awe at the coastline below.
Both east and west, the city rolled into cramped hills.

*You should spend a few days here! Think of the spice markets and
hidden alleyways you've seen in books. This place once hosted legends
like Kerouac, Ginsberg, and Burroughs.*

I shook my head. I knew that I wouldn't see much more
than this hillside. I pushed any ideas of visiting recommended
travel sites to the back of my mind and finished my meal.

A few hours later, I sat in my tent trying to make sense of
the clothes, gear, and toiletries scattered across the floor.
From the open flap, I saw a young couple return to a nearby
campsite.

I gave up trying to organize my things and stepped
outside. The pair glanced at me, so I walked over to introduce
myself.

"Have you been here long?" I asked, motioning to the
campground. It was little more than a patch of grass set
among palm trees and surrounded by decrepit hotel rooms
that had, at one time, probably been quite nice.

"Only a few days," said the man. He was gaunt with short
black hair, and the expression on his face carried a quiet air of
haughtiness. "We've been making our way up the coast of
Morocco." He proceeded to rattle off a list of places they'd
visited.

I was immediately envious, knowing they had experienced
Morocco at a depth I never would.

"Where are you from?" I asked, curious because they
both had different accents.

"I'm from Spain," said the woman, brushing back her
long black hair. "And he's from France. We're doing a gap
year, traveling a bit before going back to school and back to
work."

I became more envious. Twenty-something. Gap year.
Experiencing North Africa, not a care in the world.

"And where are you headed?" said the Frenchman as he pointed at my bike.

I hesitated. "I'm going to Ceuta tomorrow, about eighty kilometers east of here. From there I'll take a ferry back into Spain."

"Only one day in Morocco?" the man said, his eyebrow raised in indignation. "And where will you go once you return to Spain?"

"I'm heading to Geneva," I told him, not mentioning that I only had two and a half weeks to get there.

"Oh, yeah, you'll get to Geneva on your bicycle, *inshallah!*"

Inshallah is an Arabic word that means "God willing." I didn't realize it could be wielded with such sarcasm.

A slight smirk formed on the young man's lips, as if whispering, "You can't do it."

In my mind, I replied with my own smug smile, a retort that said, "Just watch me."

An awkward silence passed before we resumed our conversation. The word *inshallah* was now carved into my brain.

As I lay in bed that evening, the *muezzin* rang out the Muslim call to prayer over hidden loudspeakers, a mesmerizing sound that affixed itself to the hills of Tangiers stretching into the twilight. The sounds of near-feral dogs barking across the city reminded me I was not in Western Europe. I went to sleep fearful and excited about the next day's ride, hopeful I'd prove my new Euro-friend wrong.

I woke up in a panic.

There's no way you can do this!

I looked, wide-eyed, at the pale blue sky through the screen of my tent.

There's no way you're going to pedal your massive bike across the northern tip of Morocco.

'We've ridden four hundred miles so far.'

Somebody's going to tell you to get off the highway. Or worse.

31

'We can ride fifty miles back to Spain.'

The argument continued as I packed my things. My fellow campers were still tucked in their tent. I left the campground in the muggy light of dawn and rode back along the waterfront. I saw countless people strolling with friends, taking in the fresh sea air. It was a scene I hadn't expected, just another day in another city.

Leaving Tangiers was straightforward because all I had to do was keep the Mediterranean on my left. Under the early morning heat, as I pushed my load up a seven-mile climb, an old man saw me and gave me a thumbs-up and enthusiastic smile. Every passing car gave me plenty of room.

Around noon, I stopped for lunch at a roadside restaurant. The proprietors, a husband and wife, welcomed me inside with broad smiles. The wife pointed out the different meal options in a glass display.

I pointed to an appetizing choice, and the woman motioned for me to sit down. A few minutes later she brought me a mix of vegetables and beef served in a hot clay bowl, smiling warmly as she set the food in front of me.

I smiled back and looked down at the steam rising off my food. I picked up my fork and scooped the tasty assortment into my mouth, exhaling urgently as the first morsels scalded the roof of my mouth. By the time I left, my belly was full and my fears of riding in a foreign land had subsided.

At the top of a long descent, I snapped a photo before proceeding down the steep stretch of pavement. I savored the wind in my face as my hulking bicycle accelerated beneath me. In an instant, my rear pannier flew off my bike and the exhilaration of flying downhill was replaced by panic. The bag was attached to my rear rack via two hooks on top and an elastic cord on the bottom, and while the top hooks had detached, the cord held firmly to both the Soma and the pannier. The sudden imbalance nearly toppled me.

I evenly applied the brakes and came to a halt, an image of a Moroccan emergency room flashing through my mind. I caught my breath and put the pannier back on, duct-taping it so it couldn't fly off again. I had come within a hair's breadth of ending up seriously hurt, all because of user error.

Miles later, as I climbed higher into the hills, the urban areas drifted behind me. The land was covered with forest, and I discerned small groups of young men concealing themselves among the trees, their black faces blending in with the shadows. They were not Moroccan.

'Refugees, no doubt.'

Seeking passage to Europe, on a quest for something that actually matters.

I wondered where they slept, what they ate, and if they had access to water. My own troubles felt trite by comparison.

Emerging from those forested hills, leaving behind the secret hopes of the anonymous refugees, the city of Ceuta spread out before me like a modern medieval contradiction. I barreled down the descent to the Mediterranean, already oblivious to my near disaster that morning.

I walked my bike through the border crossing, my American passport once again allowing me to move between countries with ease. Inside the small Spanish territory, I cruised past intriguing medieval buildings on my way to the ferry terminal, ignoring my inner pleas to take a closer look. I hopped on the next boat back to the European continent, gazing at the Rock of Gibraltar as the coast of Europe emerged.

From the port city of Algeciras, I kept pedaling another thirty miles north without so much as taking a breath.

I stopped for the night at Hostal El Anon, in the town of Jimena de la Frontera, where smooth white buildings ran up and down steep, narrow streets. Views of the Spanish countryside faded into the evening air.

I washed my clothes in the shower, as I had the preceding nights, letting the soap from my body wash over them and stomping out the sweat and grime with my feet. I held each article of clothing up to the showerhead and rinsed and wrung until blisters emerged on my thumbs. I hung the clothes in the most optimal places to dry.

At dinner, the *hostal* owner gave me a taste of sherry from various barrels before I decided on the right one. The cozy restaurant, with wooden beams supporting the centuries-old structure, was the ideal end to a ride across the tip of Morocco and thirty-some miles of Spain. The beef stew fell apart in my mouth. It was worth the thirty-five-euro price tag.

That evening, however, I had trouble sleeping. It was hot and the bed was uncomfortable. I envisioned the young men in the hills of northern Morocco, asleep among the trees, their fates uncertain.

Those men are seeking the stable and secure life that for you seems to have become so tiresome.

I sat in the semidarkness, on top of my covers, listening to the jarring tones of my own inner diatribe.

Life has been nothing but good to you. Why are you on this self-absorbed adventure?

I had no response.

Instead, I thought about what Kendra was doing and wondered how I could leave her alone for weeks. She would have loved this little town and little *hostal*. I examined the walls, questioning the point of the entire trip, until sleep washed away the first fundamental doubts about my silly quest.

I awoke to a now-familiar debate.

Go visit the castle above town.

I really wanted to get on the road.

You're here. See something.

I thought about the miles ahead.

'I suppose we should see some sights.'

I put on my running shoes and forced myself upward, through the winding cobbled streets. Soon, I was looking down on Jimena de la Frontera and on Spain, meandering among the ruins of an anonymous castle that held more secrets than I could comprehend.

I spent a long time trying to understand the mysteries of the fortress until I got to the cisterns. Huge, brick underground reservoirs built to retain water in an arid land, my curiosity piqued as I peered into a dark hole that marked the outer opening.

Instead of finding any answers to the secrets of the castle, I saw too late a nest of wasps. I got stung in the face and ran for dear life.

'This is what we get for stopping to see something!'

I laughed as I held my left hand over my throbbing cheek.

Before leaving, I allowed myself an enormous breakfast. The local organic honey paired perfectly with the homemade yogurt.

I smiled with each bite, forgetting for a moment the pain in my face. My usual diet didn't leave room for such extravagances as food in the morning. Cycling for eight to ten hours a day meant that, for the first time in a long time, I could eat breakfast.

For a moment, I felt like I was on a normal vacation.

CHAPTER 3

Images of Don Quixote, sitting on his horse, lance in hand, filled my head as I left Jimena de la Frontera. I'd read *Don Quixote* in college, and his character's reputation as a delusional man lost in his own head, on a quest for something only he can understand, resonated with me now more than ever.

The famous windmills of Consuegra, thought to be those from the seventeenth-century novel, were en route to Geneva. As I pushed my hundred pounds of bicycle and gear into the mountains of Spain, I considered the disconnect between Quixote's illusions and the real world. Sometimes my own view of reality seemed as skewed as his.

Four hours of steady climbing revealed a desert landscape filled with prickly brown shrubs and searing heat. I kept my eyes on the blinding pavement in front of me, not wanting to know how much higher I had to climb.

The road eventually leveled out and tailwinds pushed me along winding mountain highways. An occasional car passed me with ample room, but otherwise I had the pavement to myself. I rode through one village after the next, tiny white buildings packed around rolling brown mountainsides. Fields of wheat added a smattering of color and expanses of towering modern windmills, spinning in the summer breeze, captivated my attention with their solitary grace and calm demeanor.

I entered a sleepy, dreary town with one small Dia grocery store and no lodging. An intrinsic loneliness enveloped the place, and I wondered if it was perpetually trapped in the muggy, hazy, in-between time of day separating late afternoon and evening.

I unclipped my black, square handlebar bag from its mount and hoisted its hidden strap over my shoulder. Inside the bag, I kept my wallet, phone, passport, and camera, both for easy access while riding and because it was the one piece of baggage that never left my side. I locked my bicycle near the front door with my u-lock and walked inside.

The cool air in the store was a welcome respite from the heat outside. I stocked up on Spanish *jamón*, cheese, apples, and carrots. After shoving my purchases into my panniers, I hopped on my bicycle and rode to the edge of town.

The land opened into olive groves as far as the eye could see, an ocean of uncertainty.

You need to turn around.

'And go where? Stay where? We haven't passed any hotels for hours.'

Silence.

My stomach was heavy with apprehension as I surveyed the scene. A slight wind blew from behind, nudging me forward, but the expanse of olive trees offered little invitation. I shook my head in dismay even as a small grin formed at the sides of my mouth. The unknown was exciting, though the knot in my stomach thought otherwise.

I stepped on the pedals and was soon surrounded by the trees. Green leaves on stubby olive branches stretched into endless hillsides and the faint scent of soil permeated my nostrils. I stopped to inspect the small stone fruits and imagined the oil waiting to be pressed out.

I passed through two small towns, neither of which had any *hostales* or *pensiones*. Miles later, a nature preserve materialized on my right. It surrounded a small lake and appeared to have plenty of cover.

'It's eight. We need to rest.'
You're going to get into trouble.
'We'll find a secluded spot.'

I walked my bike past the entry and down a path before turning into a forested area close to the water. The sun continued its descent behind the horizon and a void of darkness filled the sky.

I set up my tent and considered my options.

'Let's take a bath.'
No! Someone will tell you to leave.
'Let's at least rinse out our clothes.'
No!

I gave into fear and resigned myself to an unpleasant evening, hanging my sweaty clothing to dry on makeshift clotheslines. I wiped down my heart rate monitor chest strap with a wet wipe, removing the sweat from the plastic sensor.

Sitting on my Pearl Izumi jacket, far too warm to wear in these conditions, I ate my spoils from Dia in silence. I washed everything down with a malty Spanish Märzenbier, the subtle hops pairing well with my cheese and veggies. I inspected my favorite coat as I chewed. The reflective strips down the arms were cracking after years of wear, and the weathered sleeves brought back images of countless winter commutes between my home and school.

When I stood to stretch my legs, all sentimentality drained from my head. Moving my body reminded me how sweaty and disgusting I was.

The night was as miserable as I knew it would be, with fire ants wandering near the entrance of my tent and strange sounds coming from everywhere. One recurring noise resembled a demon straight out of the netherworld. Despite the discomfort, I eventually dozed off and awoke to daylight.

I stepped outside and picked up my bicycle shorts with two fingers, repelled by the thought of how much sweat was in them. I debated whether to shove them in a bag and use my only extra pair of shorts.

After a few moments of hesitation, I pulled out a tube of triple antibiotic ointment, smeared it into the chamois, and put on the nasty shorts. I cringed when I sat on my bike, but once I started pedaling, and started sweating again, I barely noticed how filthy I was.

*****

Ten miles from Consuegra, I turned down the worst road in Spain, with bumps and potholes to rival those in Michigan. It didn't take long for my black coffee thermos to fly out of my pannier. I bent down to retrieve it and saw numerous new dents around the lid.

I wasn't able to carry many souvenirs with me, so putting a dent in something I already had was as good as any memorabilia I might buy. I smiled at the damage and tucked the thermos under the top flap of the bag, cinching it tightly this time.

I got back on my Soma and continued, weaving around rough patches of concrete even as I absorbed the scenery. The road, the stifling, humid air, the mid-summer sun, and the anticipation of seeing something legendary all conspired to make the evening magical.

Crossing a vast plain, small white dots materialized atop a distant hillside. Mile by mile, those white dots morphed into proper Spanish windmills. Even though I'd been pedaling since morning, when I reached the hill, I sprinted to the top, not able to wait a moment longer to witness those symbols of delusion up close.

One of the twelve windmills was open to visitors, and with my two-euro entry ticket I got a self-guided tour and a free beer. The inside of the structure was a maze of circular stairs and gears that served the ultimate purpose of grinding grain. The entire top of the windmill could rotate so that the blades always faced the wind.

Stones had been placed purposefully and coated with the classic white paint shown in so many photos. I traced my hand along the smooth walls as I walked up the circular staircase to the upper level, fascinated that people had worked there five centuries earlier.

After examining the inner workings, I went outside. A hot evening breeze rolled off the plains I had cycled across. I found a spot to sit down where I could look at the other windmills. To the north sat La Castilla de la Mancha, itself a remarkable, medieval castle originally built eight hundred years ago in the epicenter of the struggle between the Muslims and Christians to control the Iberian Peninsula.

I drank my complimentary beer while overlooking the plains of La Mancha with a genuine sense of evening contentment. I breathed in the wind, noting its nondescript scent as I listened to it hum. I paused for a minute to absorb it all, a rare moment when I didn't feel any particular rush to go anywhere. My inner dialogue was strangely quiet.

The moment was fleeting, of course. It was already seven, and I didn't have a place to stay. I pedaled back to Consuegra, set on the northern base of the hillside. Rather than go to the first *pension* I spotted, I continued to the eastern outskirts of town. Once I got there, I realized the hotels were all behind me, in the city center. There had been a roaring tailwind all day, and since I didn't want to ride back into it, I kept going.

'There'll be something else up the way,' I told myself.

The next town was a depressing, in-between place with no lodging. It smelled of overcooked food and sewage, with a hint of hot concrete. I pedaled through an industrial area where the sound of a garage band blaring from an empty warehouse was the only sign of life. It was not the sort of place anyone would want to stay, much less ride through with all their worldly possessions.

Moments later I was in the countryside, enjoying the tailwind despite my predicament. At nine, as the sky darkened around me, I rolled into the town of Herencia where I located a *pension* with a phone number posted on the outside door.

After several dials, I got through to someone, but I kept using the term *cuarto* to ask about a room, rather than *habitación*, a slight difference that made the conversation impossible through the satellite connection.

As I was talking, four teenagers strolled past. I expected them to laugh at the smelly cyclist trying to find a room in their hometown. Instead, they saw my frustrated expression and inferred that I needed help. One of them called the number with their own phone. Within minutes, a woman was there to let me inside.

I entered my *habitación*, bike in hand, at half past nine. I'd ridden 127 miles, was commensurately tired, sticky, and ready to go to bed. That small gesture of kindness by a group of teenagers turned a potential disaster into a restful night.

*****

Albarracín is a postcard-worthy destination straight out of Spain's Muslim and medieval past. The remains of an immense fortress wall hover above the city, and the town itself is a maze of ancient buildings that appear to fall over the streets, creating a network of narrow alleyways where sunlight seldom touches.

Outside the city center, I found a campground, picked a site, and set up my tent. A few plots away, I noticed a touring bike leaning against a fence. Within minutes, its owner returned and, seeing me, came over to introduce himself.

"Hallo!" he said with a Germanic accent. He had sandy blond hair, glasses, and appeared to be in his late fifties. He was wearing his civilian clothes. Switching straight to English, he held out his hand. "I'm Fritz," he said warmly. "Nice to meet you."

"You as well," I said, reaching out to shake his hand. "Have you been in Albarracín long?"

41

"I arrived here two days ago," he said. "I flew from Amsterdam to Madrid." He explained in unrushed, methodical detail how he had plotted his route and his campsites for his entire trip. He maintained a leisurely pace and toured the places that normal people want to visit.

I thought about my own plans. I had yet to map out which road I should take when I left Albarracín the next day. I knew I needed to head north and east, toward Geneva, and hoped to see something interesting along the way.

Fritz invited me to go with him to the Plaza Mayor. We met a small group of people, Spanish and otherwise, who Fritz had befriended on his previous days in town. We watched a performance of traditional dancing and afterward found a restaurant to have dinner.

As we entered, we were joined by a young French cyclist, another new friend of Fritz's. He was also on a set route, visiting sites and taking his time. I sat back and soaked in the random meal in the company of an aging Dutchman and French college student.

This is the way you used to travel, back in your study-abroad days, when it was all about meeting people and experiencing things with others.

'These past two weeks have been go, go, go,' I admitted.

Why can't you slow down, like these two?

Recent articles in *Time* magazine, about the importance of slowing down and making friends, came flooding back to me. They burned in my mind like overbearing parents who always know best.

"And so I will go east, to Teruel," said the Frenchman.

What did he say?

I turned to look at him, focusing my attention on his words rather than the random thoughts in my head.

"From there, I will go to Cuenca. I hear it is an amazing city."

Amazing indeed. I had stayed the previous night in Cuenca, near the hospital, where I could see the ancient skyline. It was a UNESCO World Heritage Site and held treasures beyond my imagination. I had arrived as the sun was setting and left early the next day, experiencing nothing but the roads in and out of town.

"That will be a wonderful place to visit," I said.

"Ah, yes," interjected Fritz, "I have read many interesting things about Cuenca. You will enjoy your time."

Too bad you left without seeing anything.

The conversation continued, both around the table and in my mind. Fritz was a calming presence, measured and confident in what he was doing.

The French man was Fritz's younger mirror image, equally resolute and focused. Between the two, I remembered what normal could be.

The next morning, I hiked up the walls of the ancient fortress, hugging the sides in places where the narrow staircases offered no safety in the event of a fall. I returned to the campground at eleven and said goodbye to Fritz, a typical farewell that I have uttered to so many random people who have come and gone in the blink of an eye.

*****

Two days later I descended three thousand feet from Spain's mountains to the Mediterranean Sea. I planned to follow the coast into France, a straightforward way to navigate save for one little problem: Barcelona.

With over five million inhabitants, metropolitan Barcelona spans thirty miles from one side to the other. It is impossible to say when I entered the city, but I knew when I was in it. Traffic was stop-and-go for hours, with traffic lights every hundred yards as I passed through the city center.

At one red light I found myself stuck between two city buses, a tin can waiting to be crushed. I pulled out my camera and took a picture of each bus, the wheels of my Soma less than a foot from the respective vehicles.

'That'll make a nice anecdote to share,' I thought, shoving my camera back into my handlebar bag as the light turned green. I accelerated and hoped the bus behind me didn't run into my rear wheel. A hundred yards later, traffic came to another halt.

'There must be a better way,' I fumed, looking at the sunken freeway paralleling my own congested artery. The light turned green and I sprinted forward, only to stop before reaching cruising speed. When the light changed again, I merged across three lanes of traffic and dropped down the freeway ramp.

This is not a good idea.

Initially, I was happy with the fluid momentum the freeway offered but was soon terrified of the subsequent entrance ramps where cars flew by me on both sides at speeds that left no room for error.

After a few miles, I admitted to myself that riding the freeway through Barcelona was worse than stopping at all the lights. I ascended an exit ramp as vehicles continued unimpeded below me, speeding in smooth, happy, bliss.

Back on the main road, I could at least view some of Barcelona's remarkable architecture and watch people walking about, getting a vague sense of life in the city. It continued for hours, braking and accelerating, in the heavy evening air, soaking in the exhaust of the buses and other urban fumes as my knuckles turned white gripping the handlebars and my headphones drowned out the noise of traffic.

So this is how you see Barcelona?

I could only laugh at the ludicrousness of it all. I vowed to never ride through a major city again unless it was necessary.

I found a campground thirty miles northeast of Barcelona where I could wash my clothes and shower. There were ads at the campground for bus rides to the major tourist sites. I considered taking one the next morning so I could behave like a proper tourist for a few hours.

Of course, I didn't. I had to keep moving.

*****

On June 19th, I stayed in the town of Playa l'Escala at the Campground Riells. When I entered, I found a corner site where I could sleep in silence, surrounded by the soft pine needles covering the ground.

Instead, the Italian noticed me. He was older, perhaps in his late sixties, with white waving hair, a tall, broad build, and deep soulful eyes. Seeing my bike and my tent, he came over to talk to me, communicating as well as he could in slow Italian. I replied in Spanish, hoping some of my words would be comprehensible.

For most of the way across Spain, people rarely asked about my trip. Now here was this man, interested in who I was, in where I was going, in my journey. Our interaction was brief, and I left the campground to walk around town, find some food, and stretch my legs. When I returned to my campsite, I thought I'd go straight to bed.

Instead, the Italian man saw me return to camp. He walked over and invited me to join his crew for dinner, all of whom were from Belgium. They were in their mid to late sixties, save for one, someone's mom, who was over eighty years old and the spitting image of my long-deceased grandmother.

The Belgians spoke English and told me they came to the campground every year, set up their campers, laid out linoleum tiles as their patios, and then sat back and enjoyed the weather, the beach, the pine trees, and each other's company.

They handed me one schnapps after the next and one sizzling sausage after the next, the smells emanating from my plate making every morsel irresistible. Through it all I kept counting my calories, careful not to overstep my bounds since I'd had an easy riding day.

We talked about topics that were soon lost on me, though they elicited no small amount of laughter. I leaned back in my chair and smiled, enjoying the company of a random group of people in a random Spanish campground. When the conversation tapered off, the Italian pulled out his guitar and started playing and singing, the joviality of the moment carrying on late into the night.

Before leaving the next morning, I walked over to say goodbye to the Italian man. The others were not yet awake.

"*Hasta luego*," I said. "Until later."

The man frowned. "*Ciao*," he replied, holding his hand out to shake mine. He seemed genuinely sad to see me go. I gave a final nod and pushed my bicycle out of the campground and back to the concrete.

I pondered his melancholy as I rode away.

'Why do we become friends with some people instantly, but with others it can take years?'

Or sometimes never?

I considered those questions, and contemplated broader concepts of friendship and human interaction, while I cruised over the pavement, alone.

I also began to wonder whether my little bid to ride my bicycle around the world was worth the price.

CHAPTER 4

My only responsibility this summer was to be in Geneva before Kendra arrived, and I had a week to get there. France was the last country in my way. I left Spain via a small mountain pass where the Pyrenees mountains meet the Mediterranean Sea. After a long, winding descent, I continued north, arriving in the small community of Lézignan-Corbières as the day's heat was dissipating.

Signs pointed me to a municipal campground where I found a pleasant grassy spot to camp. I locked the Soma to a small tree and pulled my tent from the right rear pannier. I set it up and started unloading the rest of my belongings. The sky changed colors as the sun worked its way westward, and the relaxed sounds of campers scattered among the trees produced a peaceful white noise.

Hungry, I strolled through the circuitous, narrow streets to find something to eat. I left a corner kebab shop with a Max-Kebab and a sizable order of fries that I took back to my campsite. Lacking any utensils, I used a pair of twigs as chopsticks and devoured every bite.

After eating, I pulled out my Acer laptop.

Who brings a laptop on a cycling trip?

'Can you imagine editing all these photos when we get home? It'd take weeks.'

Your electronics take up an entire pannier.

I shrugged. After several long minutes waiting for Windows 10 to wake up, I pulled the SD card out of my camera and plugged it into the computer. Processing photos had become part of my evening routine. My laptop was also my connection with the outside world when I had Wi-Fi. It amazed me that I could pay my bills from Europe.

In 1996, when I lived in Leicester, email was a novelty. Now, I could check it daily, though it was rare that I heard from anyone and even rarer that I took the time to email anyone myself. Mostly I sifted through junk emails. I'd made a conscious decision to stay off Facebook for the summer, and the longer I tuned out, the better I felt.

I renamed the photos on the SD card for easy organization, copied them to my computer, and edited them. I went to bed content, my belly full of kebab and fries, and slept well, a rare delight for me.

The ensuing days became a happy meandering blur, a summer of quaint French scenery viewed from the saddle of my favorite bicycle. Tree-lined roads, rolling countryside, and countless wineries that I never stopped to visit merged into one long image in my head.

One evening, en route to the town of Saint-Martin-de-Londres, I ascended a three-mile climb as the sun made its slow descent to the horizon. Pink Floyd's "Anisina" reverberated through my headphones, the electric guitar and saxophone solos weaving themselves into the deep blue sky as rivers of sweat poured down my face. The scene ingrained itself in my head, an unforgettable memory even as it unfolded.

I camped that night, and the following nights, discovering that in France, unlike in Spain, virtually every town has its own municipal campground. I began to feel worthy of a bicycle trip as I was no longer spending every night in air-conditioned luxury but instead sleeping outside, under the stars, my air mattress holding me inches off the earth.

One night, I stayed in a small campground next to a narrow river in the village of Suze-la-Rousse, nestled in the Rhône Valley. Marked by brown brick buildings covered with traditional clay roofs, I was amazed that trucks of any size could navigate the narrow main road. Adding to the charm of this historic place was a small castle standing on a hill above town, a reminder of the region's medieval past.

I arrived around five, a few hours earlier than I normally stopped riding. After putting up my tent, showering, shaving, washing my clothes, and hanging them to dry on a makeshift clothesline, I had time to walk around and visit the castle. While the inside was closed, the grounds were open, and from the hilltop I caught glimpses of the surrounding countryside.

'Kendra would love this place,' I thought.

You should be traveling with her.

'We'll be meeting up soon enough.'

Still. This is no place to experience alone.

I did my best to ignore the last comment.

I walked back to town, where I ordered a flatbread pizza and salad at a small family-run restaurant. The owners, perhaps Algerian, worked behind the counter while their son watched television in the dining area. I waited only a few minutes before the woman handed me a bag.

I managed my best "Merci," and walked out of the shop.

A block down the road I heard a child's voice yelling, "Monsieur! Monsieur!"

I looked back and saw the shopkeeper's son running after me. After a few hand gestures, I understood they had given me the wrong salad. We traded bags and I thanked him, delighted by the exchange. While I enjoyed my summers off, sometimes I missed my fifth graders, and this small interaction reminded me of my students who had left my classroom for the final time in May.

I sat down to eat at a picnic table next to the river, enjoying the sounds of running water and the view of the castle hovering above me. I cracked a smile as I realized I was called "monsieur."

After dinner I returned to my campground with time to spare.

What now?

I furrowed my brow. My heart sank. Boredom was upon me in an instant.

What are you doing out here all alone?

I thought back to the past several days. While riding all day made me content, in the evenings, when I wasn't moving, lingering doubts, fears, and disquietude about the trip would encroach into my psyche. Tonight was worse than most, perhaps because I had a full two hours before bedtime to slow down and relax.

I opened my computer and began editing photos, something to pass the time while I waited for sleep. I clicked, cropped, and adjusted brightness and contrast as darkness fell and the sounds of the creek overtook daytime noises.

The next morning, the disquietude was still there. I packed hurriedly and pushed my loaded bicycle toward the road. The moment I rolled forward, I felt better about everything. Those lingering doubts had a hard time keeping up with me when I was moving, especially when I turned up my headphones and songs like Moby's "Porcelain" soothed my angst.

My confidence and resolve returned. I had places to go.

*****

'We need to go to Alpe d'Huez.'

You need to go to Geneva.

'But first we need to go to Alpe d'Huez.'

I opened my tent and took in the views from my campground. Situated in the Alps, the site offered uninterrupted vistas of jagged peaks. The soft grass was damp, along with the clothes I had hung out to dry.

Alpe d'Huez is the penultimate hill-climb finish featured in so many editions of the Tour de France. Anyone who knows anything about bicycle racing knows about the classic climb, which snakes its way up the side of a mountain past twenty-one numbered switchbacks.

I'd been thinking about making the detour for weeks.

'It's only seventy miles out of the way,' I reasoned. 'We've got time.'

Time to stroll to Geneva, I countered, *and see something along the way.*

'What could be more amazing than Alpe d'Huez?'

My negative self became quiet. I had a compelling point.

I put on my wet cycling clothes and was soon freezing. The ubiquitous dewdrops on every blade of grass worked their way into the vents of my shoes, compounding my discomfort. My only hope was to start pedaling and wait for the sun to emerge over the distant peaks.

Late in the morning, I stopped for an espresso and pastry at a *boulangerie*, which I'd always thought was a word Dr. Evil had made up in the first *Austin Powers* movie. Pointing to a few pastries in the glass case, I quietly counted the calories in each one. I estimated low, a conscious lie I let myself get away with because I was pedaling all day.

I passed through the city of Grenoble around noon before veering thirty miles east, uphill, to reach Alpe d'Huez, where so many outcomes of the Tour de France had been decided. I found a campground at the base of the famous ascent and set up my tent.

I left seventy pounds of gear at the campsite and, despite riding two thousand miles in the previous three weeks, attacked the climb. Rocketing upward, I counted down each numbered switchback, glancing occasionally at the wide valley below me, a mix of green and granite gracing every mountainside.

I hadn't always loved climbing hills on my bike. In fact, I'd hated them my entire life. But then, in 2009, I lost all that weight. I'd been riding uphill with the equivalent of a thirty-five-pound dumbbell strapped to my back. In five months, it was gone.

Suddenly I could fly up hills and my view of climbing changed as drastically as my self-image. With that newfound love of scaling mountains, I made a new goal for myself: win the Mount Evans Hill Climb. Set on the third Saturday in July every summer, the race starts in Idaho Springs, Colorado, at 7,500 feet above sea level and finishes at 14,130 feet, on top of Mount Evans, at the end of the highest paved road in North America.

I thought it would be ironic if the kid who constantly got made fun of for being fat could win the amateur Category 3 division. When I first looked at the winning times for my category, coming in at two hours, I couldn't believe it.

My exact words were, *That's not humanly possible.*

Discouraged, I did the race anyway. My time was 2:06.53, less than seven minutes shy of something I said wasn't humanly possible. The following year I got second place with a time of 2:01.10.

For the next two summers, I trained and trained, alone, often with my bicycle panniers filled with cement as I scaled Fort Collins's most infamous climbs. I never went out to eat or drink with friends, fearing I'd gain weight at restaurants which have no compunction about loading up their menus with notorious amounts of unnecessary calories.

In the summer of 2013, at 128 pounds, I finally attained the glorious amateur Category 3, Men's 35+, Colorado State Hill Climb Champion title.

In the years that followed, I wondered what the point of all my training was, spending one summer after the next starving myself, placing a priority on staying thin over maintaining friendships. I became so fixated on a singular objective that I didn't realize how lonely I'd become.

I achieved my goal and lost a lot more in return.

Today, however, I shook those opportunity costs from my mind. I loved to climb, and here I was scaling one of the most famous roads in Europe. Today, cycling up Alpe d'Huez, I wasn't going to let myself ponder such existential issues.

Today was all about the exhilaration of every single switchback and savoring every single moment of an activity I used to bemoan. I grinned through every painful turn of the pedals.

*****

I spent my last evening in France at a campground in the city of Aix-les-Bains, where unruly teenagers kept me up all night. Just as I fell asleep, crows and encroaching sunlight woke me. I got out of my sleeping bag, packed my things, and left before anyone else was awake.

I dragged myself through rolling hills that gradually became bigger and bigger, with steep descents and ascents of two and three miles. At the crest of one insidious climb I could see, in the distance, the giant fountain of Lake Geneva shooting into the air.

I had made it, *inshallah*.

CHAPTER 5

"Hi."

"Hi."

Big hug. Kiss. Another hug. Another kiss.

"How was the flight?" I asked.

"Tolerable," said Kendra. "I barely had time to get through the Frankfurt Airport."

"Delayed in Denver?"

"Of course."

"But you're here now."

I smiled and grabbed Kendra's hand. Our farewell at Denver International Airport twenty-six days prior had been a tearful one. It was the first time since 2003, when I left to do my graduate research in Belize, that we'd said goodbye to one another for an extended period.

Despite the tears, it was oddly refreshing to add some new emotional dimension to our marriage after so many steady years that seemed to drift from one to the next.

But it was even better to see her again.

We navigated our way from the yellow-trimmed baggage claim area to the train station. Compared to the gear I unpacked in Lisbon, Kendra's carry-on backpack and rolling suitcase were far more conventional.

We sat close together on the short train ride.

"How was your ride into Geneva yesterday?" Kendra asked.

"It was … eventful," I said. "I was riding into the city and got stuck in a traffic jam. I hopped onto the sidewalk and pedaled past the cars."

I paused, replaying events in my head. Kendra's eyes were intent on me.

"I came to a blind driveway," I said. "I slowed down and peered to my right. When I saw it was clear, I kept going. And then …"

I held up my left arm and gingerly ran my right hand under it.

"When I looked forward, it was too late. A woman had opened the passenger door of a parked car. I swerved to the right, but not fast enough. I crashed into the door."

I pulled up my sleeve to reveal a long purple bruise on my left triceps. "My arm took most of the blow. But my bike is OK!"

Kendra leaned in to inspect the damage.

"The woman said something in French. She had a horrified expression on her face. I shook out my arm and nothing appeared broken, so I gave a little wave and kept riding. It hurt so bad that I debated going to the hospital. But that seemed like a big hassle."

The train approached our station. We stepped off the car. "Even though I was in utter pain," I said, "I cruised to the waterfront and asked a kid from Korea to take my photo in front of the water fountain."

Kendra rolled her eyes. "You're considering going to the hospital and instead stop for a picture?"

"Uh, yeah! I made it to Geneva!"

We continued catching up on the short walk to our apartment building. I pulled out the key I'd gotten from the owner a day earlier and opened the door. We'd booked the place on Airbnb and hadn't noticed that our ninth-floor apartment didn't have air-conditioning. Geneva was not known for hot summers, but our visit coincided with the worst heat wave in recent memory.

With the windows open, the breeze cooled the apartment, and we had ample space for our things, including my Soma. We were also close to the World Health Organization, where Kendra had scheduled meetings to find practicum sites for her graduate students.

The next morning, we walked to the nearest bus stop. Kendra examined the schedule and determined which bus she would need to take to her first appointment. Then, both feeling the need for a little exercise, we hiked the entire route, past various United Nations offices and ending at the World Health Organization, a nine-story building resembling a glass beehive.

I was more than content to walk. I could ride my bike next to buses in any locale, and yell at the drivers when they cut me off, but I rarely considered taking one anywhere. I was scared of doing something wrong, like paying incorrectly or missing a stop. I was impressed that Kendra could show up in a foreign country and figure out how to ride them. She was far braver than me.

We spent the afternoon walking through the city, admiring architecture ranging from medieval, Romanesque, and neoclassical to the somewhat comical apartment blocks in the Grottes district, where buildings ballooned in Daliesque fashion with no parallel or perpendicular lines.

We ate dinner in a small park next to Lake Geneva, something we never did back home. We spread out an assortment of bread, cheese, ham, olives, and veggies on a towel. I popped the cork on a bottle of wine, the familiar sound followed by the scent of red Rhône.

"Drinking in a public park. Can't do this back in the States!" I declared.

I handed Kendra a plastic cup. We toasted our good fortune and enjoyed the scenery.

Over the next four days, Kendra visited potential practicum sites while I rode my bicycle in the French countryside. Our plans from the previous year had worked out, in a slightly unexpected way.

From Geneva, we went to Rupperswil, Switzerland, where we visited Alex, a friend of mine from Leicester. He was German and, like me, had studied in England as an exchange student. Having lost touch for a number of years, Alex and I reconnected on Facebook. I knew he was married and had a few children, but beyond that I knew little about his life.

We navigated our enormous black diesel Opel station wagon to his home, following the directions he had texted. My Soma lay flat in the back of the car, fuming over the humiliation of driving anywhere. I, however, was quite content to cruise along the freeway at the touch of an automobile pedal, a novelty after tenaciously pushing my bicycle pedals up innumerable hills in the past three weeks.

We turned into Alex's modest Swiss neighborhood, full of suburban detached homes with fenced-in yards and garages. It was so familiar and so different from our neighborhood in Colorado. We parked in the driveway and knocked on the front door.

"Hallo!" said Alex, reaching out to shake my hand and pulling me in for a hug.

"It's so good to see you!" I said. "This is my wife, Kendra."

"Nice to meet you," said Alex. "Please come in."

Alex showed us through his spacious two-story home and led us outside. Deep green grass covered the backyard and a variety of vegetables sprang to life in fertile plots of soil. Flowers bloomed along a wooden fence.

"My wife will be home soon," Alex said as we walked back into his house.

"What does your wife do?" asked Kendra.

"She's a nurse, in intensive care."

I remembered visiting Alex in Switzerland, in 1996, after leaving Leicester. An image of him at the hospital, where he was doing his medical residency, resurfaced in my head. He was so young in those days. Now, he had a beard and his hair was showing signs of gray. He held both in a regal way. Age had been good to him, and I hoped he thought the same about me.

"I'll show you to your room. I need to get my son and daughter from day care soon. You're welcome to come along. It's around the corner."

"Certainly," I said, somewhat curious to see a Swiss day care. "Grab us before you go."

Kendra and I unpacked our things and settled in for a one-night stay. A few minutes later, Alex knocked on the door. We walked a few blocks with him to the day care, housed in a small brick building that blended with the surrounding homes.

Inside, the sound of kids crying and cooing flooded our ears. The whole scenario could have played out in any country anywhere, but here in Switzerland it held a certain mundane fascination for me.

Alex's wife, Irene, was at the house when we returned. She had picked up their eldest daughter, who looked at Kendra and me with bashful eyes, unsure what to make of the strangers in her home.

Alex fired up the backyard grill and soon we were sitting around the dinner table eating brats and burgers. Alex and I reminisced, telling our wives about our many adventures in England, from hikes in the countryside to the time we ran from a group of drunken English college students. It felt refreshing to be surrounded by family and friends. It had been a long time since I'd had dinner with a group of people.

You need to do a better job at maintaining friendships.

'It is easy to let them slip away.'

I considered how lives can come together so closely for a time and then drift apart again.

I pushed those thoughts out of my head and rejoined the conversation, savoring the company and the moment of normalcy.

We left the next morning, out of Rupperswil and out of Switzerland, passing the next few days in random towns in Germany and Austria before arriving at our planned destination of Slovenia. We spent a week there, first in Bled, a small town with a castle overlooking a picturesque lake, and the remainder of our time in Ratez, surrounded by Slovenia's wine country.

I rode my bike each morning and Kendra went for a walk. We spent our afternoons sightseeing like conventional people and eating at restaurants. I was grateful European portions were smaller than their American counterparts.

As the days passed, yellow and purple bruising materialized up and down my left triceps, a reminder of my incident with the car door and a reminder that I would soon return to my bicycle trip.

After a relaxing week in Slovenia, we started our return to Geneva, across northern Italy. "Are You With Me," by Lost Frequencies, blared from the speakers of our Opel as we sped down the Italian freeway.

We found a small, quirky hotel in the town of Sirmione our first night, a few blocks from the massive Lago di Garda, a tourist destination that we haphazardly discovered. Our host was an aging woman as fascinating as the strange paintings that graced the hallways. Between my rudimentary Spanish and her Italian, we communicated well.

"We lucked out on this place," I said to Kendra over dinner, a meal of assorted seafood within sight of the lake. "And the parking was easy."

We hadn't booked any rooms for our three-day return to Geneva, instead trusting to fate that things would work out. The next day we circumnavigated Milan and drove into the Alps, certain we'd find a pleasant place to stay. As the day wore on, our hopes diminished.

We entered a valley with mountains towering on both sides. While the views were pretty, lodging was limited. As the sun disappeared behind distant peaks, the stress of our failure became apparent. We approached a random motel next to the highway and its traffic. A small village sat on the other side of a rapid, narrow river, accessible via an old stone bridge.

It was too late to keep going, so we checked in. Neither of us said much as we unpacked our belongings. Our room was austere, but comfortable, with two twin beds and an en suite bathroom. Outside the window, we could see the valley and the highway snaking its way through myriad turns and bends. We could also hear the incessant traffic.

Nonetheless, the small village held a certain allure in the early evening light. Pastel buildings, painted in shades of white and yellow, offset the shrub-covered granite cliffs. At the top sat the ruins of a fifteenth-century castle, a single tower and crumbling wall visible for miles. A path arched upward from town, winding its way along the hillside to the castle.

"Let's check it out," I said, eager to leave the spartan hotel room and the sounds of cars driving past our window.

Kendra nodded.

We navigated through the narrow streets and found a footpath that started underneath someone's laundry line and went steeply up, between two apartment buildings. Within moments, we were above the town, peering down on brown clay roofs and the river making its way down the valley. Our hotel took on its own majestic image the further up we walked.

Despite the steep ascent, we made it to the castle in fifteen minutes and were soon exploring the ruins.

"This would be a perfect place for dinner tomorrow!" I exclaimed. "We could have a final picnic full of our usual food."

"That's not a bad idea," Kendra admitted.

After touring nearby towns the next day, we once again ascended the path to the castle and spread out our assortment of ham, cheese, bread, olives, and wine.

Evening set in and we ate our meal in the ruins of the fifteenth-century structure. The valley reflected the rays of the descending sun, and soon we forgot about every other aspect of our lives, even the fact that Kendra would be returning home in two days.

"And we didn't even plan this one," I pointed out. "I think this may be the best dinner I've ever had with anyone."

Kendra smiled. "Agreed."

"The best-laid schemes ... or lack thereof."

We finished our meal and found a comfortable spot to sit. Kendra leaned into my arms so we could both take in the views, together.

Two days later, Kendra and I posed for a photo in the lobby of our hotel in Geneva. In the picture, Kendra is standing in civilian clothes, suitcase in hand, ready to fly home. I'm holding my Soma, decked out in full cycling gear, ready to ride south and west, to rendezvous with the Tour de France.

After taking the photo, I leaned my bike against the wall outside. We hugged a final time, a long one that didn't ease the pain of the impending separation.

"It's only two and a half more weeks," I said with forced enthusiasm.

"It'll go quick."

I could tell she was trying to sound upbeat.

"Good luck meeting up with the Tour," she added. "I hope you find a good spot to watch it."

"I'll take lots of pictures for you."

"I can't wait to see them."

We looked at each other.

"Well ..."

"I'm going to head over to the shuttle," said Kendra. "Be careful. No more running into car doors."

"I won't." I tried to smile.

"Bye. Love you."

"Love you too."

One more hug.

I grabbed my bike and swung my leg over the saddle. I gave Kendra a final wave before I turned the corner and was out of sight, navigating my way out of Geneva the same way that I had come in.

CHAPTER 6

I'm not into sports. I've always hated watching football, baseball, or basketball on TV. It's made for some awkward conversations over the years.

Professional cycling is the only sport I enjoy, perhaps because I started racing my bike at fifteen and understand its tactical complexities, or because I've read books about individual riders and know their backstories, sacrifices, and occasional moral failings. Whatever the reason, today I was willing to wait five hours to witness a stage of the greatest cycling race on the planet.

I parked on an uphill stretch of road outside the small city of Aubenas, France, a two-day ride southwest of Geneva. Scores of fans lined the hill, waiting in anticipation. To pass the time, I read, strolled along a creek, and watched a family play a heated game of Pétanque. They cheered each time someone tossed a metal ball into an imaginary circle.

Finally, the Tour arrived. Cars and trucks, adorned with mascots ranging from stuffed animals to a man pedaling a stationary bike, drove past the crowd. Fans rushed to the side of the road to catch the hats, candy, bracelets and other souvenirs tossed from the vehicles. At the end of the parade, a car sporting a giant lion, the symbol of the Tour de France, materialized and disappeared over the hill.

Ten minutes later, a breakaway of ten riders cruised past, followed by the peloton, the main field of riders. I glimpsed the race's leader, Chris Froome, in the yellow jersey. The sound of shifting gears and spinning wheels hummed through my ears. The crowd cheered.

After the peloton came the team vehicles, logos splattered over their hoods. Countless wheels sat on top of every car, waiting to assist riders with flats or other mechanical issues.

A few straggling cyclists struggled up the hill ahead of the broom wagon, the final vehicle in the show that had a literal broom attached to it. Altogether, the spectacle lasted thirty minutes.

'Well that was worth riding two hundred miles out of our way!' I declared.

It's amazing you could sit around for half the day.

I gathered my things and squeezed past a traffic jam that stretched for miles. I was soon pedaling through rolling hills dotted with pine trees that reached into the evening horizon. Groves of lavender lined the road, delighting my eyes and nose, and a tailwind propelled me toward northern France.

I was aiming for Normandy, where I would catch a ferry to England. I covered five hundred miles in four days, thanks to favorable winds and the incapacity to stop riding. I stayed my final night in France in Port-en-Bessin, seven miles east of the Normandy American Cemetery on Omaha Beach.

That evening, after emailing Kendra, I walked to the bluffs above town where German bunkers and artillery mounts sat in measured silence. I planted myself on a patch of grass atop a small cliff overlooking the coast. I pulled up Pink Floyd's *The Wall* on my Sansa MP3 player and listened to the entire album while trying to comprehend the horrors of the Allied invasion of Normandy.

Finally, you're relaxing.

'If pondering the Battle of Normandy while listening to *The Wall* is relaxing, then yes.'

Still, you're taking a moment to sit down and think about things.

'We've been thinking about things nonstop since we started pedaling. When do we not think?'

Yes, but you're thinking while sitting. Like people are supposed to do.

The first drops of rain put a quick end to the pointless conversation. I didn't want to leave, but I didn't want to get wet either. I took one last look at the German artillery bunker. The soldiers who manned them didn't have the choice to simply clear out when the weather became unpleasant. I reached my hotel as raindrops started finding their way through the fabric of my clothes.

The next morning, I left my gear in my room and rode seven miles west to Omaha Beach and the Normandy American Cemetery. It was humbling to be surrounded by the perfectly aligned crosses, and I reflected on the sacrifice made by the souls who lay beneath the sea of white marble.

I walked to the beach where people rode horses, flew kites, and enjoyed the sandy beauty of the tragic place. Granules of sand slid between my toes as I walked toward the water. I dipped my feet in the Atlantic, the frigid water sending minor shock waves through my system and waking my senses.

I returned to my hotel, packed, and headed toward the city of Ouistreham, where I planned to catch a ferry to Portsmouth, England.

What time do the ferries leave?

'No idea.'

What if they're full? What if they don't leave until tomorrow? You need to find a bicycle box to fly your bike home. You need to figure out where you're staying in England. You need to …

The front end of my Soma started wobbling. The chatter ceased. A knot formed in my stomach. I slowed down and dragged my bicycle onto the sidewalk, glad the gray skies hadn't produced any rain.

I pulled off the front right pannier, which was hanging oddly, and saw that a two-inch, stamped metal mounting bracket on my front rack had snapped. Without the bracket, I couldn't attach the rack, and without the rack, I couldn't attach a pannier. I examined the damage, saw that half of the bracket was usable, and screwed the now-too-short piece back into place, leaving the rack pointed awkwardly, but functionally, upward.

Don't forget to bring spare brackets next year!

'Noted.'

I arrived in Ouistreham at noon and headed straight to the ferry terminal where I learned that the next boat wasn't leaving until eight in the evening. I bought my tickets and then found a campground where, for two euros, I was able to shower and wash my clothes.

Since I now had wet clothes, I found a park not far from the terminal. I strung up a clothesline over a picnic table, hung my things to dry, and hoped that no overzealous police officers would tell me to take them down.

While my clothes were drying, I called my dad. He still lived in Lansing, Michigan, in my childhood home, but also owned a condo near my brother, north of Grand Rapids. He'd purchased it shortly after I'd left for Colorado.

"Hi, Dad, it's Tom."

"Ohhhh, hiii, Tom."

My dad had a particular way of greeting me when I called. He dragged out the "Oh" and ever so slightly did the same with the "Hi."

"Where are you?"

"I'm in Ouistreham, France, in Normandy, about ten miles east of Omaha Beach. I visited the cemetery there."

"Is that the one where all the American soldiers are buried?"

His question surprised me. I inherited my love of history and geography from him. I expected him to know the significance of Omaha Beach.

"Yes. It was amazing. There's so much history there. Now I'm waiting for a ferry to England."

"You're heading back to England? Have you been there since college?"

"Only once, and only to London, in 2002. When I came back from the Peace Corps."

"Oh, right. Well, it will be good to go back, I'm sure."

I waited for him to ask how the riding had been going, but he didn't. He loved bicycling as much as me, even if his leisurely rides rarely took him more than a few miles from home. I got a vague sense that he didn't remember I was on a bicycle trip. After an unusual moment of silence, I changed the subject.

"How are things back in Michigan?" I asked.

"Oh, they're fine. I'm keeping busy. I still take Avery and the triplets to school and other activities. I'm up at the condo a lot."

Avery, fourteen, was my oldest niece. The triplets were three years younger.

"I'm sure the kids like having grandpa around. How's everything with the condo?"

"It's fine," my dad said, "but I'm having trouble with my computer. When I try to use my email, it keeps saying I have the wrong password. It keeps changing."

"Maybe you've forgotten it?"

"No, I'm pretty sure they're changing it."

I wasn't sure who "they" were. "You could write your password down," I suggested, "but keep it safe if you do."

"I suppose," my dad replied with a confused tone.

"I'm taking an overnight ferry," I said, changing the subject again. "I'll sleep on the boat."

"Very good! You won't need a hotel tonight."

"Yeah, hopefully I'll get some sleep."

I glanced at my drying clothes.

"I should go," I said. "I have to take care of my laundry. I'll call you again from Colorado."

"Have a good trip," said my dad.

"Bye."

I hung up, thought momentarily about my dad's passwords, then turned my attention to the pseudo campground I'd set up in the park. Ominous clouds approached from the west and I was again thankful it wasn't raining. When my clothes were dry, I packed them, strolled around town, found a grocery store, and otherwise kept myself occupied.

When boarding time arrived, I was ushered to the motorcycle entrance where I took a remarkable picture of my bicycle surrounded by motorcycles. Half were streamlined sport bikes and half were old-school European motorcycles. The owners were just as diverse, with a group of young college-age men hovering next to their high-speed machines and grungy, older English guys standing near their collector's bikes.

I smiled.

I love it when I'm so out of place I can't even try to fit in.

*****

The boat hummed beneath me and small waves crashed against the hull as I watched the coast of France disappear. A faint scent of rain blew from the west where massive storm clouds flashed with lightning and lumbered eastward.

Within minutes, raindrops engulfed the ship and I retired to my room, which resembled the inside of a movie theater. Rows of plush chairs faced forward, but no one sat in them. Instead, passengers reclined in dark corners, or on entire rows of seats, in anticipation of the long night ahead. I did the same and was soon lulled to sleep by the rocking movement of the boat.

In the morning I brushed my teeth and went to the deck where I saw the coast of England fast approaching under patchy clouds.

'We're coming home.'

I thought back to my days in Leicester. England holds a certain malaise, a certain cloudy mood emanating from its stoic brick buildings and manicured greenery. Sometimes I feel like I fit in better with the melancholy of England than the bright sunshine of Colorado, where there seems to be a certain expectation that you remain upbeat and outgoing.

As the boat pulled into the dock, I thought about this summer's finish line, envisioning my bicycle in front of a large sign at London Heathrow Airport. It was less than a week away.

I was in high spirits as I disembarked the ferry. I approached the border patrol station with my passport in hand, expecting a warm welcome. Instead, the agent glared at me.

"Where have you been traveling?"

"Well, um, France, and Spain, and ..." A list of all the places I'd visited over the summer rushed through my head. "Switzerland," I added, leaving out at least five other countries.

The guard drilled me with more questions, each more accusatory than the last. Then he asked something unexpected.

"Where are you planning to stay?"

"I figured I would find something."

He raised an eyebrow and gave a faint, bemused smile. "You are aware that school just got out yesterday for the holidays? You'll be lucky to find a room anywhere."

"Oh," I said. I hadn't expected my good fortune running out. "I'll figure something out. It's early yet."

"Suit yourself." The agent shrugged and stamped my passport.

I was home again.

I headed north, passing out of Portsmouth and into the proper English countryside, where I passed a white sign with bold letters that read "World's End. Please Drive Safely."

In the midafternoon, I reached Winchester, home of the fabled round table of King Arthur. I checked several hotels, but at each one I was told, "Sorry, mate, we're full."

Clouds from the west signaled impending rain. At a chain hotel on the outskirts of the city, a sympathetic receptionist was kind enough to call a few hotels in the area for me. She found one ten miles away with one room left. I thanked her and dashed out of the building.

An hour later, I rolled up to a solitary brick inn situated next to the highway. I checked into a pleasant room and, after unpacking, hopped on my bike and cruised a few miles to the nearest pub.

'It's about time we had some proper English beer!'

I ordered the maltiest ale they had, savoring every sip even as I calculated that it contained three hundred calories. I read the menu multiple times, but the only thing that looked appetizing was the fish-and-chips.

You're going to be that American who orders fish-and-chips at an English pub, aren't you?

'What else is there?' I countered.

I ordered it, against my inner rumblings, and was disappointed when it arrived. It was a high-quality dish, not the sketchy side-of-the-road fish-and-chips I'd hoped for, the greasy meal from my past that I'd scarf down at eleven at night after a rainy Leicester evening at pubs with my friends.

Nonetheless, it was my first warm meal in days. I ate every bite.

Back in my room, I got online and researched where to go next. I settled on the town of Stroud, in the Cotswolds region. With its rolling hills and stone fences, it seemed like a nice place to spend a few nights, and I'd never been to that area of England before.

I went to bed proud I'd booked a room in advance.

The next morning, even with my hood pulled over my head, and my helmet on over that, I could feel the cold drops of rain pounding down.

Why did you book a nonrefundable room sixty miles away?

I put on my winter gloves, which had sat scrunched at the bottom of a pannier the entire summer. I watched my exhale condense in front of my face, glanced back at the cozy little inn, and pushed forward into the drizzle.

Flying down hilly, narrow English roads with cars gliding past my right side under a steady rain that soaked everything wasn't my idea of fun, but I had a tailwind the entire way, making the trip tolerable and quick.

I entered Stroud under rainy gray skies. Pavement curved in every direction and green pastures dotted the surrounding hillsides, interspersed with redbrick row houses and postindustrial factories. My hotel, an old, dreary building six stories tall, was next to the railway station. I watched people enter the depot and contemplated sitting in a warm train for the final push to London.

Instead, I locked my grime-covered bike outside my hotel, checked in, and rushed upstairs. My room was clean and modern, and I immediately turned on the shower, waiting for the water to heat. I'd been dreaming of a hot shower all day.

My smile disappeared as the water didn't get beyond warm. After four hours of riding in the cold, English drizzle, I got a tepid shower to thaw my bones.

I spent three nights in Stroud, and the typical English angst I remember from my time living in Leicester hit straight away. Usually I enjoy being by myself; I love the solitude. Here, though, I felt a slight tinge of loneliness too, but that bittersweet kind which is so typical of me. If ever there was a place that personified my character, it was this random town of Stroud, England, a place I'd never heard of twenty-four hours earlier.

The rain let up the next two days, and I was able to ride a few times through the not-so-gentle rolling hills. I hiked a few times as well, happy to be on English trails again, with their signs that led through people's property and down hidden staircases through town and into beautiful stretches of countryside.

Stroud was one of those in-between towns that I like to experience, a real kind of place most tourists will never visit.

Yet I had my doubts.

Why don't you want to go to the warm places that everyone else goes to? Who travels somewhere and pays to be miserable?

I sighed when those questions materialized, again and again, and wished that I wanted to go to all those pleasant locales and relax. And yet, I was happy here, in my own overcast kind of way.

I couldn't figure it out.

*****

Two days later I rolled up to a "Welcome to Heathrow" sign. I had ridden from Lisbon to London via northern Morocco and Geneva, touring 3,057 miles in thirty-eight days.

I stayed at the Marriot next to the airport for three nights. It was inexpensive by London standards, and next to a tube station. From my hotel window I watched, transfixed, as one plane after the next came in for a landing. I understood the plane-spotters in the area, people who would stand for hours recording the various planes descending from every corner of the globe.

My first day in London, I found a sporting goods store where I procured a bicycle box to carry my Soma home. I walked the mass of cardboard a mile back to my hotel under a rare sunlit sky, questioning how I would find a bicycle box the following summer in a country where no one spoke English.

After securing the container in my room, I went to another store and bought a duffle bag to bring the rest of my gear back to Colorado. It was a far simpler task, but one I knew I'd have to repeat in the years to come.

In the ensuing days, I settled into a routine, cycling in the morning and sightseeing in the afternoon. I revisited my favorite places, including Hyde Park, Covent Garden, St.

Martin-in-the-Fields church, and the Bag O'Nails pub near the Victoria bus station.

Most importantly, I visited the streets around St. Paul's Cathedral. When I arrived in England in 1995, at the age of nineteen, I stayed at a nearby hostel. I would walk down to the River Thames daily to think about my new predicament, about being abroad for the first time, alone, and going to a new university in Leicester.

Across the Thames sat the massive, decommissioned Bankside Power Station, its single smokestack, composed of blackened brick, towering above the river. It was designed by Giles Gilbert Scott, the same architect behind the Battersea Power Station on the rail line to Gatwick Airport, made famous by the album cover of Pink Floyd's *Animals*.

Back in 1995, I thought the Bankside Power Station would make a fitting art gallery. In 1999, the building was, in fact, turned into the Tate Modern Art Gallery, and the Millennium Bridge was constructed so pedestrians could easily access it from the north side of the river.

Underworld's "Born Slippy," the trance anthem for the film *Trainspotting*, reverberated through my headphones as I gazed at the scenic stretch of the river. The song had become one of my favorites in the spring of 1996, and now here I was nineteen years later, sitting in the same spot, listening to the same music, almost as though I hadn't grown or matured one little bit despite all the lives that had transpired since then.

Bass and vocals battered my eardrums. I swayed with the synthesizers of Underworld's classic sounds, feeling like I was twenty again, my head swirling with possibilities. I thought of the summers to come and the roads ahead.

I grinned. Even at thirty-nine, there was still a lot of life left in me.

I was no longer a middle-aged guy rambling on about a dream. I wasn't going to sit idly by and watch life dissipate in front of my eyes. I was already plotting a course for the following summer and was already stressing about how far I could make it.

'To Istanbul?'

Maybe.

'To Georgia?'

Hardly.

At the end of it all stood Shanghai, its glorious skyline filling the night. I knew if I could ride there, making it the rest of the way around the world was a foregone conclusion. I was going to find that elusive something, that answer to it all, that epiphany, somewhere out there. I just needed to get to Shanghai.

Thinking about the summers ahead left me stressed and worried, but the stress felt good and the worry felt good. It was like the start of a bike race—one foot clipped into a pedal, heart pounding, wondering if I'd crash and how painful it would be, hoping I'd make top ten, or maybe even win. The uncertainty fueled me.

I knew that next June, I'd waltz through the airport of some foreign country with my helmet casually hanging off a pannier that was strapped across my shoulder, not unlike Don Quixote carrying his silly lance.

I'd be someone again. I'd have purpose again. Things were only going to get better from here.

I was sure of it.

Unpacking the Soma, Lisbon International Airport

East of Tangiers, Morocco

The windmills of La Mancha, Consuegra, Spain

Suze-la-Rousse, France

Picnic dinner in northern Italy

Boarding the ferry, Ouistreham, France

PART II: 2015-2016

Music differs from travel.
When you travel, you are trying to get somewhere.
In music, though, one doesn't make the end of the composition, the point
of the composition. If that were so, the best conductors would be those
who played the fastest, and there would be composers who wrote only
finales. People would go to concerts just to hear one crackling cord,
because that's the end.
Same with dancing. You don't aim at a particular spot in the room
because that's where you should arrive.
The whole point of the dancing is the dance.

-Alan Watts

CHAPTER 7

A month after returning home, I was back in the classroom, standing in front of a new group of students. But they weren't looking at me—they were looking at each other. I could hear them whispering.

"Do you think he notices?"

"I don't know. He hasn't said anything."

"Maybe he's mad."

"Maybe he doesn't realize we have on fake musta …"

"Pull out your papers from yesterday," I said. "Can one of you summarize the passage we read?"

I turned to a student directly in front of me. "How about you?"

She looked back at me, unable to speak. Small giggles emanated from the smile on her face. She tried to cover the paper mustache taped to her lip.

I glared at her.

The other students snickered, their mustaches hanging at odd angles on their faces.

"Well?" I said, shaking my head and suppressing a smile.

The student paused for a moment before announcing, "Mr. Sweeney, we're wearing mustaches!"

My eyes widened in mock surprise.

"I thought there was something different about you!"

The kids laughed, and I smiled one of my rare, genuine smiles.

I imagined myself at a staff meeting in a professional boardroom where the adults had surreptitiously put on paper mustaches, secretly hoping their boss would notice.

"That was a good one!" I said. "Now can we get back to summarizing the text?"

I can't say I did my best at fostering academic growth that morning, but it was moments like these that made me love teaching. Most days, I enjoyed coming to school, a good thing because Sarah Milner Elementary was where I spent the bulk of my life, my real life, not the silly summer adventures floating through my imagination.

This year I had twenty-three generally well-behaved students on my roster. My teaching partner, Clara, had a similar number.

Watching the fifth graders play outside at recess one afternoon, Clara remarked, "They're so rough with each other. But they never complain about getting hurt."

"They're resilient," I replied.

"And hard workers."

"And fun. They have a tight bond."

Clara nodded.

"This is like a rest year," I joked. "An opportunity to recover from some previous ones. I'm going to enjoy it while it lasts!"

Clara smiled. "Me too."

We watched the kids play a few more minutes before pulling out our respective whistles and calling them inside in one tandem motion.

Clara had come to Sarah Milner the previous school year. She had succeeded Denise, who had been my teaching partner for two years. Denise had stepped in after Robbie, my partner for two years, retired. And Robbie had followed Ursula and Suzette, who had been my teaching partners my first year at Sarah Milner, after I left my previous team at Lincoln Elementary so many years earlier.

Clara and I had similar approaches to teaching, blending social studies and science content into reading and writing instruction. We both believed in challenging kids to think for themselves, to advocate for themselves, and to be curious about the world.

Most importantly, Clara had a good sense of humor. In a job where data matters, every minute counts, and you're always upsetting someone, laughter is key to long-term survival. Meetings with Clara were always productive and hilarious.

We worked closely with Laura, our fifth-grade paraprofessional, who helped small groups of students in both of our classrooms. Rounding out the team this fall was my first student teacher, Jerod. Mature, even-keeled, and confident, he contradicted every image I'd ever had of a millennial. Sometimes, I thought he acted more like an adult than I did. He was everything I was not at that age.

I loved being around my students and my team. Sarah Milner felt like home, even if my mind was always somewhere else.

Of course, my job wasn't all roses and sunshine. I was a teacher, after all, and that meant I was torn in twenty directions at any given moment. The second the bell rang, all insanity broke loose. I had to check homework, smile graciously at the picture someone had to show me at that exact moment, do attendance, remind students to turn in a permission slip, talk to the parent who popped in to ask something I had emailed about the day before, and start class.

For someone who had a hard time sitting still, a hard time slowing down and enjoying the scenery, the constant jump from one thing to the next left me bewildered. And yet, over the years, it also became my normal. I didn't feel right if I wasn't doing ten things at once, even on my days off.

It didn't help that I spent every spare moment burning off my excess calories. I was up by five every morning and, after showering, I stepped directly into my cycling gear so I was ready to ride the moment I left the bathroom.

By five thirty, I was on my indoor bicycle trainer in my garage. I had built a computer stand over it so I could work and pedal simultaneously. I was out the door by six for my hour-long bicycle commute to work. My return home took another hour or more. Most days, I wasn't home until five thirty in the evening. If I could eke out another hundred calories here and there, I would, and those extra minutes added up.

I hadn't missed a day cycling to school in four years, regardless of the weather or temperature. I put in 150 miles on a slow week, with plenty of climbing. For most of my cycling life, I'd focused on intervals and speed training to prep for local races. Now, I simply rode, day after day, in anticipation of summer trips when I would ride for weeks on end at a measured, steady pace.

My weekends became a mess of things I had to do, a limitless list of unnecessary necessities that amounted to nothing important. It always started with sitting on my indoor bicycle trainer. On my computer, I'd open ten tabs, ordering something from Amazon while simultaneously looking up the lyrics to a new song before checking the weather. Then I'd jump to the latest headlines on BBC News before resuming my work on a social studies unit or entering grades. By eleven, I'd go out for an actual ride before returning home to do housework or run errands.

To relax, I'd read four books concurrently because I couldn't focus on any of them for more than a few minutes. Even sitting still, I couldn't sit still.

Every weekend, the same conversation would replay.

You need to call Russ.

'I know. We should text him.'

But he might want to do something.

I knew if Russ wanted to do something, I wouldn't be able to ride and burn off my calories.

'Good point. Except that we should go out with friends. Remember that article?'

I'd recently read another report about the importance of strong social networks. According to several studies, people with solid community support live longer than people who are alone.

You should text Russ now.

'We should.'

I hesitated.

But you can't let the fatness return.

My Excel spreadsheet loomed heavy in my mind. I couldn't disrupt my routine.

'Let's get in touch next weekend.'

But next weekend rarely came. I couldn't deal with the uncertainty of it. I had to burn calories, and to do that I had to keep riding. I ceased going out with whatever friends I had left. Instead, I threw "likes" at their posts on Facebook. It seemed like an adequate substitute for the real thing.

*****

In December, I turned forty. When I walked into my classroom that morning, my desk was covered with confetti. A giant "40" hung on the wall. Post-it notes were everywhere, each with strange equations written by fifth-grade hands. They all equaled forty: $2 + 5 = 40$, $6 \times 9 = 40$, $(7 - 8) + 4 = 40$.

In my periphery, I detected a pair of eyes peering around the corner of my classroom door and heard muted laughter. I turned.

"I waited so long for you to leave yesterday!" announced Clara.

I thought back to our conversation, after school, when she asked me when I was going home.

"That's why you were asking! It wasn't because you hoped I'd go home early and enjoy my evening?"

"Not entirely," she replied.

"Sorry I kept you waiting. You really outdid yourself."

"I had to find a way for the kids to wish you a happy fortieth birthday!"

"You'll be there soon enough," I retorted. "I hope you're around so I can return the favor."

Clara grinned and I smiled. It was a nice surprise.

Despite the angst I'd been feeling the previous year, I didn't view myself as old. I was younger than most of the Sarah Milner staff and I'd ridden across half of Europe. I commuted to school by bicycle, twelve miles each way, through every kind of weather imaginable.

Forty didn't fit with my self-image.

"Just make sure the kids don't sing 'Happy Birthday' to me."

"We'll see," said Clara as she laughed her way out the door.

A few weeks after the birthday incident, as his student-teaching placement at Sarah Milner was coming to an end, Jerod announced he was applying to teaching jobs in Colorado, Arizona, and through the Peace Corps. I wasted no time writing recommendation letters. I remembered being his age, fresh out of college, ready to start the next chapter in my life.

As I typed, it dawned on me that I would never make decisions of that magnitude again. My days hopping lives were done. I doubted Kendra and I would ever leave Fort Collins, on to a new adventure.

Maybe you are getting older, I thought.

I couldn't shake that notion as Kendra and I made our annual Christmas drive to Michigan under typically bleak and gray skies.

I noted the leafless tree branches when we pulled into the driveway of my dad's condo, swaying in the December wind. Frigid temperatures muted the scents of home.

We knocked on the door before turning the knob and walking inside.

"Ohhhh, hellooo," my dad said as we entered his condo, the tuft of black hair on his receding hairline standing on end. "Tom! Kendra! How are you? How was the drive?"

"Traffic wasn't too bad," said Kendra.

"But the drive was as long as ever," I added. "How are you?"

"Well …," my dad said, "things are mostly fine, although the sliding back door won't open, and the porch on the house in Lansing needs to be painted again."

I examined my father. At eighty-two years old, he was doing well. He managed his own finances, went to church every Sunday, walked four miles each day, and helped with his grandkids. But the years were showing more clearly each time I saw him.

"My computer isn't working," he added.

"What's wrong with it?" I asked.

"I can't log into my email. They keep changing my password."

"Who keeps changing your password?"

"Well, I think it's Yahoo. They keep changing it. My computer keeps changing it."

"So, is it Yahoo or your computer?"

"Well, I don't know." My dad gave a frustrated wave toward his laptop. "It doesn't work. Every time I try to use it, it asks for a password. And I don't remember it."

"Well," I said, "Yahoo is a website. Your computer has a separate password. All your emails are stored elsewhere …" I pointed at the ceiling and beyond. "Wherever Yahoo's servers are located."

My dad stared at me.

I don't think there's much point explaining the cloud to him.

'Didn't we have this conversation with him last summer?'

At that picnic table in France.

"I don't think Yahoo is changing your passwords, or your computer," I pointed out. "Did you write them down anywhere?"

"Well, no. But they keep changing them."

I exhaled slowly.

"Let's look at your computer later," I said, eager to change the subject.

That night, I mentioned the password situation to my brother.

"It might be time to give his laptop to one of the kids," was Kevin's only suggestion.

"I suppose he got by most of his life without one."

We left it at that and set about making plans for the rest of the holiday, deciding what stupid movies we were going to watch together, what time we'd all celebrate Christmas, and when Kendra and I would leave for Omaha to see her parents.

I forgot all about my dad's password situation.

*****

In January, I bought plane tickets to Geneva. I planned to pick up where I left off and return home from Istanbul. I was worried about returning home from Istanbul because I wasn't sure if I could get that far, and because I was apprehensive about going to Turkey in the first place. The previous October, terrorists killed over a hundred people at a peace rally in Ankara, Turkey's capital, and on January 12th a suicide bomber murdered ten tourists in Istanbul.

I booked my tickets anyway.

Despite my hesitation, I couldn't wait to return to Geneva and to my journey, and Turkey wasn't the only country that had suffered suicide attacks in recent months. With that decision made, I turned my attention back to my ordinary life.

I started an online graduate program in March, and between that and teaching the days blurred past, each one a sprint to finish a virtual discussion post or help my fifth graders understand new concepts. I spent my teacher plan time responding to emails, organizing field trips, making copies, and responding to more emails.

Even as school became a haze of assessment and curriculum design, I couldn't stop thinking about flying back to Geneva. I was simultaneously excited and nervous. I wouldn't be meandering across the French countryside this year.

On February 17th, twenty-six soldiers were killed at a traffic light in Ankara, and in March a car bomb there massacred thirty civilians. Another bomb in Istanbul killed four, including two Americans. The civil war in Syria loomed in my mind too.

What would it take for a van to pull up beside you and take you into the heart of ISIS territory?

'Not much,' I acknowledged.

I wondered what Syria was like and pictured my face plastered across CNN while I told the world how well I was being treated.

It didn't help that *Lonely Planet*, my go-to guidebook since I was twenty, pointed out that travelers of both genders reported being sexually assaulted in eastern Turkey.

Going across Turkey is stupid.

'It's either Turkey or Ukraine into Russia. Or just Russia.'

My options were limited.

Please don't camp this summer.

'Agreed.'

In April, I called United Airlines and rebooked my return flight to the United States from Athens, instead of Istanbul. If I did get to Istanbul or, hope beyond hope, made it all the way to Tbilisi, Georgia, I could book a connecting flight to Athens.

I shared all my hopes and fears with Kendra, but when my colleagues asked about my summer plans, I gave evasive answers about flying back to Geneva and heading east, perhaps to Greece. I didn't need the additional pressure of publicly declaring my intentions to ride across places like Turkey that would never come to fruition.

I had enough self-doubt as it was.

*****

Six weeks before school ended, Clara came into my classroom and sat down. I knew what she was going to say. She had moved to Colorado two years earlier and since then home values and rent in the area had skyrocketed, making it difficult for a teacher in Loveland to find a decent, affordable place to live.

"I'm moving back to Washington," she said. "I don't have a choice. It's impossible to stay here and make ends meet."

"I wish things were different," I said. I tried to find comforting words, but I was already thinking about hiring another teaching partner. Clara and I had clicked, and it was going to be hard to replace her.

"I think you'll be happy back in Washington," I said. "Your family's there."

Some days I questioned why I had left Michigan.

"Let me know what I can do to help," I added.

There wasn't much else to say. We had two good years teaching together, fun, productive years.

My principal posted the position for a new fifth-grade teacher.

We interviewed countless potential replacements, but none seemed right. One morning my principal handed me a resume.

"Her name is Rachel," he said. "She's interviewing for second grade, but said she'd be interested in fifth as well. Her principal recommended we interview her."

"All right," I said with a shrug, cursorily glancing at her paperwork. "Let's call her in."

The next day, we offered Rachel the fifth-grade position. She visited Sarah Milner on the last day of school for a whirlwind tour. We agreed to get in touch in July to plan for the coming school year. I said goodbye to her, and a few hours later said a final goodbye to Clara, a scenario that was becoming all too familiar.

That was the last I thought about Clara, or Rachel, or school, for a long while. Instead, I imagined the roads ahead. I worried and fretted and calculated every possible outcome until the day I got on the plane to Geneva.

Only then did all my hopes and fears cease to matter.

I was going to ride east, like I'd told everyone, at least to Athens, perhaps to Turkey, and maybe even to Georgia, *inshallah*.

Tom Sweeney

THE ROUTE: 2016

Daily Log

2016		
June	Miles	Description
Wed 1	114	Geneva to 10 miles west of Brig, great tailwind.
2	104	First 20 miles in 5 hours, to Simplon Pass in the rain, freezing descent into Italy.
3	125	Somma Lombardo to Sermione, Italy, on Lago Garda
4	111	Sermione to Oderzo, Italy; rain all day, but flat
5	115	Oderzo, through Slovenia, ending 5 miles east of Rijeka, Croatia
Mon 6	102	Rikjeka to Vrelo Korenicken, Croatia, in Plitvicka Jezera National Park
7	122	Vrelo K., Croatia, to Banja Luka, Bosnia, jeep trails kept things interesting, as did the mine field
8	102	Banja Luka to Tuzla, Bosnia, swerved because of a dog, almost died, so did the driver
9	132	Officially 1030 miles in 9 days, Tuvla, Bosnia, to just south of Belgrade, Serbia
10	122	Belgrade to Aleksinachi (Aleksinaci?), hot and humid, mostly flat and rolling, some hills
11	127	Aleksinach, Serbia, to Sofia, Bulgaria. Nice tailwind last 30 or so miles
12	119	1400 miles in 12 days, Sofia to Parvomay, Bulgaria
Mon 13	127	Parvomay, Bulgaria, to halfway between Babaeski and Luleburgaz, Turkey, rolling hills
14	105	From the hotel above to the center of Old Town Istanbul, rained on twice; lots of traffic
15	85	Istanbul to Sakarya, Turkey, awesome tailwaind, 50 miles to get out of the Istanbul traffic
16	105	Sakarya to Gerede,s, three passes, hard, felt good. Sea level to approx 5000ft
17	110	Gerede to Tosya, flatted, new front tire at 1905 miles. Winds favorable
18	110	Tosya to Havza, Turkey, flat rear wheel. Feeling the miles now, legs are dragging
19	122	Havza to Fatsa, Turkey, on the Black sea, hills to start, downhill, then 60+ miles flat, headwinds
Mon 20	142	Fatsa to the far side of Trabzon, hotel by the airport
21	136	Flat tailwind, Trabzon airport to just north of Batumi, Georgia, to the Oasis Resort Hotel
22	80	Oasis hotel to Kutaisi, Georgia. Flatted in first four miles. Lots of headwinds
23	94	Kutaisi to Gori; drafted tractor-trailor through tunnel, flatted four miles from end
24	74	Gori to Tbilisi, had to go to the airport before hotel. 2699 miles total. Arrggh.
25		25 miles, around Tbilisi, one of the worst places ever for a bike; then 8 or 9 miles walking
26		"Easy" 8.1 miles straight up, near hotel; then lots of walking and museums again, 675/225.
Mon 27		Ride 28+ miles, south of Tbilisi, then west; then hikeed around Turtle Lake, and to city center
28		Ride to Tsk-something, the 8 mile climb from Sunday; good to have a solid last day on the bike.
29		Recumbant bike, treadmill at Holiday Inn Attica/Athens, Greece, very sluggish
Thurs 30		Recumbant bike, treadmill at H.I. Attica/Athens. 2 hours walking around Athens.

CHAPTER 8

I arrived at Geneva International Airport bleary-eyed but ready to ride. I changed into my cycling clothes in a bathroom and threw away the T-shirt and boxers I'd been wearing since leaving my house.

My bike box and bags arrived unscathed. I looked around to make sure there weren't any security guards nearby, then set up a workshop in a corner of the baggage claim area, assembled my Soma, affixed the panniers, and discarded the cardboard box and duffel bag.

I pushed my loaded bicycle through customs and into the waiting summer sun. I pedaled to the spot where, a year before, a kid from Korea had taken a picture of me in front of Geneva's fountain, my arm throbbing from that unfortunate encounter with the car door. I smiled and thought briefly about the park where Kendra and I had dinner.

Soon I was out of the city, pedaling away from my memories. I followed the southern sunlit shores of Lake Geneva for forty miles before veering south, into a valley and into the Alps.

Unlike the previous summer, when I wasn't sure how far I could pedal each day, this year I wanted—and needed—to cover a hundred miles a day. I planned to cycle across northern Italy and into the Balkans, passing through Slovenia, Croatia, Bosnia and Herzegovina, Serbia, and Bulgaria before

93

entering Turkey. If everything went smoothly, I had just enough time to reach Georgia.

Even though I hadn't slept much on the plane, I managed to ride a hundred miles my first day. I found a room at a roadside hotel and, after showering, washing clothes, and otherwise getting situated, I picked up my phone and dialed Kendra's number.

"Hi!" said Kendra. "Where are you?"

"In Switzerland, near a town called Brig."

"How's the weather?"

"Today was sunny, maybe seventy degrees. I got too much sun on my arms."

"You need to wear sunscreen."

"I do, every day. Multiple times a day. I just forgot one little spot on my arm." I rubbed the tiny red patch on my wrist. "How are you? Enjoying your freedom yet?"

"I'm adjusting to an empty house and taking care of all the chores." Kendra's sarcasm was as finely tuned as my own.

"Sorry about that. I'll make it up to you someday!"

We talked a bit longer about my route for the next day and about her job before the inevitable goodbye arrived.

"Wear sunscreen tomorrow!"

"I will. Love you."

"Love you too. Be careful."

Click. The silence hung in the air. I opened my Acer laptop and edited the day's photos before going to bed.

I awoke to the patter of raindrops, a steady light drizzle outside the window.

So much for sunscreen.

I bundled in my Pearl Izumi coat and pulled a rain jacket over it. I put my gear into plastic trash bags before placing it all in my waterproof panniers. The road climbed steadily to Brig, but after passing through the city the gradient increased sharply into the mountains, a distressing reminder that the pavement likely followed a medieval goat path.

The rainfall was steady. With temperatures hovering in the mid-forties, I observed every exhale dissipate under countless drops of rain. Fog covered the road, at times reducing visibility to thirty yards. Occasional breaks in the clouds revealed breathtaking views of Swiss mountain streams, lonely cabins, and winding roadway.

It took me four hours to travel thirteen miles, topping out at le Col du Simplon, a mountain pass situated six thousand feet above sea level. Walls of mossy green climbed out of the valley and merged into towering peaks.

The rain increased as I descended into Italy, my arms shivering uncontrollably as I struggled to maneuver the hundred-pound mass beneath me. My hands became numb in my wet cotton gloves. The ninety-minute descent left me more exhausted than the climb, but at the bottom I found myself in the foothills of northern Italy.

At lower elevations, sunlight broke through the clouds, the air grew warmer, and I dried out. My bike looked up at me with a filthy grin, not unlike a dog that had been rolling around in a pile of mud. It was a mess of road grit and grease on my second day of riding.

I self-consciously proceeded down the shore of Italy's exquisite Lake Maggiore where vintage hotels and gated villas lined the small patch of land between the highway and the waterfront. I spent the night at an inn above a pizzeria on the outskirts of Milan.

My planned route across northern Italy, south of the Alps, would take several days, and would mirror the route Kendra and I had driven across last summer on our return to Geneva. Primarily industrial, riding through this region of Italy was like visiting Colorado but never veering off I-25 and away from the smog of Colorado's Front Range.

The weather didn't help matters. Rain came and went each day, coating my bike in layers of dirt and grime. I got a flat on my third day out of Geneva and had to seek shelter from the drizzle under a business awning, the filth of the tire turning my hands black.

Leave it to you to ride through the worst part of Italy.

'It's an unfortunate necessity.'

My logic didn't help my mood. I was anxious to reach Turkey, to confront months of disquietude and fear.

I pushed my thoughts aside and pedaled through one random town after the next. One afternoon, I grew agitated as homes, businesses, and traffic became progressively more congested.

A traffic light turned red.

Oh, come on!

'What's the deal?'

My opposing halves were both upset.

The light turned green and I proceeded forward, only to be stopped by another red light.

This is ridiculous!

'It wasn't this bad earlier. What's going on?'

I hit another red light.

Seriously!

I struggled to figure out what had changed.

'It's the roundabouts! They're gone.'

I thought of all the roundabouts I'd gone through that morning and the previous days, and last summer, flying through them with fluid ease, merging between cars and trucks. Now, I was squeezing my brakes every few minutes to wait for a stupid traffic light.

I considered the significance of my revelation, and for much of the afternoon pondered whether traffic lights contributed to road rage, and whether a study had been done comparing drivers' moods in areas with roundabouts to those of drivers who have to stop every five seconds for a red light.

That evening, irate, I entered Sermione, the same lakeside town Kendra and I had visited. I stopped to see if our lodging from the previous year, the one with the little old lady and eclectic paintings, had a room, but it was full.

I checked multiple hotels, becoming wetter and dirtier, until I found one with a vacant room. I washed my clothes in the shower and hung them to dry on hooks, door frames, and furniture around the room.

Afterward, I sat on the balcony and ate a dinner of bread, cheese, and ham, with a side of prepackaged salad. Darkening clouds meandered over the lake, engulfing it in shades of black. I thought about the hotel where Kendra and I had stayed, together. It was strange to be in a familiar setting under such different circumstances.

I watched the clouds break apart and wondered if it would rain the next day.

On June 5th, I crossed a sliver of Slovenia before passing into Rijecka, Croatia, on the Adriatic coast. I stayed at one of the many family-run *pensions* lining the hilly roads on the outskirts of the city. The elderly couple who lived there offered me a shot of homemade schnapps while I checked in. I pulled out all the German I knew trying to communicate with them and instinctively opened Google Translate on my phone.

Your apps don't work without an internet connection.

I glanced at my phone.

'But it is working. Google Translate works.'

I clicked on my settings to see if my phone was connected to Wi-Fi. It was not. I pulled up Google Maps. My eyes widened. The little blue dot hovered over the house in which I sat, pinpointing my location with chilling accuracy.

It took you five days to figure this out?

'This changes things.'

I grinned and let my new reality sink in while I translated a few German words to use with my hosts. I would have translated directly to their language, but I wasn't exactly sure what language they spoke.

*****

Bosnia and Herzegovina is one country, and it is beautiful. That was apparent the moment I crossed the border. I passed a small village set among rolling green hills, with the small, forested mountains of Croatia gracing the background.

Contrasting this beauty was graffiti, on the side of a building, which read "Remember Srebrenica," an homage to the 1995 massacre of eight thousand Bosniaks by the Bosnian Serb army. It was the first of many signs that the haunting wounds of the civil war were still fresh.

Yugoslavia was formed in 1918 following World War I and was composed of the nations of Bosnia and Herzegovina, Serbia, Croatia, Slovenia, Macedonia, and Montenegro. In the early 1990s, the country erupted into civil war, with the Serbian dictator Slobodan Milošević capitalizing on the nationalistic sentiments of the Serbian people, both in Serbia and those scattered around Yugoslavia, to justify attempts to expand Serb territory. This resulted in military offensives throughout Bosnia and Herzegovina. Existing ethnic tension between Muslim Bosniaks and Orthodox Serbs—tensions dating back to the 1400s—only added fuel to the atrocities committed on all sides.

The initial scenery belied the nation's tragic past. I gazed at the rolling hills, small mountains, and beautiful puffy clouds. I noted the many postcard-perfect Orthodox churches scattered across the countryside and the modest homes gracing tranquil farmsteads.

Yet the further east I rode, the more uneasy I felt.

Where are all the people?

I hadn't seen a single person for hours.

'And why are so many of the houses gutted? Were they bombed?'

I considered that possibility, but as I examined each empty home, I noted that the frames were intact. It was the roofs, windows, and doors that were missing, like they had been systematically removed.

The beautiful rolling hills under the puffy white clouds were suddenly, eerily, quiet.

Keep pedaling. Enjoy the clouds.

I stocked up on groceries in the small, nondescript town of Sanski Most. After loading my panniers, I pulled out my paper map. I was aiming for the city of Banja Luka, but the route was circuitous, veering miles south before turning north again.

Not satisfied with my options, I opened my now-functioning Google Maps. According to Google, there was a road that went directly east to Banja Luka. I followed my app, watching the small city fall away behind me. The road changed from pavement to a hard-packed white gravel road.

Um ...

'It's fine. The gravel is smooth.'

We have time to turn around.

'We'd have to backtrack five miles. No way.'

The gravel road progressed steadily uphill. I passed a war memorial where I paused to read the names cast into the side of a metal plate. The words written on the plaque meant nothing to me, but the date, 1995, told a story of fresh wounds.

Several miles later, the white gravel was replaced by brown dirt.

Um.

'We're not turning around. If Google Maps says this road goes to Banja Luka, then it goes to Banja Luka.'

Two miles later, the roadway became a muddy mess. I walked my bike around several impassable puddles. I rounded a curve and the road became a literal jeep trail, two tracks rising steeply up the mountainside.

How's your faith in Google Maps now?

'We'll get there.'

But I wasn't so sure. Unlike the main roads, which I assumed curved around the mountains, this tertiary path apparently went over them. I kept going forward. The tracks were gradual enough for me to keep pedaling.

At the top of the mountain, I reached a clearing where a massive sign towered over the road. It had the word "Mine" written in four languages on it and included a map of the area. The map was littered with little red *X's* marking the explosives. I was in a minefield. I scanned the surrounding forest, wondering where the nefarious traps were hidden, thankful I didn't have to pee.

I methodically moved forward, beginning my descent down the other side of the mountain. The dirt road was better, but I still had to maintain a smooth trajectory on my narrow tires.

When I reached real pavement again, after several hours, I saw Orthodox churches like the ones to the west. But I also saw mosques in every little town I passed. Churches and mosques. And full houses. And a mountain and minefield to separate them from the silent pillaged homes and Orthodox-only churches on the other side.

Something had happened here, in this region. Something horrible. I could only surmise who had done what to whom, and who had fled their homeland, if they were lucky enough to get away at all. The place felt haunted.

Darkness descended around me as I entered the city of Banja Luka. My odometer registered 120 miles for the day, far more than anticipated.

After a twenty-minute search, I found a hotel where a surly receptionist gave me keys to a room with no hot water. That evening, I emailed Iris, a friend of mine from my days in Leicester. Her mom was from Bosnia but had passed away years before the war.

Iris replied an hour later to tell me that she had spent a lot of time as a kid in Banja Luka and that her mom was buried in the city. She recommended a restaurant to me as well, although I never made it there.

In her email, full of memories, the city sounded like a happy place. Now, as I peered out my hotel window at the people walking around, I couldn't help but speculate whose side they had been on, which political demagogue they had followed, and which neighbor they had turned against.

It wasn't only the hotel water sending chills down my spine that evening.

*****

The CDC recommends travelers to rural areas of Eastern Europe and Asia get the rabies vaccine. The three injections cost over a thousand dollars and are not covered by insurance.

'Just be careful,' was my prevention strategy. 'Assume that every dog is unleashed and wants to bite us.'

That's not much of a plan.

'We'll be fine.'

Late one afternoon in central Bosnia, on a flat stretch of two-lane road, I came across a lone farmhouse where a giant dog barked and jumped, outraged at my presence. I could hear the vicious snarls despite the bass vibrating on my earbuds.

I veered toward the other side of the pavement to put as much distance between me and the canine menace as possible. I didn't bother to look behind me. I could always hear cars coming, even with my headphones blaring. Car tires make a surprising amount of noise. Besides, no cars had passed me in ages.

As I moved into the middle of the road, I heard the screech of tires behind me. I didn't turn my head around. Instead, I waited for the impact. In the brief instant between hearing the sound and recognizing what it meant, I didn't want to see it happen. I kept my head forward and prepared myself for the inevitable. There was no internal dialogue, no arguing, no thoughts about what to do.

I accepted a simple fact. I was about to get hit, and then I was going to die.

In an instant, from the corner of my left eye, I saw a car skid to the opposite side of the road, nearly careening into a small ditch.

I was still upright. I was still on my bike. I was still alive.

A family emerged from the house to view the commotion. The dog continued to bark, but I realized then that it had a thick chain around its neck. I looked at the family before glancing back, to my left.

An old Volkswagen reversed out of the embankment. After a bit of maneuvering, it pulled onto the pavement and came to a stop in front of me.

The driver, in his late twenties, emerged from the car. An older man, presumably his father, got out of the passenger side. Both were screaming at me.

I was mortified and embarrassed. I didn't know how to say "sorry" in Bosnian or Serbo-Croatian. Instead, I held my palms up, to express regret, apologizing in English. I kept my distance.

The younger man screamed for several minutes. When he quieted down, the older man screamed at me. When the older man finished, the younger man resumed.

"Sorry … sorry … sorry …," I uttered in English. I felt like the biggest fool in the world. They almost went sailing off the road because of me.

They yelled a few moments longer. The only word I could comprehend was "*Idiote!*"

The younger man, realizing that I couldn't understand them, calmed down first. He got back into his car, but the older man shouted a few more times.

I stood, dejectedly, a wave of fight-or-flight hormones reducing my well-trained legs to jelly.

"Argh …" The old man threw up his hands, finally realizing his tirade was having no effect on the idiot tourist.

He needn't have bothered. I was already screaming at myself.

How stupid are you? Why didn't you look back? You could have died because you're too arrogant to turn your head!

And so on.

I felt weak in the knees as I pedaled forward, shame literally slowing down my pedal strokes.

Just what Kendra needs—a call from the US embassy in Sarajevo, informing her that her husband perished because he was scared of a dog.

I pedaled, tears welling at my own hubris. It was then that I began to internalize something I hadn't detected before. Roughly every mile, on the side of the road, were memorials with people's faces on them and the dates they had died, victims of car accidents.

It could have been my face on one of them. Worse, it could have been the image of the driver and his dad engraved in one.

I examined every face on every marker the rest of the day.

That same week, an irate motorist near Kalamazoo, Michigan, sixty miles from where I grew up, intentionally rammed a group of cyclists with his truck, killing five and injuring four. Witnesses say his brake lights never came on as he ran through the pack of riders.

Yet here I was in war-torn Bosnia and Herzegovina, where a man almost died to avoid hitting me. With a heavy heart I continued eastward, unworthy to be pedaling.

Toward the eastern edge of Bosnia, new concerns became apparent. Cars scooted by me emitting clouds of black smoke. I could taste the acrid waste on my tongue. Entering the city of Tuzla, I rode into an opaque cloud of smog that smelled and tasted like paint thinner. The beauty of the Bosnian countryside was countered by a libertarian approach to emissions regulations.

Between the fumes and my encounter with the car, I was more eager than ever to move past the Balkans and onward to Turkey. Only Serbia and Bulgaria remained between me and the source of all my fears.

CHAPTER 9

The Serbian landscape was flat, dull, and uninspiring. The muggy midsummer heat, coupled with a lack of sleep the previous night, exacerbated the disheartened unease that enveloped me as I entered the former heart of Yugoslavia.

In one village after the next, groups of young men sat outside small houses, apparently unemployed and bored. I watched them watch me and prayed that I didn't get a flat tire.

Cruising onward through barren stretches of farmland, I pictured their morose faces, full of resignation. I considered the gravity of my near accident in Bosnia. I counted the miles ahead, the distances overwhelming me.

I burst into tears.

You don't need to be here.

I continued pedaling even as I wiped the salt water from my face, my sunglasses clouding with errant teardrops.

'We're not in France anymore.'

You're not a tourist anymore.

Through it all I kept moving, keeping my eyes open for hotels. I needed to rest and absorb the change in circumstances. Around six, I found a hotel on the outskirts of Belgrade. From the entryway, I could just make out the skyline of the city center. After showering, I walked down a nearby country road where fields of corn swayed in the breeze. After watching the stalks dance in mesmerizing unison, I called Kendra.

"Hi," I said, trying to sound upbeat.

"Hi," she replied. "Where are you?"

"Southeast of Belgrade. In Serbia. I had a long ride today, 132 miles."

"Wow! Why so long?"

"There aren't many hotels in Serbia. Croatia had a lot, and Bosnia had its share, but here, there aren't any."

"I wonder why," said Kendra.

I wondered too.

"What's it like there?" Kendra asked.

I thought about the drab landscape, the unemployed young men, and the heat. But most of all, I thought about the car in Bosnia and the screeching tires. I thought about putting my head down and waiting for the impact.

"It's flat," I said. "And hot. I think a lot of people are unemployed." I paused, debating whether to mention the car. "I can't wait to get to Bulgaria," I added.

All I knew about Bulgaria was that the country produced respectable wine. I figured it would be more developed than the nations that once comprised Yugoslavia.

"Is your hotel nice?"

"Actually, it is," I said, glad to change the subject. "And it's only thirty dollars for the night. There's a big restaurant downstairs too."

"What do they eat in Serbia?"

"Um, that's what I'm here to find out!" My mind shifted from the turmoil of the past few days to dinner.

We talked a few more minutes before saying our goodbyes. I started toward the hotel, taking a few final glances at the rows of corn glowing in the setting sunlight.

*****

I wasn't surprised when the two-inch stamped metal bracket on my front rack mount broke, although I hadn't expected it so early into my tour. It was the same fixture that snapped in Normandy. I thought back to the rainy little town in northern France and the weathered sidewalk next to the redbrick wall where I'd fixed it.

I opened my saddle bag. I kept my tools and spare parts in it, and I had specifically bought extra brackets in Fort Collins prior to leaving this summer. I reached into my tool bag, knowing the pieces of metal were in there, somewhere. I dug around some more, and more, and more.

You idiot!

'What?'

They're in the garage. In Colorado. In that small box.

'Crap!'

I pictured the little cardboard container, sitting on my workbench.

I shook my head and unscrewed the broken half of the stamped metal. I pulled the bracket tight, to half its size, and reattached it so the pannier sat at a peculiar angle, like it had last year. I vowed to find a hardware store so I could buy a new bracket and fix it correctly this time.

On the west side of Sofia, Bulgaria, I found a Mr. Bricolage hardware store, Europe's answer to Home Depot. Walking in transported me home. Beef jerky and gum graced the checkout lanes and every imaginable home improvement tool covered the shelves. I located stamped metal brackets in the door-repair aisle. I handed eight brackets to an employee who wore an apron identical to the type everyone at Home Depot wears. He scanned the small bar codes.

I slid my credit card through the reader to pay and laughed internally when I realized I had crossed Croatia, Bosnia, Serbia, and now Bulgaria without any local currency in my pocket. I had charged every purchase across four countries.

The clerk handed me a receipt in a voiceless transaction. I walked out of the store beaming with pride at my renewed foresight.

I glanced at the time as I stepped outside. It was nine, the evening sun had long since disappeared, and only a faint sliver of twilight remained. I hopped on my bicycle and pedaled into central Sofia, desperately searching for a hotel.

*****

I'd created a playlist before leaving Colorado entitled "Crossing the Border," anchored by the song "Do it, Try it," by M83, because I thought that when the time came, I'd have to psych myself up to cross into Turkey.

Instead, when I reached the eastern edge of Bulgaria, I couldn't wait to leave. The roads were a mess of potholes and the towns destitute. The extreme poverty made me worried for my safety, riding as I was with all my worldly possessions affixed to my bicycle.

By the time I got to the Turkish-Bulgarian checkpoint, jumping a queue of hundreds of semis on a rainy Tuesday morning, I had no reservations about entering Turkey because I was so relieved to leave Bulgaria.

The rain tapered off the moment I crossed the border. I entered the city of Edirne where pedestrians meandered into shops of every kind. Little red Turkish flags fluttered in the wind. When I passed to the eastern side of town, with cars streaming by me, I stared at the road in glazed confusion.

Turkey has bike lanes?

'Appears so.'

The pavement was smooth and bright, and the traffic well-ordered. I threw myself into the stream, another anonymous element in the scenery.

That evening, I scrolled through Facebook in an air-conditioned hotel room.

'Bri and Aaron are in Istanbul?'

Bri was a former third-grade teacher from Sarah Milner. She and her husband were doing an around-the-world trip and would be in Turkey's largest city two more nights.

'We should hang out with them.'

The thought of speaking to someone in English, in person, was appealing. Other than talking on the phone with Kendra, I hadn't spoken to anyone since leaving Colorado.

You could take a picture with them and they'll post it on Facebook.

I had a policy of not posting photos until I got home.

People would know you're in Istanbul.

'That's hardly a reason to race there. It's kind of pathetic, in fact.'

But still.

'Look,' I said to myself, 'it would be cool to see Bri and Aaron in a random place like Istanbul. And it might make up for all the Friday Afternoon Club get-togethers Bri organized after school that we never attended. But Facebook should not be a reason to race anywhere.'

Yet deep down, the thought of a post on Facebook propelled me forward. That impulse troubled and confused me. I messaged Bri to tell her I could meet up with them, provided I had decent tailwinds.

*****

My freshman year of college, I took a course on Western civilization. I liked it so much I dropped out of the civil engineering program and switched my major to history.

One place that stood out in the class was the Aya Sofia, formerly known as the Hagia Sophia. An Eastern Orthodox Cathedral built in the year 537, it was overrun by the Muslim Ottomans in the mid-1500s and turned into a mosque. Centuries later, it was converted again, this time into a museum by the secular Turkish government. How one building could survive so much upheaval was beyond me. How it could survive so many years at all was unfathomable.

And yet, here I was, getting a photo of my Soma with the Aya Sofia in the background. I had ridden from Lisbon to the center of the Ottoman Empire.

After letting that moment of glory sink in, I wandered a few blocks away, following Google Maps to a side street filled with cobblestones. I walked my bike down the narrow lane until I found the hotel where Bri and Aaron were staying. I had no problems booking a room there; with all the terrorist activity of the previous months, Istanbul was empty.

After settling in, I walked down the hall and knocked on their door. Bri opened it and gave me a big hug. Aaron reached out his hand.

"How are you!" I asked.

"Good," Bri said. "We've been here four days, so we're taking it easy. We fly out tomorrow."

I considered the idea of spending four days somewhere. It sounded so pleasant, though I wasn't sure I'd be able to handle it.

"Where are you headed after this?" I asked.

"Johannesburg," said Bri.

"Wow!" It wasn't often someone told me they were flying to South Africa. "And after that?"

"Mozambique," said Aaron. "Then Thailand, Cambodia, and Vietnam."

"I'm jealous!" I replied.

"How is your trip going?" said Bri. "Where did you start this summer?"

"Geneva," I said, before listing all the places I'd pedaled through.

We continued our conversation into the warm evening air. We visited the courtyard of the Blue Mosque, built in the early 1600s, a majestic and still-functioning place of worship. We snapped a few photos together and I secretly wondered how long it would take Bri to post them on Facebook.

We had dinner at an upstairs restaurant where we admired the view of the city center, the Blue Mosque towering above the ancient streets.

"It's Ramadan," said Bri, "so most restaurants don't serve food before sundown. Except in the tourist district."

I glanced around the dining area and realized it was empty. That would change as the sun set and locals filtered in to eat after a long day of fasting.

After dinner we strolled outside, passing groups of police officers in the central market. I glanced their way, wondering if they were scared, knowing they were targets for Kurdish separatists, ISIS terrorists, and who knows who else. I was impressed with their bravery, sitting there and watching for signs of trouble even as they were being watched themselves.

We continued to an outdoor market where lights hung in delicate patterns, creating a calming ambience. The place was bustling with locals yet oddly quiet. I'd never been there before, but I could tell it was usually full of tourists. Based on the headlines from the past year, I sensed a constant trepidation that a bomb would go off. My unease was not wholly irrational, and it saddened me that violence was on my mind the entire evening.

We made it back to the hotel without incident, and I slept well at the epicenter of all my fears and consternations.

The next morning, I visited the inside of the Blue Mosque and the Basilica Cistern, an underground chamber full of water, longer than a football field, that had been built in the sixth century during the reign of Emperor Justinian I. Since I avoided cities as much as possible after my foray through Barcelona last summer, I was grateful Bri and Aaron had given me a reason to stop so I could see something.

Of course, there were plenty more sites to visit, but I couldn't delay. Looking at the calendar, I had time to get to Georgia, but that meant another eight hundred miles across Turkey. If I slowed down and thought about it, I might chicken out and turn around toward Athens and my flight home. I couldn't lose a beat. I had to keep riding east.

I said goodbye to Bri and Aaron and within minutes was on a ferry across the Strait of Bosporus, which separates western and eastern Istanbul. I enjoyed the tranquil motion of the boat as it lurched toward the opposite shore, the open breeze hitting my face as central Istanbul fell away.

When I got off the ferry on the other side, I smiled from ear to ear.

I was in Asia.

CHAPTER 10

At fifteen million inhabitants, Istanbul is the fifth-largest city in the world. Like Barcelona the previous year, I spent the afternoon concentrating on buses pulling in front of me and cars entering and exiting the divided expressway from never-ending entrance ramps. My hands perched on the brake levers for hours.

The mundane technicalities gave me an immediate focus that pushed away any worries about cycling across eastern Turkey. By the time urbanity drifted away and traffic subsided, I was too frazzled to worry about the uncertainties ahead.

I covered eighty-five miles before checking in at a chain hotel off the highway near the city of Sakarya. Clean and modern, it had a back patio where I could lock my bike. There was a well-stocked grocery store down the street inside an enormous shopping mall.

Snug in my hotel room, I took stock of my situation. I was past Istanbul and had two weeks left before my return flight from Athens. Tbilisi, Georgia, was nine hundred miles to the east.

'It's time to book our ticket.'

Are you sure?

'Sure as we'll ever be.'

I opened my laptop and navigated to the Aegean Airlines website. I typed in my information and, after a moment's hesitation, booked my flight from Tbilisi to Athens.

'Now all we have to do is get to Georgia.'

Easier said than done.

I sighed and got ready for bed.

I awoke ready to tackle the expanse of the former Ottoman Empire. I started my day with breakfast at the hotel buffet, which spanned three counters and included eggs, sausage, toast, fruit, cereal, yogurt, cheese, and more. My eyes gleamed as I piled food on my plate, grateful that I was again burning enough calories to have breakfast.

The divided highway curved through countless hills and wound its way up long, mountainous passes. Cars and semis moved into the left-hand lane when they passed me even though the shoulder provided ample room for my bicycle. I took in the beautiful scenery, where short deciduous trees emitted a different shade of green from the rolling patches of grass covering the hillsides.

One morning, in the small town of Hendek, I slowed to a halt at a stoplight situated at the intersection of the primary highway and a residential street. Waiting for the light to change, a chubby man sporting a full beard and camo fatigues, topped with a Turkish flag headband, approached me. He smiled broadly as he reached out to shake my hand.

The light turned green. I wanted to continue riding but I couldn't be rude. Through gestures and fragmented English, he invited me to see his "guest book" that was, he pointed, in the apartment on the opposite corner.

The man was the embodiment of all my fears about riding across Turkey. In my mind, he was one of the militants the media kept writing about or one of the sociopaths I'd read about in *Lonely Planet.* And he was inviting me into his home.

I glanced at the front door that faced the busy corner. Outside, a few people sat around, idling away the morning, casually glancing my way.

'Those people will know we're going inside,' I reasoned.

No! This is stupid! You're going to die. Or you'll be put on some terrorist watch list by association.

'Calm down.'

After sizing up the situation and noting that the wide window of his apartment opened to the busy sidewalk, I decided to check out whatever it was he was talking about.

What if you don't have the option to leave? What if ...

But I had already locked my bike. I followed the man inside. The front room was a normal living area with conventional furniture. A long hallway extended toward the back of the building. Several bicycles hung from racks attached to the ceiling. My new friend showed me his favorite one, a silver aluminum road bike. Then he pointed to his belly and noted that he didn't ride it too much. I smiled.

He pointed to a workbench full of computers and radio equipment. Two monitors were turned on, and one had video footage of the street. I assumed he had seen me approach the intersection on the screen. A large ham radio, with more dials than I could count, sat disheveled next to a mess of electronic gear.

'All markings of an introverted hobbyist.'

Or a jihadist!

I rolled my eyes at my own paranoia even as I glanced at the front door, my only escape.

The man handed me a journal. I opened it up and saw pages of comments. The word *host* came up a lot and various countries were written next to peoples' names.

He offered me some tea, but I declined as politely as possible. I felt bad about refusing the offer.

'I think he's simply a nice guy who wanted to meet us.'

Fine! But seriously, don't drink the tea.

'Agreed.'

The man kept muttering something about his different Facebook *groupus* as if he collected "friends" to follow him. He showed me around his place a bit more, but I sensed the ticking minutes and told him I needed to leave.

"Teşekkürler," I said. "Thank you." I was impressed with myself for bothering to learn some basic Turkish on

Babbel.com, especially after fumbling my way through the Balkans for the past ten days.

The man gave a heartfelt goodbye, and I left without incident. I kept thinking about his Facebook *groupus* as I continued into the Turkish heartland.

Turkey is an amalgam of spectacular scenery ranging from rice paddies reminiscent of Vietnam to forested mountains to rolling, grass-covered hills typical of Central Asia. I pedaled across them all, stopping only to drink coffee from my dented thermos and scarf down snacks at abandoned buildings and anywhere else that offered shade.

Back on my bike, I would think away the hours while the scenery and my carefully composed music playlists kept me company.

My mind jumped from one thing to the next.

'That was an interesting tea stand.'

You should have stopped.

My negative self never skipped a beat. My memory shifted just as fast.

'Remember when all the students cleaned their desks last year, and one student tipped over their desk.'

Images of the scene floated past, replaced by a snapshot of my pie-shaped room at Lincoln Elementary where nothing quite fit. That scene was replaced by childhood images of my fifth-grade classroom in Lansing and my fifth-grade teacher.

A tree on the side of the road caught my attention.

In the next instant, I wondered what Kendra was doing.

'What time is it in Fort Collins?'

How many miles have you gone today?

I looked at my odometer.

'What will school be like next year?'

Why weren't you more proactive about getting a job out of college?

'I don't know, but Tucson was quite the experience.'

You were an insecure jerk in college.

I thought of my friends from those days, long gone.

You said some horrible things to people.

I tried to think of something else.

Peace Corps too. You were immature back then.

'We did all right with AmeriCorps though. And grad school—mostly.'

Still.

'We've learned from our mistakes.'

The next moment I wondered if Bri and Aaron had posted their picture on Facebook yet.

How many miles have you gone today?

'Not enough.'

There's no way you're going to get to Tbilisi.

An image of myself popped into my head, sitting on the couch playing video games and shoving Doritos into my mouth.

'We're not that kid anymore, at least.'

You're only a few steps away from being that kid again.

'Where will we stay tonight?'

I hope your spokes don't break.

'Remember that time we floated in the Dead Sea?'

You were miserable back in those days.

'We should replace the bike chain soon.'

And so on.

The conversations never ceased, hopping from one thought to the next. Sometimes I'd step back, listen to the nonsense, and shake my head at the confusion.

Through it all the steady circular motion of my legs turning the cranks continued. The movement of the bike soothed me and eased the chaos. Songs like "Wide Open," with Beck's calming, mellow voice streaming into my head, placated my inner ramblings. Random moments, like the day I got a flat and changed the tube next to a field of poppies waving in the afternoon sun, would shake me out of my daydreaming.

I rolled into the small city of Gerede early one evening. Cresting one of the city's many hillsides, the *adhan*, or Muslim call to prayer, emanated from hidden speakers affixed to myriad mosques and echoed throughout the valley. I steered to the shoulder and planted my right foot on the ground, savoring the extraordinary moment. The warm evening light blanketed the surrounding mountains in muted shades of deep yellow. I popped out my headphones and listened to the melodious voice.

The stress of finding a hotel I'd perceived only a minute earlier was momentarily displaced by the spectacular scene. I didn't mind sleeping on the ground if necessary. It was a small price to pay for sitting on the saddle of my favorite bicycle in the middle of Turkey as the afternoon faded to evening and the sounds familiar to one-quarter of earth's inhabitants echoed in my ears.

An hour later, I reflected on the moment from the comforts of a hot shower, happy I got both.

I enjoyed a similar moment in the city of Tosya where I stayed in a hotel sitting all by itself on a hill overlooking the skyline. It was a stunning night, with twinkling lights and white buildings stretching into distant hills.

I climbed onto a spiral fire escape on the fourth floor for a better view of the cityscape. Wind gusted around me, knocking me in all directions. The sky had turned dark enough to see stars dotted across the celestial canvas. It was a dreamlike evening in an otherworldly place.

In Turkey, those magical moments kept coming, one after the next. After a few days of cycling across Anatolia, I forgot I was supposed to be afraid.

Turkey, it turns out, is an amazing place, and bicycle friendly.

*****

As I neared the Black Sea, Röyksopp's "Running to the Sea" became the song of the week, the entrancing vocals and rhythmic beats filling me with confidence that I was going to make it to Georgia.

Fatsa, home to a hundred thousand people, was my first stop on the coast. I had no problem finding a hotel in the city center, and I was allowed to carry my bike to my room rather than lock it in the lobby. After unsystematically unpacking my panniers, I took a photo of my things scattered on the floor, struggling to believe it all fit.

I didn't have my tent this year, but I did bring a sleeping pad and a small sleeping bag in case I needed to sleep outside. I had two sets of everything: cotton T-shirts, cycling T-shirts, underwear, short socks, regular shorts, cycling shorts, cycling jerseys, and bandanas. My Pearl Izumi winter jacket, rain jacket, windbreaker jacket, insulated vest, windbreaker vest, gloves, arm warmers, leg warmers, hat, and two sets of gloves were included for various degrees of inclement weather.

Toiletries included all the usual items, including sunscreen, antibiotic ointment, and first aid materials. I also kept a round of ciprofloxacin in a plastic bag in case I needed a quick fix of antibiotics.

My electronics gear consisted of my camera charger, spare MP3 player, Acer laptop and its charger, two electrical adaptors, and an assortment of USB cords and cables. I also had spare batteries for my Polar heart rate monitor watch.

I had folders containing various papers, including receipts, map fragments, torn-off labels, and whatever else I could later glue into a journal that I would someday find interesting to peruse.

And of course I had the cards Kendra sent with me, to open on specific dates. I always looked forward to opening them, to see what she had written months before in anticipation of where I would be at a certain date. She included a few pieces of my favorite gum and sudoku puzzles that I never had time to solve.

In my handlebar bag, I carried my cell phone, wallet, passport, regular glasses, and camera, as well as a guidebook that I'd tear apart as I went so it became lighter as the trip wore on. My trunk bag held a full set of tools and spare parts, including two extra chains, two sets of tires, and four out of the seven extra inner tubes I started with.

To get away from the mess, I walked to a pier that jutted into the Black Sea. Countless men and their kids thrust their fishing lines into the water, oblivious to the solitary, white American taking pictures. Families strolled around, and I found a bench where I could sit comfortably and call Kendra.

"I think I might pull this off!" I announced.

"Great! How far away from Georgia are you?"

"I'm 250 miles from Batumi, which is right across the border. I should be there in three days."

"I knew you could do it!"

"Well I'm not there yet."

"But pretty much."

"Yeah, I suppose." I didn't want to project any sort of overconfidence. That's when everything goes wrong. I changed the topic. "How's everything back home?"

"Well, I had three meetings today, one with my team and two with prospective students …"

As Kendra talked, I glanced at the pier, the setting sun illuminating the backs of the fathers fishing with their sons, the long poles and lines reflecting glints of sunlight.

Too bad Kendra isn't here right now.

"And the garden is covered with weeds, which has kept me busy. There are more bald patches in the lawn."

I smiled. I didn't miss the lawn.

"I wish you could see all the people fishing," I replied. "You'd love the scene."

"Yeah, but I don't think I'd feel too safe in Turkey."

"Probably not," I agreed, "although I thought the same thing until I got here. It's funny how being somewhere can make you forget all your fears."

"I suppose. But there are other places I'd like to go. Like Scotland."

I smiled again. "We'll go there someday!"

Our conversation, stretching across six thousand miles, weaved and meandered. Families walked past me, enjoying each other's company.

"Well, I should stock up on some food. And I passed a liquor store a few blocks back. They're hard to come by in Turkey. I'm going to get some beer!"

"Sounds like an exciting evening. My day is just beginning."

"Hope it's a good one. Love you," I said.

"Love you too. Bye."

From Fatsa I followed the rugged coast all the way to Georgia. Like Morocco, I only needed to keep the sea on my left. The highway hugged some rocky bends but went straight through others, the bicycle shoulder all but disappearing through the tunnels ranging in length from a few hundred feet to a mile.

The longer ones terrified me.

You're going to die! This is how Princess Diana died!

'Keep pedaling. This might be the last one.'

But they were never the last one. I kept my head down and put my faith in Turkish motorists, who continued to pass me with ample room.

I flatted one afternoon and realized I was down to three spare tubes. I used Google Maps to navigate my way to a nonexistent bicycle shop in a small town south of the highway. Giving up, I worked my way back to the highway, passing through the middle of an open-air market, dodging pedestrians on the busy street.

Behind my sunglasses and helmet, in all my weird cycling gear, I stood out more than ever, yet I felt like I was in uniform, stoically maneuvering through the Turkish scene. I looked at the trinkets spread out under dusty tents, peddlers and customers everywhere, and soaked it all in before winding my way back to the highway.

Forty miles from the Georgian border, I saw a cyclist. I could tell from a distance that she was a tourist. I pulled alongside her and gave a small wave. We both moved to the side of the road.

"Hallo!" she said with a smile.

"Hi!" I said, reaching out to shake her hand. "On your way to Georgia?"

"I am," she said. "I'm hoping to meet a few Dutch cyclists in Batumi. I'm going to cycle across Armenia with them. I don't want to go there alone."

"Have you ridden all the way across Turkey by yourself?" I asked.

"Yes, I started in Germany."

"How has your trip been across Turkey?"

"It's a beautiful country," she said, "although I've been yelled at by the men everywhere."

I considered her statement for a moment. For as worried as I was about riding across Turkey, here was this twenty-something German woman who had just done the same thing.

"Where are you heading today?" she asked.

"I'm not sure how far I'll get. Maybe Batumi, maybe further."

"If you see two Dutch cyclists, can you tell them I'm on my way?"

"Absolutely," I said, though I doubted I would run into them.

We took an obligatory selfie together before getting back on our bikes and continuing in the same direction, separately.

As I pedaled, I considered all the fears that had consumed my mind for so long. In hindsight, they were all a waste of energy. I turned my attention to the rocky shoreline and the road, which stretched and curved around rocky cliffs. I looked at my odometer and did some math in my head.

'Georgia should be around the next bend.'

I picked up the pace.

CHAPTER 11

After receiving the third degree from a surly Georgian border agent, I went to change money at a busy exchange kiosk. I pulled up next to two cyclists, none other than the Dutch tourists the German woman had mentioned.

They eyed my Soma and its racing wheels.

"Looks like you're traveling light," said the man in accented English. Tall and lanky, in his mid-fifties, he had a sturdy mountain bike outfitted with wide tires. His wife's bike was similar.

'We're traveling *fast*,' I thought, calculating that I'd ridden nine hundred miles across Turkey in eight and a half days.

Consider that, my Dutch friends!

Rather than vocalize my thoughts, I reached out to shake their hands.

"I passed a German cyclist about an hour ago," I said. "She asked me to tell you she's on her way."

"Oh good," the woman said. "We were hoping she'd catch up to us."

"We're staying in Batumi tonight," added the man. "We have reservations at a hostel. You should join us if you'll be staying in town."

"What's it called?" I asked. I hadn't spoken to anyone since I left Bri and Aaron, and the prospect of hanging out with a random group of people for an evening sounded appealing.

They wrote the hostel name on a business card and handed it to me. The card had a photo of them in traditional Dutch clothes. "That's our blog address at the bottom," the man said. "We've been blogging about our trip."

You should blog!

'When would we have time to blog?'

I thanked them both and said I would try to find the hostel.

On the way to the city, I stopped at the Gonio Fortress, which is purported to house the gravesite of Saint Matthew the Apostle. Georgia is one of the oldest nations in the world, and was the first country to officially adopt Christianity in the fourth century, so it's plausible he's buried there. The earliest evidence of wine is also found in Georgia, with jugs dating back eight thousand years.

I wandered around the ruins, admiring the thick stone walls and turrets standing against the backdrop of lush green hillsides. It reminded me of an image from a medieval history book, but the site itself dates to Roman times, an eastern stronghold of the former empire.

I felt an ironic sense of pride for soaking in some culture only nine miles into Georgia. After leaving the fortress, steady traffic followed me into Batumi, and once I entered the city itself the congestion became intolerable, with cars merging in every direction while emitting noxious black fumes. I was reminded again about what happens when governments don't have, or don't enforce, air quality regulations.

Google Maps led me to the street where the hostel should have been, but I couldn't find it. Frustrated by the heat and the traffic, I worked my way out of the city and kept going. I ascended a long climb and made my way through a narrow tunnel with only one lane in each direction.

You're going to die, for real this time.

I put my head down and pedaled.

On the other side of the tunnel, I consulted Google Maps. It showed only one option for lodging, the Oasis Hotel Resort, in the small hamlet of Chavki, next to the Black Sea. It was a proper, gated resort, and I was more self-conscious than usual walking into the lobby, sweaty and smelly, and asking for a room. I balked at the sixty-dollar price tag but splurged when I realized it included dinner and breakfast.

Like all the guests, I was given a wristband granting me access to the dining hall. Several imposing buildings, housing the guest rooms, towered over the grounds. After cleaning up, I went to the cafeteria where I found myself surrounded by Russian families. Most of the adults looked miserable as their kids whined, cried, and threw tantrums.

'American families and Russian families aren't so different,' I thought with a smirk, the lyrics of Sting's song "Russians" scrolling through my head.

I was glad to eat alone.

After dinner, I went swimming in the Black Sea, making a proverbial victory lap in the water.

You have four hundred miles to Tbilisi. Don't get overconfident.

I dove under the water and came out smiling.

'Whatever. We got this.'

I gazed south at the silhouette of Batumi, ten miles away. I was glad I wasn't stuck in the congestion and noise, but sad that I wasn't hanging out with a random group of people. I sighed.

The next morning, tall trees, intermittently lining the road, greeted me as I began pedaling east into a faint headwind. Free-range cows meandered, greedily munching on the abundant green grass. Flattened cow dung covered the roads, and I vowed to wash my bike before boxing it up to fly home.

Two days out of Batumi, I dropped down a ten-mile-long canyon that snaked its way east. It bottomed out and I started going back uphill, a slight headwind hindering my already slow progress.

Spinning in my lowest gears, averaging six miles per hour, the wind continued to taunt me. A lack of sleep the night before made the situation insufferable.

Two miles from the top of the climb, a tractor trailer lumbered past me. I jumped into its draft—the area of low pressure following a moving vehicle—and felt myself surge forward. In a pack of cyclists, someone riding in the middle expends 60 percent of the energy that the lead riders put forth. Riding behind a semi, even uphill, has similar advantages, particularly into a headwind. The psychological benefit for me that afternoon was immeasurable.

A van followed the tractor trailer, there to make sure the vehicle passed safely to its destination, and I was now tucked between the trailer and the van. As we approached the top of the climb, the gradient flattened out and a sign for a tunnel appeared to my right, indicating that it was two kilometers long. With only one lane in each direction, I debated my options.

'We should keep drafting the truck! The van driver will know we're there!'

Are you crazy! You need to let them pass through and then go through on your own!

'If we do that, other cars will pass us, and they won't know ...'

Too late!

We had all entered the tunnel. I was two feet behind the trailer. The pavement was smooth, and I stayed tucked in the trailer's draft.

If you hit a pothole ...

'There won't be any potholes!'

My heart raced.

'Please don't let there be any potholes.'

You have zero reaction time.

'Neither does the driver behind us.'

I knew the van behind me would run me over if I fell. I bit down hard on the tip of my sunglasses, which were clenched in my teeth. It was the only place I could hold them once I entered the tunnel.

Every worry in the world, every anxiety, every bad memory, every happy memory, indeed, every memory, disappeared. One hundred percent of my attention was tuned to the trailer and the pavement in front of me. I was truly living in the moment, practicing mindfulness in the only way I knew how.

I grinned a serious, no-nonsense kind of grin, all the while my sunglasses sticking out of my mouth. My eyes affixed themselves to the back of the trailer, and the concrete zoomed beneath me.

Gradually, the truck's speed increased. We maxed out at twenty miles per hour, my hands turning white as they gripped the handlebars, fingers poised over the brake levers, my eyes never veering from the metal frame in front of me.

The world appeared to stand still.

Amid the quiet intensity, I heard a small European engine rev and saw a streak of red zoom past the van, past me, and past the tractor trailer, leaving behind a cloud of exhaust. I couldn't believe it. Before the shock of that audacious move fully registered, we were out of the tunnel and a long descent opened before us.

The truck was moving at twenty miles per hour, and suddenly the very vehicle that kept me safe through the mountain became annoying. I flew around it, like the crazy motorist in the darkness, and bombed downhill at forty miles per hour, burning the adrenaline that had built up in my system.

Toward the bottom of the descent the landscape flattened and an ancient castle appeared to the south. I spotted a bicyclist riding uphill in the opposite direction. I slowed down evenly, pausing the momentum of my two-wheeled boat. After looking behind me, I crossed the road and introduced myself.

"Hello!" I said, the thrill of the past ten minutes rushing through my veins. "Where are you headed?"

"I'm on my way back to Istanbul. My name's Mustafa. Where are you from?"

I reached out to shake his hand. "My name's Tom. I'm from Colorado, in the US. Where have you been cycling? Only in Georgia?"

"Oh no, I was doing a tour of Iran."

"Wow! That must have been beautiful." I'd seen images of Iran, and between the mountains and valleys imagine the place is a cycling heaven.

"Oh, it was. Are you heading there?" He paused, realizing I had told him I was from the States.

We both gave an awkward laugh. A bicycle tourist faux pas, to be sure.

I smiled. "Someday, maybe. For the moment I'm planning to fly home from Tbilisi."

We chatted a bit more and then got on our bicycles.

"Be careful at the top of the climb," I told him before we parted ways. "There's a long tunnel up there. It's kind of scary."

*****

I'd read a news article years before about an architectural revolution in Georgia. Postmodern structures of all sorts were going up around Tbilisi, contrasting with the existing Baroque, Soviet, and myriad other design styles dotting the country situated at the crossroads of Asian and European cultures.

The article featured a picture of a rest area, of all things, with concrete branching out like tree limbs to form a roof and glass walls to reflect the sun. When I'd read the piece, Georgia was just some foreign country that I'd never visit, an interesting place to learn about.

Yet here I was cycling past the only photo in the article. *Too bad you don't have to pee. Maybe then you'd stop to see it.*

'We can see it from here. Besides, it's late. Fixing that flat back there slowed us down.'

I was down to two spare tubes, which wasn't helping my mood.

I rolled into the city of Gori, hometown of Joseph Stalin, around eight, settling into a hotel as a light drizzle started coming down. I sat on the balcony, a cozy smile filling my cheeks, content that I had a warm place to sleep and only fifty miles to ride the next day.

In the morning, I went for a brief walk around Gori, taking a few extra minutes to read the historical markers outside the Joseph Stalin Museum. I hadn't realized Stalin was Georgian, not Russian, until I read about it in my guidebook. Satisfied to learn something, I returned to my hotel, packed, and embarked on the final stretch to Tbilisi.

Rolling hills covered with waving grasses created a welcome juxtaposition to the dull gray clouds that filled the sky. I followed Google Maps across meandering back roads, through random small towns and over more flattened cow poop, arriving in Tbilisi around noon. Acrid smoke and heavy traffic marked my push to the finish line.

Although the hotel I reserved was on the west side of the city, I proceeded another ten miles east to the airport, because the following year I would leave from there. I couldn't have a ten-mile gap in my ride.

I rode past the terminal and back toward the highway. I stopped to take a picture of a signpost that had an arrow pointing left to central Tbilisi and another pointing right to Baku, Azerbaijan. I took a moment to consider the sign, knowing that it would be stuck in my head for the next eleven months.

After the obligatory detour, I headed to the center of town, dodging cars and city buses, holding my phone in one hand so Google Maps could guide me to the Vake Hotel, where I was shown to my first-floor room. It had a sliding door that opened to an outdoor patio, complete with a swinging chair and surrounded by high rocky walls on two sides. It was an ideal place to relax for the next four days.

After unpacking, I checked my odometer to see how far I'd come from Geneva. When I got to the total distance screen, I stared in disbelief, countless obscenities bubbling up within me. My odometer read 2,699 miles.

'Seriously?'

Could you maybe have checked your mileage before arriving at the hotel!

'Enough! Stay calm!'

The screaming in my head dipped to an inaudible diatribe.

'We rode here from Geneva and arrived unscathed. We can deal with one mile.'

I shook my head, an ironic scowl forming on my lips.

'We can deal with one mile,' I repeated as I unpacked my things.

*****

Prior to my arrival, I had researched lodging in Tbilisi that was within walking distance of several bike shops. My first day in the city, I walked into one and held up a list of phrases on my cell phone to the salesman. I pointed to the one that said "bicycle box" in Turkish, Russian, and Georgian. He went to the back of the store and returned with a large cardboard container that would carry my Soma back to Colorado. Later, I bought a cheap duffel bag from a street vendor to get my panniers home.

After that, I established a schedule that I followed for my remaining days in Tbilisi. Without a routine, I knew the voices in my head would start hammering my psyche, leading me into a melancholic haze.

I rode each morning and had breakfast when I returned. I would chat with the English-speaking receptionist for a few minutes before walking around like a proper tourist, fascinated by the aging Eastern European cars inhabiting the city and the outdoor markets that sold old Soviet propaganda and Russian cameras.

I gazed at the dichotomy of architectural styles, a mix of postmodern architecture interspersed with medieval castles, ancient Orthodox churches, and Soviet-era apartment blocks. Dunkin' Donuts was popular in Tbilisi, and each time I passed one I stared in fascination at the name written in the strange Georgian alphabet, which appeared to me a mix of Hindi and Aramaic.

I hiked a few times in the hills behind my hotel, and even forced myself to learn how to ride the city buses, inspired by Kendra's ability to navigate the bus system in Geneva the summer before.

Other than a growing impatience to return home, things were good. I had no pressing concerns and, after cycling twenty-four solid days, I needed the rest. I felt calm and collected, secure in the routine I had built, and while I did occasionally feel a bit of lingering melancholy wandering through the city alone, it never became more than a dull ache.

I woke up at two thirty in the morning on June 29th to catch my flight to Athens. I turned on the news and gaped at the headlines, which showed twenty-something dead at Ataturk Airport in Istanbul the previous day in an apparent terrorist attack. I would have been flying to Istanbul if I hadn't changed my return ticket to Athens.

I warned you something like this would happen.

I stared at the screen, understanding now that my caution wasn't idle paranoia. It was prudent thinking.

'Changing our tickets was a wise move. But let's not be so happy about it. A lot of people are dead.'

I alternately packed my belongings and watched the horrific news before turning off the TV and lugging my things outside to a waiting taxi.

The driver strapped my bike box to the roof of his sedan, a horrifying, yet fitting, end to the summer. Lightning illuminated mountainous storm clouds in the distance, but we made it to the airport without getting wet. Once in the terminal, I saw that two flights to Istanbul were canceled.

Multiple televisions projected the tragic news. A bomb had torn through the front entrance of Ataturk Airport, and the scene was utter mayhem.

My flight to Greece was right on time.

During my two days in Athens, I visited all the major sites, including the Parthenon as well as the Agora, where a young man named Plato fell under the influence of a philosopher known as Socrates. I made my way to the harbor where even my semi-colorblind eyes could appreciate the intense blue of the water. Tourists lined up to board ships to magnificent Greek islands, and I wondered why I wasn't joining them, with my wife.

A few days later, I looked out the window of the plane as it gained speed and lifted off from Greek soil, trying to absorb the magnitude of what I had accomplished. I had pedaled from Geneva, Switzerland to Tbilisi, Georgia, in under a month. My eyes fixated on the ground below as Athens fell away, a hazy mix of smog, mountains, and white buildings. Maybe it was because I was too tired, or perhaps because I was simply eager to go home and see Kendra, but the scope of what I had done was lost on me.

As the plane reached cruising altitude and I hid behind my headphones, I also considered that I was glad to have this year out of the way. It was neat to ride through so many unique places, but my heart wasn't in any of them. I wanted to pass through them to the real adventure of the Asian steppe.

I leaned back and let out a sigh. In the back of my mind, I pictured the sign at the Tbilisi airport, with the arrow pointed right, to Baku, Azerbaijan.

'Next year we're going to go right!'

There's no way you're going to get a visa to Azerbaijan! Or Kazakhstan or China, for that matter!

'It'll work out. We'll make it happen.'

Doubtful. Something always goes wrong.

I laughed at myself. Despite all my self-doubts, I knew I'd be back next summer, ready to keep going.

First, however, I had to get through another year of my real life.

The highway south of Brig, Switzerland

View of the Adriatic Sea, Croatia

Minefield, west of Banja Luka, Bosnia & Herzegovina

The Soma in front of the Aya Sofia, Istanbul

Poppy field, central Turkey

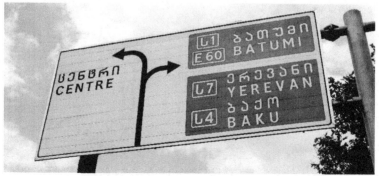

Sign at Tbilisi International Airport, Georgia

PART III: 2016-2017

And all the time that thing is coming –
It's coming, it's coming, that great thing,
the success you're working for.
Then you wake up one day about 40 years old and you say,
"My God, I've arrived. I'm there!"
And you don't feel very different from what you've always felt.

-Alan Watts

CHAPTER 12

"What did you do over the summer?"

I looked up from my computer. Rachel sat a few desks away from me, thumbing through a stack of social studies material that I'd piled in front of her.

"Well, actually, I rode my bicycle from Switzerland to the Republic of Georgia." I felt ridiculous saying it out loud.

"Oh," said Rachel, not sure what else to say. It was our first official planning session, and we were still exchanging obligatory new-colleague pleasantries.

"I rode across Western Europe last year," I added for context. "This year I pushed further east, across the Balkans and into Turkey and then to Georgia."

"Well that's more interesting than my summer," Rachel said with a smile.

"I made it just in time," I continued. "Two weeks after I left Turkey, protests erupted across the country and the military attempted a coup."

Rachel nodded. It was on the news daily, with scenes of protesters across Istanbul waving flags and riding tanks. The coup failed, and the president cracked down on anyone he deemed responsible, which appeared to be everyone, in effect establishing a police state across the country.

I paused to consider the gravity of it all and wondered what happened to the bearded man in Hendek.

"I hope things return to normal there soon," I said, oblivious to the fact that American tourists would soon be barred from entering Turkey at all.

I asked Rachel about her summer before we turned our attention back to planning our first social studies unit.

"Our incoming fifth graders have a reputation for being challenging," I said, "and we'll have twenty-seven kids each. It's manageable, but still …"

I was hopeful as we welcomed students in August. I needed another good school year, and I hoped Rachel would stick around for a while. That she had wanted the second-grade position weighed on my mind. I also needed a school year where I wasn't consumed by work and cycling, where I could reconnect with friends.

Things didn't go as planned.

In the classroom, some students were soon talking back in ways that reminded me why I didn't teach middle school. A few came to blows on the playground, physical altercations I had only experienced a handful of times in my career.

None of my teaching tricks, from rewarding positive behavior to taking away recess, made a dent. Rachel handled it all remarkably well, but it was not how I'd wanted school to go for either of us.

And then things got worse.

In late September, my phone rang. I glanced at the caller ID and saw that it was my brother.

"Hey," I answered.

"Hi, how's it going?" Kevin asked.

"Good. Busy." I could tell by my brother's tone that something was wrong. "What's up?"

"Well," he started, "this afternoon Dad was late to the kids' soccer game. And we both know he's never late to anything."

I frowned. "Yes."

"I asked him why he was late, but he kept saying, 'I can't tell you.' The more he said that the more I pressed him."

My brother was a Michigan State Police lieutenant, and I pictured him pulling out his best interrogation techniques.

"He finally told me he would get in trouble if he told anyone. So I asked, 'If you told anyone what?' And that's when he said some people had called him and said they were from the IRS."

My stomach dropped. My legs went weak.

"They told him he owed back taxes and that he had to wire them money or they'd put him in jail."

I didn't reply. I didn't know what to say.

"I asked Dad how many times he'd sent money to them. He thinks it was three times, but he couldn't remember exactly. He gave them about $12,000. Today he got another call and was rushing around trying to gather money to send them. That's why he was late."

Tears welled in my eyes.

"I'm going to take him to the headquarters tomorrow and file a report. We'll never get the money back, but at least we caught it early. He'd started liquidating his mutual fund to pay the people."

"I'm glad he was late to that game," I mumbled.

"Me too. Now we need to come up with a plan to protect his savings. Let's talk more tomorrow."

"OK." My bottom lip quivered and I uttered a quick goodbye.

I stood in my living room and stared at the wall for some time before walking into the kitchen to inform Kendra.

The worst part about the situation was that even after Kevin filed a police report, my dad remained worried about being sent to jail and felt like he needed to pay the taxes.

It was all unexpected and horrifying. My father had amassed considerable savings and had been close to giving it all away. It was a far cry from forgetting his Yahoo passwords the year before. My brother and I agreed it was time for him to downsize to one home and safeguard his finances.

The house in Lansing sold in October. My childhood home, where I had lived from age four to eighteen, the house where I used to play in the sandbox and climb my favorite tree on those muggy Michigan afternoons, my only true home for thirty-seven years, had traded hands.

I took it in stride, in my adult way, but I had to face the reality that my family was disappearing. My mom lay silent in a cemetery backed against the Grand River in Lansing, having lost her fight with cancer so long ago. Now my dad was slipping away too.

*****

"What's that?" I asked.

"What?" said Rachel.

"That thing on your phone. The extendy thing."

"That? It's a PopSocket." She said it like I should know.

I nodded like I did. "What's it do?"

"You can hold your phone with it. Or prop it up to take pictures."

"Oh," I replied, intrigued by the little piece of plastic attached to her iPhone.

I pulled on it and it popped open. I gave a confused smile.

How come you've never heard of this, Mr. Technology?

I didn't have an answer. I was used to being up to date on the latest tech. I was using USB drives to carry my files home when other teachers were lugging crates full of lesson plans to their cars. For the past two years I didn't need a USB drive; all my files lived in Google Drive, in the cloud, a concept I couldn't explain to my dad.

Yet here was Rachel, with her PopSocket.

At twenty-two years old and fresh out of college, Rachel listened to music I'd never heard of, said "solid" instead of "cool," and frequently used Pinterest, a website I couldn't understand. She had recently started a new career and had moved into a townhouse with her high school boyfriend. She went out with friends on the weekend.

Where did your life go? Became a daily question.

When I was twenty-two, I worked at Lee's Cyclery, unable to find a professional job, before transplanting myself to Tucson. I was hired by a temp agency before finding stable employment as a pizza delivery driver.

As bad as that was, I had my whole life ahead of me.

From Tucson, it was off to Mongolia, then Atlanta, and then Ann Arbor before moving into a townhouse in Fort Collins with Kendra, so full of hope for our own future together.

What do you have now? Only a lot of stories from your twenties and thirties. What have you done recently?

'These days,' I admitted, 'it's counting calories and working all the time and wondering ...'

If you'll ever feel hopeful again.

I was keenly aware these feelings were all classic signs of middle age, but that only made it worse, because my internal struggles proved I was old. The expanding bald patch on my head didn't help matters.

A return to my reclusive habits compounded my melancholy. Between sitting in front of my computer and my excessive cycling, I didn't make good on my vow to reconnect with friends. I thought about it every weekend.

'We should call Russ, or maybe ...'

Who? Who would you call?

'Um, Dave?'

You haven't talked to Dave in two years.

I couldn't believe it had been two years.

I plopped down on the couch next to Kendra and opened my computer. I clicked on my Facebook bookmark.

Click. "Like."

Click. "Like."

Click. "Like."

'See, we have friends.'

My heart sank.

Desolation and isolation enveloped me as I sat on my couch and tried to digitally connect with other living beings.

I turned to Kendra. "We should go out with people."

"Yeah, we should. Who do you want to call?"

"I don't know," I said. "Do you have any ideas?"

"What about Sarah Milner people?"

"They all live in Loveland. I don't want to go all the way back there. Besides, they have their own thing."

"Well, I don't have anyone from work …"

We both looked at each other.

"It's too bad we don't have friends we can just call and go out with anymore," said Kendra.

"It always takes weeks to coordinate anything with anyone," I said, staring at the floor. "And the plans always fall through."

Kendra made a face. "I know. But I don't know what to do about it."

"Well, we should stay in anyway. I need to go to work tomorrow. I have a lot to catch up on."

It was a poor excuse, though there was a glaring amount of truth to it. I did have an overwhelming list of things to do at school. My most recent online graduate class added one more layer to everything and gave me one more reason not to go out.

The realization that I had dug myself into a hole crept from my subconscious to my conscious. By mid-October, a familiar knot clawed at my insides, raking the lining of my stomach. I felt like I did on those lonely mornings in my cold Soviet-era apartment block in Mongolia. I was empty, anxious, and despondent, every waking moment. It was a pronounced change from the past several years when I felt nothing at all.

Whatever was bothering me wasn't limited to work or friends or my dad. Something was unsettled, an intense disquietude I hadn't detected since my twenties. Something was off.

I tried riding it out, taking the long route to school in the mornings, fast, or cycling home via the foothills in the evening, my thoughts spinning faster than my wheels, but that didn't help. Moby's "Are You Lost in the World Like Me?" came out that fall, and it seemed a fitting anthem for my present situation.

In all the darkness, the only light was a sign that pointed right to Baku. Each morning, as I crested the highest point of Shields Street between Fort Collins and Loveland, the two cities I thought were my homes, I'd contemplate the upcoming summer.

There's no way you're even getting to Baku! I doubt your Azerbaijani visa is valid.

I'd purchased a visa for Azerbaijan through an online travel agency. For seventy dollars, I received a pdf document that purportedly granted me entry into the reclusive authoritarian nation.

If you do get in, you've got to find a bicycle box in Baku and make your flight across the Caspian.

'At least we have our ticket for that.'

If you call an online reservation through SCAT airlines a real ticket.

I cringed.

And what are the chances you'll get into Kazakhstan? Or China?

'Those visas are legit. They're glued into the passport and everything.'

Even if you ride across Kazakhstan, there's no way they're going to let you into China at some random border crossing.

I pedaled harder. For all my pessimism, I believed that things would work out. I imagined pedaling into Urumqi, the largest city in western China, four hundred miles east of the Kazakh border and my de facto goal for the summer.

Somewhere in my brain, though, Urumqi wasn't far enough. I had greater ambitions.

You don't really think you can make it to Lanzhou, do you?

Lanzhou was a thousand miles past Urumqi. I didn't answer. I knew Lanzhou wasn't good enough either.

Xi'an? You're dreaming!

'All we do is dream.'

Xi'an was another four hundred miles past Lanzhou, and only a thousand miles from my end goal, Shanghai.

You'd have to ride a hundred miles a day across Central Asia to get to Xi'an.

To ride there, everything would have to go perfectly. As unlikely as it was, it was possible, and if it was possible, then I was free to dream about it.

I grinned and pedaled faster, my heart rate monitor recording every elated pump of blood through my veins and every calorie burned.

*****

In early November, I flew home to help move the remaining items from my dad's house to his condo in Rockford, five miles from my brother. I took photos as we cleaned, documenting every nook and cranny, every lamp, end table, and countertop that I would never see again.

I spent a few final minutes in my old bedroom, staring at the windowsill where I often sat and longingly looked westward, toward Colorado, where I believed my real life would begin.

On our last day at the house, I stood with my brother and dad on the front steps.

My dad looked out at the lawn and said, "It was good to have lived here as brothers."

Kevin and I glanced at each other, unsure how to interpret his unusual statement.

"Maybe he thinks of us as his brothers," whispered Kevin. "Or maybe he isn't sure who we are."

I shook my head. My dad had already forgotten why we were selling the house, about the IRS people and the taxes.

"Maybe it's his synapses misfiring," I whispered back. *Maybe none of it means much at all.*

After moving everything out of the house, I set up a few of my dad's accounts for online payments. His electricity bill was the only thing we left for him to pay each month by check as he'd done all his life.

I returned to Colorado and left my brother to deal with everything else.

*****

One Friday in December, I made a point to go out with a few teachers after work. I thought about Bri and knew she'd be proud of me.

Rachel and I talked about school, and then she asked me a question I hadn't anticipated.

"Are you going to continue your ride this summer?"

I hesitated. The previous year, I'd been careful not to tell anyone about my aspirations to pedal across Turkey. My goals for the upcoming summer were even more absurd.

"Well," I said, "my plan is to fly back to Georgia and ride into Azerbaijan. From there I'll take a flight across the Caspian Sea to western Kazakhstan. Then I'll keep going, possibly to China."

"Wow. That's impressive!"

"I haven't done any of it yet. Besides, I probably won't even get into China."

"Things will work out!"

"I hope so. I guess the worst thing that will happen is that I don't make it anywhere. There are worse outcomes" I gave a halfhearted grin. "What about your summer plans?"

Rachel smiled. "Jay and I are going to Australia."

"Cool! Any ideas which cities you'll visit?"

"Sydney," Rachel said softly. "I've always wanted to go to Sydney."

I listened as Rachel told me the details of their upcoming travels, happy to have diverted attention away from my own ridiculous ambitions.

Of course, once I told her my goals, I started telling other staff members. From there, it became common knowledge, and the prospect of failing publicly gave me one more thing to worry about.

A few weeks later, I made my Christmas drive to Michigan. For the previous eleven years, after my mom died, I made a point to spend Christmas Eve with my dad. We followed our family tradition of going to Mass at the Gothic

Revival cathedral in downtown Lansing, eating Little Caesar's pizza for dinner, and then watching the movie *Scrooge*.

This year, we went to a sterile church near my dad's condo, where the new-home interior contrasted starkly with the expansive domed ceiling and towering stained-glass windows of Lansing's cathedral.

Walking back to our car after Mass, I scrutinized my father's gait, watching his left hip falter with each step. He appeared so frail and thin, not the energetic man I knew growing up.

"Are we ordering pizza and watching *Scrooge* tonight?" I asked, as though the answer were obvious.

My dad turned to me with puzzled eyes. "I guess so. Why do you want to watch *Scrooge?*"

"Well," I hesitated. "It's what we always do."

My dad resumed walking. "I have my frozen dinners. If you want to order pizza, you can."

I had no desire to order pizza. I hadn't wanted any since I'd started counting my calories in 2009. But I still ate it with him every Christmas Eve.

"I'll figure something out," I said as my dad unlocked the car.

You've come home faithfully for the past eleven years and he doesn't remember any of it. What was the point?

I didn't know. I wasn't sure of much anymore.

That evening, my dad had his frozen dinner and Kendra and I scrounged food from the fridge. Afterward, I put *Scrooge* into my dad's VHS player. The three of us read while it played. I cast glances at the aging man sitting next to us, not sure if he could understand the book he was reading.

Kendra's eyes caught mine. "I'm sorry," they said.

I gave a weak smile and shrugged.

From Michigan, Kendra and I went to Omaha to visit her family. They lived on a tree-lined street which dropped to a tranquil park. Over the years, I had become more acquainted with the city than I had ever imagined I would, taking cold morning rides on the city's bike path or exploring the surrounding hills of the Missouri River valley. In the evenings, I enjoyed made-from-scratch dinners courtesy of Kendra's mom.

I left for Fort Collins on New Year's Eve, but Kendra stayed behind to spend a few more days with her parents before flying back. Driving home alone, across the entirety of Nebraska, I pondered what 2017 would bring.

At seven in the morning on New Year's Day, I hopped on my Trek racing bike and rode to Denver in frigid temperatures, taking a few photos from the steps of the mile-high capital. From the tiers of concrete, I gazed for a few moments at the majestic Rocky Mountains hovering in the blue midday sky, a stately reminder of why I moved to Colorado.

Returning home, I visualized myself riding across the Central Asian steppe, wondering how it would all turn out. I rode 130 miles and watched the sun rise and set from the saddle of my bicycle.

I started the new year with a sliver of hope.

*****

That hope diminished once school resumed. The defiant behaviors increased, and we couldn't figure out how to change them. I felt ineffective at best and considered the possibility there was someone out there who might do my job better than me.

Outwardly, Rachel remained optimistic, but I knew the behaviors were wearing her down. I wondered whether she would return to fifth grade the following year. The thought of having to interview someone new, just as we were settling in as a team, was too much to contemplate. Sia's "Bang My Head" became my go-to song of the season. I listened to it over and over.

One evening, Kendra walked into the living room and detected my glum face.

"What are you doing this weekend?" I asked her, as though she might have some magical solution to my melancholy.

"The usual. Getting groceries in the morning. Going to Animal House to walk dogs."

A tinge of guilt passed through me. I rarely helped at the dog shelter. I was too busy riding.

"And you?" Kendra asked. "Why don't you call someone?"

"You know," I mused, "we could leave Fort Collins and no one would even notice."

"Where would we go?"

My mind sped across a map of the United States. We wanted to maintain an eight-hour radius around Omaha so Kendra would always be within driving distance of her family. "We're not moving to Kansas," I said.

Truthfully, I considered a college town like Lawrence a possibility. It was somewhere new, somewhere we could start over.

Kendra sat down next to me. I glanced around our living room, noting the deep shades of red and green that we had painted the walls when we moved in, vibrant colors we wouldn't dare use now that notions of resale value nagged at our adult conscience.

"We don't know anyone in Fort Collins anymore," I said.

"Perhaps it's time to find a job here. You might meet people who live near us."

"But Sarah Milner is like a second home. I have tenure. I have a good team. I don't want to leave just to get a job a few miles closer to home."

Kendra looked at me.

"Plus, I don't want to give up my commute." I silently laughed at my attempt at a joke. "If I'm going to make a change, let's move somewhere new. Maybe a new state. Or a new country."

"I'd have to quit," Kendra pointed out. "There are insurance issues to think about."

"And I've been paying into Colorado's retirement program for years," I added. "If we leave, I won't get much from Social Security."

I thought back to 1999, when I drove my red Geo Prism, stuffed with all my worldly belongings, to Tucson with no idea of where I would live or what I would do. Now I was talking about mortgages, health benefits, and retirement plans.

Pathetic.

"I think you should consider finding a job in Fort Collins. Why move somewhere new if you haven't given our home a chance?" She ran her fingers through my hair, kissed my head, and walked into the kitchen. "Think about it," she said as she left the room.

Home?

I considered the word. With each passing day, I increasingly felt like I lived in two cities but didn't belong in either one.

"I think I'll head to work tomorrow," was the best answer I could muster.

A few nights later, I clicked on a Facebook link to a video called "Why Your Life is Not a Journey." Set to music, with imagery from the movie *Tree of Life*, it contains part of a speech by Alan Watts, a British philosopher with an interest in Eastern religion.

In his speech, Watts states, "You wake up one day about forty years old and you say 'My God, I've arrived. I'm there!' And you don't feel very different from what you've always felt."

The words rang true. I had a good home, a wonderful wife, a fulfilling job at an excellent school, but I was as unsure of myself and my choices at age forty as I was when I was twenty.

I incessantly berated myself for it.

Why can't you be happy doing what normal people do?
Why do you have this urge to do all these stupid things?
Aren't you a little old to be so conflicted?

Will a summer riding across the hinterlands of Central Asia really change anything?

The only question I came close to answering was the final one. Deep down, I believed cycling all that way would change things.

Especially if I got to Xi'an.

I replayed the Alan Watts video again and again. His speech followed me throughout the spring, as did the unease and melancholy scraping at my insides. It was as though I was reliving my twenties, not sure of who I was or where I was meant to be.

Music from my youth reverberated in my head, songs like Bruce Springsteen's "No Retreat, No Surrender" and "Born to Run," and "A Murder of One," by Counting Crows. When I heard them, my soul would expand with the crazy notion that something more is out there, waiting for me just over the horizon.

It was like I hadn't grown up at all.

Every week I read more articles stating that we should be more mindful and live in the moment, and that people with close social networks are healthier and have longer, fuller lives. Those studies compounded my guilt.

If the research is correct, that means you and Kendra are destined to die soon, very soon, and it will be a sad, lonely death.

I laughed at my nonsense, but in a way it wasn't funny.

For the first time in my life, I questioned why Kendra and I had moved all the way to Colorado when our families were back east. My departure from Michigan into the western sunset had turned into a reality that lacked any of the mysticism I'd anticipated and included none of the close-knit friendships I'd assumed I'd make.

*****

In May, Sarah Milner Elementary held a walkathon to raise money for new laptops. Minor back issues had forced me to give up running several years earlier, so I intended to walk during the event. Instead, the moment someone said, "Go!" I ran as fast as I could.

After thirty minutes, my right knee began to seize, but I kept running until the walkathon ended ten minutes later. I hobbled across the blacktop, my knee screaming, "Why? Why?" at me in near panic.

I assured myself it would be OK.

For the next week, my knee was tolerable if I pedaled with smooth strokes and didn't put much pressure on it. I didn't worry about it. I had plenty else to do as the school year ended. That included showing Rachel where I kept all the materials in my room.

"My science supplies are up here," I said, opening one of my yellow classroom cabinets. "And over here is my reading stuff. Social studies is in that cabinet there." I pointed above the sink.

Rachel gave me a quizzical look.

"In case you need anything over the summer," I said.

Of course, I wasn't showing her around so she could use my materials for planning. She had her own things. As we moved from one shelf to the next, I thought of the car in Bosnia, the one that almost ran me over. I wasn't being melodramatic; I was being practical. I'd given all my online passwords to Kendra. Why not tell my teaching partner where I kept my spare scissors? It might save everyone a lot of hassle if things didn't go as planned.

"So, I think that's it. Sorry again this year was so challenging. Next year will be better!"

Rachel laughed. "I'm sure it will."

I appreciated her optimism and was glad that she'd be returning.

"Have a great summer," I said.

"You as well. Good luck and be careful!"

Rachel walked back to her room, and I loaded my things onto my Soma for a final ride home. I cranked up "We Don't Know," by The Strumbellas, on my MP3 player, singing along to lyrics echoing themes of confusion, loss, and hopeful longing. Under bright blue skies, they were a fitting end to an upheaval of a year.

As the foundations of my real world cracked around me, I looked to my ride as some kind of salvation. It had become everything to me. All else could fail, but the ride had to succeed. I had to get to China.

Anything less was existential failure.

THE ROUTE: 2017

Daily Log

2017		
May	**Miles**	**Description**
Mon 29		Power walk around Munich airport
30	108	Tblisi to Samkhir, Azerbaijan, really hot by the end
31	121	Samkhir to Kurdamir, flat as it can get, tailwind much of the way
June	**Miles**	**Description**
Thurs 1	121	Kurdamir to Baku, tailwind until the final 21 miles
2	0	walk 2.5 hours around Baku, Azerbaijan; did a bit of sightseeing
3	94	Atyrau to Maqat, Kazakhstan, tailwind, pavement great until it wasn't
4	116	Maqat to just NE of Nogayty, almost all on jeep roads, knee killing me, camped
Mon 5	126	Campground above to Kyndayagash, knee getting worse on the hills; pavement better though
6	60	Kyndayagash to Aktobe, knee really, really bad
7	136	Aktobe to truck stop motel east of Karabutak; knees miraculously better, roads flatter, tailwind
8	125	Motel above to random campsite under an overpass on M32, in the desert now
9	120	Campsite above, to Aralsk, a fast 120 miles through the Kazakh desert
10	137	Aral to Baykongur (Toretam), flat and with a tailwind
11	121	Flat, headwind, from Toretam to Chaghan, where I stayed at a truck stop hotel
Mon 12	120	Chaghan to just east of Shieli, to the strange but quaint roadside hotel; sunscreen running low
13	130	Hotel above, stopped at Sauran Fortress, then thirtieth miles past Turkistan, camped by highway
14	159	Campground to Taraz, into the mountains with a major dustorm pushing me onward
15	102	Taraz to Merki, flat, headwind most of the day, later storms, terrifying lightning
16	140	Merki to about 100 miles west of Almaty, camping off the A2 at Kilometer marker 137
17	80	Campsite to central Almaty, traffic a nightmare
18	119	Almaty to ??!!, 119 miles east, under the highway, after the new highway took me off my map
Mon 19	90	Campsite under highway to Korgas, China, riding into a heartbreak of a headwind
20	90	Korgas hotel to campsite under highway about 25 east of Lake Sayram Hu
21	130	Campground to junction of M30 and Highway 124, where I found a hotel and a good restaurant
22	145	From wherever I was yesterday to Hutubi, China
23	70	Into Hutubi, looking for ATM; then to Changji and then to Urumqi
24	110	Urumqui to Turpan, known for it's raisins. Two flats
25	107	Turpan, 106 miles east to random truck stop after hitting a killer headwind and hill at mile 85
Mon 26	107	Highway hotel, uphill into gusting headwind, 3 hours to do 20 miles; ended in Liushuquan
27	124	Liushuquan to campsite in a gulley resembling Tattooine 62 km from Xingxingxia
28	100	Campsite from last night to...Liuyuan, felt good, but four flat tires...keep picking up metal shards
29	107	Liuyuan to the next campsite, another flat at mile 20, headwind and uphill whole way
Fri 30	102	Campsite to Jiaguyuan, headwind and uphill, flat at 20 miles again, used spares until mile 90
July	**Miles**	**Description**
Sat 1	136	Jiayuguan to campsite under a bridge, after seeing the Great Wall in the morning
2	110	Campsite to Yongchang, over a 20 mile climb, raining and cold all day
Mon 3	118	Campsite to Tianzhu, last 12 miles with the Gansu Highway Patrol
4	120	Tianzhu to Lanzhou, then 15 miles further east to a crossroads hotel
5	94	Whereever I was yesterday to Tongwei. Rained first half of the day
6	125	Tongwei to about 60 miles east of Tangshui, in some random village on the river
7	119	Random mountain village to Zhouzhi, about 60 miles from Xian
8	61	Zhouzhi to Xian!
9		Exerbike at Sheraton, walked around Xian all day today too.
Mon 10		Ride around Xian, almost 2 hours, easy, then lots of walking
11		Ride to the Tomb of Emperor Jindi, north of central Xian, 30 miles total, flat, easy
12		Exerbike at the gym at the Sheraton, light weights, lots more walking too
13		Exerbike at Sheraton 1:15; walked at least 15 minutes at airport in San Fransisco

CHAPTER 13

A remix of Iggy Pop's "Lust for Life," from the *Trainspotting II* soundtrack, pounded through my headphones as I pedaled away from Tbilisi International Airport, leaving behind another bicycle box and duffel bag. In the morning darkness, I snapped a photo of the sign from last summer, the one that pointed left to central Tbilisi and right to Baku. I couldn't believe an entire year had passed.

I rode through the industrial outskirts of the city, terrified by the invisible growling dogs haunting every business front. I was soon out of the city and pedaling up the rolling green hills of the Georgian countryside.

Forty miles and four hours later I was within sight of the Azerbaijani border crossing where a sign, written in Georgian and English, read "Good Luck!"

I approached the checkpoint with wariness, passing a long queue of semitrucks before arriving at a huge gate. It looked like the entrance to a luxury home, not a country.

An armed guard in military fatigues waved me toward a kiosk where a border patrol agent waited with a hostile frown. I pulled out my passport and a printout of the visa I had downloaded from the internet and handed it to him.

There's no way it's valid.

'It'll work.'

The agent eyed me suspiciously and pointed at my MP3 player. I gave him an earbud and played a song to convince him it wasn't a secret microphone. *There aren't any direct flights from Tbilisi to western Kazakhstan.* The guard gave me a long, cantankerous stare. I prepared for the worst.

He scrutinized my visa, then my passport, and then me. Without warning, he pulled out a stamp, pounded my documents, and handed them to me. He waved me forward.

Another guard opened a second gate and motioned me through, a genuine welcoming smile spread across his young face. He closed the gate behind me and there I was, in Azerbaijan, free to ride wherever I wanted across the totalitarian state.

I passed countless vineyards and enjoyed long, open stretches of highway. The E60 cut straight across the middle of the country, with two full lanes in each direction, and descended from an elevation of two thousand feet at the western edge of Azerbaijan to a hundred feet below sea level at the capital city, Baku. A strong wind blew out of the west, pushing me onward.

On my second day in the small nation, the temperature crested a muggy ninety degrees. I stopped at a gas station in the midafternoon, paid an outside attendant for a few bottles of water, and hurried to leave. I avoided going inside where numerous men sat at tables sipping tea.

I was walking back to my bike when a young man approached me with a broad smile. He appeared like so many others in Azerbaijan, with black hair and eyebrows, the trace of a goatee and beard, and moderately dark skin. He held out his hand to shake mine, introduced himself, and motioned for me to go inside and have some tea. I couldn't say no.

I felt self-conscious as I walked toward the door. My sunglasses were perched on top of my shaved head. I had on a smelly, torn, gray and black jersey. My cycling shorts accentuated my shaved legs, which glistened under a mix of sweat and sunscreen. And Donald Trump's executive order barring citizens of seven Islamic nations from entering the US was making headlines around the world.

The moment I walked inside, every conversation ceased and every head in the café turned in my direction. Twenty Muslim Azerbaijani men stared at me.

"As-salamu alaikum!" I declared with a broad smile and wave. An awkward moment passed, milliseconds. It felt like an eternity.

The men gave muted waves back, a few mustered a smile, and then they returned to their conversations.

I sat down with my new friend, and he ordered tea. I didn't speak a word of Azerbaijani, and he spoke no English, but we had an entire conversation through hand gestures, talking without talking. He asked me if I'd been chased by dogs and whether I was married.

We took a selfie together, and before it got awkward, I took my leave. My host insisted on paying. I squandered fifteen precious minutes of riding time for one of the most memorable experiences of my life.

I arrived at the Caspian Sea the next day. I parked my bike and walked to the black and tan sand so that I could touch the foamy water. It was warm on my fingertips.

Standing on the water's edge, I could see the skyscrapers of Baku jutting out along a peninsula. I took a few obligatory selfies before turning north into an infernal headwind.

Forty miles later, I reached the outskirts of the capital city. Oversized and manicured homes, brand-new roads, and a golf course showed how wealthy the country had become off of the reserves of black gold beneath its surface. I navigated my way through Baku traffic, an amateur endeavor after cycling across Istanbul the previous summer.

After settling in at a nondescript hotel, I found a small bicycle shop and bought another box to pack my bike for the hour-long flight to Atyrau, Kazakhstan, the next day. I was proud of myself for streamlining the process and having the foresight to translate the phrase "bicycle box" into Azerbaijani, Kazakh, and Chinese.

During the short trip across the Caspian Sea, I gazed out the window, watching the evening sun cast the water in a quiet, warm glow. The descent into Atyrau offered uninterrupted views of the flat, sprawling city filled with fenced-in houses that resembled the *hashaas* of Mongolian towns.

I got off the plane on the tarmac, walked through passport control with no problems and assembled my Soma in the tiny terminal. I stuffed the bicycle box behind a staircase and discarded yet another duffel bag before making my way to a nearby hotel where I fell into a deep sleep after a whirlwind four days.

*****

I stopped in front of a road sign on the eastern outskirts of Atyrau. It was painted in familiar, reflective tints of gray and white. Written in both the Cyrillic and Latin alphabets were the distances to several cities, including Aktobe, my first destination in western Kazakhstan. It was only 360 miles away.

I scanned the road in front me, a flat stretch of concrete beckoning me forward. I grinned and pushed down on my pedals. The pavement started off smooth and the shoulder provided ample room for the occasional passing car. A tailwind propelled me past flattened grasslands and small stretches of salt flats.

'If all of Kazakhstan is like this, we'll be hitting Shanghai before the end of summer!'

I saw my first camels that morning, grazing near a deserted gas station. Some were Bactrian, with two humps, while others were the single-humped dromedary variety.

Why are there single-humped camels here?

I'd only seen Bactrian camels in Mongolia. Observing single-humped camels in Central Asia distorted my worldview.

You need to look that up later.

'Noted.'

I turned up my music and cruised along in happy bliss, glad camel species were my primary concern for the day.

And then the pavement disappeared. A harsh gravel underbelly emerged, pounding my bike and belongings and reducing my speed to six miles per hour. The pavement returned in sections, but disappeared again, leaving me worried about the remaining two-thousand miles of Kazakhstan.

Two tedious hours later, a man in a beige Toyota SUV slowed to a halt and rolled down his window. He had distinctive Kazakh facial features, with dark hair and wide cheekbones accentuating his broad smile.

"The road," he told me in English, "washed out last year. Now it's nothing more than broken concrete."

I frowned.

"How far is it like this?" I asked, not wanting to hear the answer.

"Maybe three hundred kilometers."

I did the math in my head.

That's 180 miles!

"Do you want a ride?" asked the man. "Past the bad part?"

I shook my head. I thought about all the times people had offered me a lift on snowy days commuting between Fort Collins and Loveland. I couldn't take their help then, and I couldn't imagine accepting any now.

"Thank you," I said, "but I'll ride. Slowly."

"There is a town up ahead," he said, pointing down the highway. "Maquat, with a hotel. Be sure to continue into town, not on the highway around it."

"Thank you so much." I reached out to shake his hand.

"Are you sure you don't want a ride?" he offered again.

I shook my head. "Thank you. But I have to ride." I knew my words sounded silly to him.

He started his truck, gave a final wave, and pulled away.

The moment his vehicle was gone, I noticed clouds had drifted overhead. I pushed eastward. The pavement returned and disappeared, along with my optimism. I turned up my headphones to drown out the creaks and groans emanating from my baggage racks. I reached Maquat just as thick raindrops came tumbling out of the sky.

Maquat was a small town full of angular, dull apartment blocks. I veered into the center of the city, searching for the hotel the man had mentioned, the drizzle clouding my sunglasses and making it difficult to see anything. Maquat's residents had long since taken cover inside and I felt a sense of abandonment on the desolate street.

I had translated the Kazakh word for hotel on Google Translate many times before leaving, and it always gave me the Russian word, гостиница (*gostinitsa*). I can read and write Cyrillic fluently, having learned it in the Peace Corps, so I rode through town looking for a *gostinitsa*.

After twenty minutes riding up and down the main street, I saw a few people sheltering under the awning of a building. I pulled up to them and asked, "*Gostinitsa?*"

One of the men nodded and pointed to an intersection a few blocks away. I thanked him in passable Russian, having used Babbel.com again this year to learn the basics, and rode in the direction he pointed. I still couldn't find the hotel.

As a wave of frustration swept over me, a truck pulled up. Two young men, perhaps eighteen, peered at me through an open window. I thought they were going to harass me, but the driver asked me, in English, if I needed help.

"I'm looking for a hotel," I said. "Someone said there was one nearby."

The driver pointed behind me to a two-story imposing white structure that resembled a school. I read the word қонақ үй (*konak ui*) written in massive block letters on the left side of the building. I figured that was the name of the hotel.

I parked my Soma outside and the two men led me through a set of double doors at the front of the building.

Inside was an expansive and empty foyer. We passed through it and went up a flight of stairs.

At the top, a woman sat at a makeshift reception area. The driver translated for me, explaining the different price options for the rooms. I paid the woman and walked back outside with the two young men. We took a selfie together, an instant classic, my muddy sunglasses perched on my wet hair, a glimpse of rainy pavement behind us, and three huge smiles spread across our faces.

I thanked the men profusely before they left. I locked my filthy, mud-covered bicycle in the front entryway, barely able to look at it, and proceeded inside.

The room was austere, with no towels or toiletries, but it only cost eight dollars for the night. I unpacked, showered under a cold stream of water, shaved my face and legs, and washed my clothes. Then I called Kendra to tell her, as best I could, where I was.

The sun had come out and I went outside, wandering past the aging apartment buildings, broken sidewalks, and kids playing. It reminded me of Mongolian cities, and was surprisingly comforting, like returning home after a long time away.

I found a grocery store and stocked up on necessities. I was impressed by its selection of German, Eastern European, and Kazakh beer, as well as liquor from all over the world, including whiskey and whisky, vodka, brandy, and gin.

I returned to my hotel and ate a dinner of cheese, bread, and sausage on the front steps, washing my meal down with a malty Kazakh ale. The sky turned brilliant shades of blue and yellow as the sun descended. I waited for the first stars to appear before retiring to my room.

The highway out of Maquat the next morning began as beautiful black asphalt. Within a mile, however, the pavement crumbled away and the road once more became a washed-out mess of gravel. On either side of the fragmented highway, scattered jeep trails emerged, cut by drivers trying to find a better route.

The jeep paths were smoother than the road, and I navigated the beautiful singletrack with relative ease. But with seventy pounds of gear on my narrow tires, I worried about the beating my wheels were taking.

It was impossible to stay in one line, as the tracks would crisscross with other tracks, and where one would fizzle out into a mess of mud and rocks another would appear. Several times I pushed my bike through areas of sand, the bottom of my bicycle rims disappearing beneath the brown crystals.

The weather remained cool and overcast. Small grasses swayed to the north and south, and droves of horses congregated around watering holes.

Occasionally, a vehicle passed me and I gave a wave. In the midafternoon, a lumbering cargo truck pulled next to me and four Kazakh men hopped out. In any other country I would have been terrified, but they grinned as they approached me, cell phones in hand to take a picture. We posed together and then, as abruptly as they materialized, they got back into their truck and continued onward.

Later a car stopped, and two men got out. One of them offered me a carton of liquified yogurt. I thanked him and we took a selfie before he, too, disappeared. I tasted the sour drink but decided it was not the best cycling food, though I appreciated the gesture.

The wind picked up as the day wore on, and the sunny skies were replaced by thin gray clouds. I savored the pleasant drop in temperature even as I speculated on where I would stay for the night.

Towns marked by a black dot on my map were small and didn't have any accommodations. They did have cell towers though. I paused on the outskirts of a village as evening descended to text Kendra and let her know I'd be camping that night.

A few miles later, I found an area of washes that, while close to the road, provided a few hidden campsites. I set up my tent and laid out my cycling shorts to air dry, relieved to put on regular clothes. I ate, edited photos on my laptop, and then climbed into my sleeping bag.

'We made it 116 miles today!'

If I could get through roads like these, I reasoned, I could get through anything.

*****

I woke up the next morning with a small pain in my knee. It had bothered me a little the previous day, but this morning the discomfort was more apparent. I shrugged in denial and set out.

The pavement fluctuated with no rhyme or reason, with smooth stretches morphing into jagged areas of potholes and gravel.

The knee pain grew worse. I kept pedaling through flat, dull scenery, semi-green grasses contrasting with thin gray clouds.

Late in the morning, I spotted something to the left following me. I turned my head and saw a scrawny, pathetic dog with big paws and a pronounced rib cage trying to catch up to me.

It was young, adorable, and save for a few dilapidated buildings half a mile away, alone in the middle of nowhere. I tried throwing some cereal in the opposite direction, hoping she would leave, but the dog was more interested in me than the food.

"Go on!" I yelled.

She stared at me, smiling the way dogs do, her tongue hanging to the side of her mouth.

I tossed more cereal and tried pedaling away. My heart was breaking at the sight of her. She ignored the food.

"Go!" I said, more forcefully this time. I surveyed the distant structures, hoping someone would step out and call for her.

The buildings were silent.

I tried to pedal away. The dog followed.

'Someone in those buildings owns her,' I told myself.

I thought of my own dogs, long since gone. I thought of the many foster dogs Kendra and I had taken in over the years.

The lonely canine continued after me.

I considered my options before picking up a rock. Tears pooled behind my eyes.

Don't do it.

'What else can we do?'

The animal backed away. I scanned the nearby buildings again.

'Someone must live there.'

I was unconvinced.

I stepped away. The dog followed.

I hesitated and tossed the rock, toward the dog but not at her.

She cowered for a moment before continuing toward me, without a sound, her pleading eyes peering into mine.

I threw another rock, off right. She planted all four paws on the ground.

I lobbed another, off left.

I moved away.

She didn't follow. Instead, she looked at me with sad, longing eyes.

I hopped on my bike and pedaled furiously away. I glanced back to see if she was following me, but she had turned around, dejected.

Tears flowed from my eyes. The immensity of that dog's situation left me hollow. She had so much love to give but couldn't find anyone to reciprocate. She couldn't control the world swirling around her. I was overwhelmed by the lost souls like her treading those in-between spaces. I was utterly useless.

What's the point of this ride? I screamed at myself. *You're fulfilling some pointless narcissistic desire ... You should do something to help others this summer ... maybe volunteering at an animal shelter ... Why are you here?*

'I don't know,' I shouted back. 'I don't know why we're here.'

I looked up at the cool, colorless skies and kept pedaling. The tears flowed for miles, and when I approached a Kazakh cemetery under late-morning clouds, where Islamic crescent moons reached upward from their brick enclosures, more emotions erupted.

How many of those people have grown up and lived and died in these remote little villages?

I examined the headstones dotting the landscape, metal lunar shapes hovering over dusty gravesites.

How many people dreamed of something more but weren't able to do anything about it?

My eyes flooded again. Halfway around the world, I felt the same lingering, acidic anxiety that had followed me around the past school year.

'I thought we were doing better.'

Through the inward wailing, I rolled forward. When I calmed down enough to consider the day, it occurred to me that the chaos of landing in Georgia, pedaling across Azerbaijan, hopping another flight across the Caspian, and setting out again was a momentary diversion.

Now, there were no more logistics to work out. I had pushed my emotions aside in my rush from Tbilisi to Atyrau, but with that leg of the trip over, I now had a lot of time to think. I was in for the long haul.

Simply seeing a sad little dog or passing a Kazakh cemetery was enough to bring the memories of the previous year, of school, of my dad, of the isolated weekends, to the surface. The familiar knot had returned and all I could do was try to pedal away from it.

I was grateful for the road conditions, as they demanded my utmost attention and distracted me from my intermittent malaise. At times, the highway was diverted so construction crews could repave mile-long stretches, and I would follow lines of huge trucks through dusty detours.

Two hundred miles after the first signs of cracked pavement, paved surfaces became the norm. But as the highway pavement returned, the hills became bigger and the pain in my knee became worse.

When the short hills became long climbs, the outside of my right knee started to moan. Then it started to scream. Then it seized. I began using my left leg to complete the pedal stroke my right leg should have been pushing.

How could you have been so stupid, to run in the walkathon?

I didn't have a good answer.

This won't get better.

'It has to.'

Tears welled in my eyes, again.

I made it to the town of Kyandagash and stayed in a small roadside hotel, where the word *Gostinitsa* was clearly displayed outside next to the words *Konak Ui* in equally large letters.

A Russian van, identical to the ones people drive in Mongolia, was parked next to the building. I examined the familiar gray paint and abrupt curves of its design. A reel of memories streamed through my head.

After a thoughtful moment, I stepped into a small store. It could have been any country shop in Mongolia, with candies, tasteless bread products, and random other things behind the counter. After stocking up, I headed to my room, which was at the top of a flight of stairs. Pain seared through my knee with each step.

The next morning was chilly. Gray skies lingered, further darkening my mood.

'Please, knee,' I pleaded, 'be better today.'

Instead, it grimaced at me as I set the mass of steel, panniers, and water bottles in motion. A headwind hit me at once and reduced my pace to a crawl. While the hills I feared never materialized, cranking on my pedals into the relentless wind punished my knee as much as any incline. It screamed all day. At times I burst out crying, continuing to pedal even as my sunglasses became a blurry mess of tears.

I arrived in Aktobe six slow hours later. I checked into a hotel, then went for a walk. I was amazed that white Russian faces nearly equaled the number of Asian Kazakh faces. I meandered through an outdoor bazaar, found a grocery store, and otherwise forgot about my knee for a while.

On my way back to my room, I called Kendra.

"Hi!" Kendra said.

"Hey," I responded, trying to sound cheerful.

"Where are you?"

"I'm in Aktobe," I said. "It's the first major city I've seen since I left Atyrau."

I gazed at the drab apartment buildings and leafy green trees lining the manicured streets as I strolled with my phone to my ear.

"Did the roads improve?" Kendra asked.

"They did, eventually. And I made good progress on the jeep trails. They didn't slow me down too much. I'm hoping the pavement will be OK from here. I'll be on the only major highway between Moscow and Almaty."

"That sounds promising," said Kendra.

"I hope so. I could use a break."

A sharp pain in my knee screeched at me. I hoped Kendra couldn't hear.

"How's everything else going?"

"Good. I stocked up on groceries." I hesitated. "My knee has been bugging me a bit."

"I'm sorry. Is it bad?"

"I'm sure it will get better," I answered before changing the subject. "How's Gracie?"

Gracie was a shy pit bull with heartworms that we were fostering. We'd gotten her in May, and of course I fell in love with her like I did with all our foster dogs. I smiled at the thought of her laying upside down waiting for a belly rub.

Kendra sighed. "She follows me around nonstop, and on walks I can't trust her with other dogs."

I knew Kendra was not enamored with Gracie like I was, and I knew Gracie probably wouldn't be home when I got back.

"That's a lot for you to deal with on your own. Sorry I'm not there to help."

"It's OK," Kendra said.

It's not OK, I thought.

"How's work?" I asked, changing the subject again.

Kendra talked while I listened, shuffling my heavy groceries from one hand to the other. Soon I had circled the block and was gazing at my ten-story hotel.

"Well, I should go back to my room and eat dinner. I need to make plans for tomorrow."

"How far do you think you'll make it?"

"We'll see. There's not much east of here."

"Call me tomorrow if you can, or at least text."

"I will. Love you."

"Love you too. Bye."

Click.

I shifted my groceries again and walked into the hotel lobby. I took the elevator to the sixth floor and walked down the hallway to my room, where cigarette burns littered the carpet. I gazed out the window at the communist-era city planning, full of rectangular apartments. After a moment considering Kazakhstan's Soviet past, I sat on the bed.

This is it.

'We've failed.'

Your knee is done.

'There's no way we can make it a hundred miles a day. We'll be lucky to make it to Urumqi.'

You'll be lucky to get ten miles.

I wanted to scream or cry or punch something. I stared at the pile of gear lying on the bed, then put my head in my hands, thinking it all through.

"No," I said to myself. "You're not done. You're going to leave here early tomorrow. If you can only ride ten or twenty miles a day for the next six weeks, so be it."

That does sound better than sitting around and moping.
'We'll at least make it to Almaty.'
I looked out the window again.
"You're going to keep going east," I declared. "No matter what."

CHAPTER 14

I set out the next morning under dreary skies, my mood matching the dark clouds. I softly pushed on my pedals, thankful the wide boulevards leading out of Aktobe were flat.

A soft tailwind nudged me forward into never-ending grasslands. I took three Advil ten miles into my ride, the pain in my knee an all-too-apparent reminder that I was only a few steep hills away from coming undone.

The road, which began as a divided, two-lane-in-each-direction highway, soon diminished into one lane each way. The shoulder disappeared for miles at a time, but I was happy to have pavement.

A few hours into my ride, the two-inch metal bracket that held my front rack in place, the same bracket that broke in northern France two summers ago and in Serbia the previous summer, snapped, no doubt a result of two-hundred miles of jeep trails.

I put my bike on its side.

'We're prepared this year!'

I dug through my saddle bag and removed a Ziploc filled with spare parts. I pulled out two brass-colored brackets, fresh from Mr. Bricolage's home improvement store in Sofia, Bulgaria.

I grinned at my wise planning, and the memories of Sofia and Normandy, contemplating how the three summers were so connected. Fifteen minutes later, I was on the road, a smudge of grease on my hands the only evidence I'd paused at all.

Around four, I pulled off the highway, sat down, and removed a squished bag of bread and a block of warm cheese from my trunk bag. I gazed south where faint patches of blue broke through the horizontal stratus clouds and Kazakhstan stretched out before me. The breeze carried a delicate scent of grass and dust. I watched the tall grasses and tiny scattered flowers of the steppe sway in the delicate wind while I nibbled my food. My favorite bicycle lay next to me.

'You know, it doesn't matter how far we make it. Sitting here under the afternoon Kazakh sun makes it all worthwhile.'

I stretched out my legs and let myself enjoy the moment long enough to finish eating. I washed down three more Advil before pushing my bike to the highway, not wanting to waste the strong tailwind.

My bike reached cruising speed.

You know full well it does matter how far you make it. It matters plenty.

I sighed.

'Yes, it does. But it was still a nice spot to eat.'

I suppose.

Two hours later, as the sun began its downward motion toward the western horizon with only a stray line of clouds blocking the view, I rolled into an expansive parking lot filled with semitrucks. I cruised past the massive rigs, noting the license plates from Latvia, Russia, Poland, France, and more. It was astounding to think that many of the trucks had passed me earlier in the day, each one giving me a respectable amount of room.

Past the semis were two buildings. One was a truck stop, with a small store, restaurant, and gas station. To its left was the hotel I'd been hoping to find. I paid the equivalent of six dollars for a brand-new room that, while lacking amenities like towels or soap, had hot water, clean sheets, and a safe place to lock my bike.

As I unpacked, a small wave of euphoria hit me.

'We rode 120 miles today. How's that for a bad knee?'

You're lucky there weren't any hills.

'Everyone's entitled to some luck now and again.'

I showered and washed my cycling gear before meandering outside. To the west, the sun was making its daily exit from the sky. I walked among the hulking rigs, feeling the heat of the cabs, the engines warm after a heavy day's work. Remnants of diesel fuel filled my nose.

I made my way toward the cafeteria when two classic black cars with Estonian license plates caught my eye. The contours of the automobiles were familiar, but I couldn't place them. Several older Kazakh men inspected the cars as well. I snapped a photo and walked to the cafeteria.

Inside, I grabbed a tray and got in line, elbow to elbow with burly Eastern European truck drivers. I pointed at a variety of pickled vegetables and grilled meats. A woman wearing a hairnet piled my plate high with unknown but appetizing food.

At the checkout, the clerk stated the price in Russian. I had learned my Russian numbers through a hundred, but Kazakh currency is in multiples of a thousand. I handed the clerk a large bill and hoped it was enough, a ripple of relief flowing through me when he counted out my change.

I set my tray on a table and looked around. It could have been any truck stop anywhere in the world. Truckers, some by themselves, others in pairs, sat at the fast-food-style tables, painted in tacky shades of red and blue. None of the drivers noticed me. To them, this was simply another day on the job. To me, it was remarkable. I savored every last bite of my warm meal.

My belly full, I stepped outside. Stars appeared in the twilight sky. I crossed an open field and wandered through a Kazakh cemetery, examining the towering cement walls and Islamic crescent moons with fascination and curiosity, rather than the tears and sorrow from the previous day. I considered the anonymous souls inhabiting the grounds with an inner calm I hadn't perceived in a while.

I walked back to my hotel room, with its bright yellow walls, and dug through my scattered belongings to find my map of Kazakhstan. I also pulled up Google Maps on my laptop via the hotel Wi-Fi.

Unlike last year, Google Maps on my phone was not working at all without Wi-Fi. I assumed it was because I was in exotic countries beyond the reach of Verizon. The few times I'd tried to pull up my location, it offered only a vague sense of where I was in Kazakhstan.

Examining my paper map and the map on my computer screen, two names caught my eye: Aralsk and Baikonur. I had read about Aralsk in graduate school because it was home to one of the world's worst environmental disasters, and I knew about Baikonur because it was the home of the Soviet space program.

Aralsk was only 250 miles away and Baikonur another hundred miles past that. Breaking the distances into sections and setting goals for the next three days lifted my spirits. With my plans set, I emailed my photo of the two black cars to a friend of mine who was interested in classic automobiles.

I climbed into bed at a reasonable hour, only to be woken at two in the morning by a group text from my principal about extra-duty contract hours. I felt so disconnected from work, and the disconnect felt good. I silenced my phone and went back to sleep.

*****

Thick clouds greeted me in the morning. The air was cool, and a few sprinkles dotted the pavement.

Put on your jacket.

'The windbreaker is fine.'

You're cold.

'Another layer now means more laundry later.'

Then quit complaining about being cold.

'We're both complaining.'

I was not in a good mood.

I became even more annoyed when a young police officer flagged me down. I knew what he wanted even before he pulled out his cell phone. I forced a smile and pulled in front of his white police car.

As I put my right foot on the ground, an SUV came speeding down the road. The officer motioned for the vehicle to stop. He walked up to the window.

The elapsed time on my heart rate monitor ticked by as the policeman wrote the driver a ticket. I stared at the white squad car. Five minutes passed.

You have a lot of miles to cover.

Ten minutes passed.

These minutes add up.

Frustration welled.

The SUV drove off, and the officer approached me. He held up his phone and we took a few selfies together as though we were old friends.

Twenty minutes after being flagged down, I was pedaling again. The sky was dark, but the rain had ceased.

I rolled into a solitary gas station thirty miles later. It was a two-story blue building surrounded by a mix of grassland and desert steppe. Parked outside were the two mysterious black cars from Estonia.

As I approached the building, I saw a tall, burly Estonian man standing in the door. He looked at me and said, in a drawl, "Welcome to the big city!"

I was surprised that he spoke English, and that he could speak it with such sarcasm.

I laughed and gave my own hearty, "Hello!"

We shook hands. I had to crane my neck upward to look at him. He had pale skin and wore an expression that was hard to read.

"What kind of cars are those?" I asked.

"They are Volgas, Soviet KGB limousines," he said. "Every Soviet spy movie you have seen has them."

"That's why they're so familiar." A rush of nameless communist-era movies rolled through my brain. "Where are you going?"

"We are driving them across Asia into Uzbekistan and Turkistan."

"Wow!" I tried to map out the route in my head.

His three friends walked toward the exit and pulled him out the door with them. He gave me a short wave.

"Bye!" I replied.

Wait!

I watched them pile into their respective black sedans.

Don't you want to talk some more?

I heard the engines turn over and caught a whiff of exhaust as they roared away. I thought back to Portugal and Spain, where I'd met groups of cyclists out for an adventure together. I thought about traveling with friends, about the joys of shared experience.

Then I remembered what it was like to move at other people's pace and listen to them snore all night.

'There's something to be said for traveling alone,' I told myself.

Still ...

Dust from their tires danced in the air. I went into the store to stock up on food and water.

After the gas station, the tall grassland was replaced by arid steppe that, mile by mile, turned to rocky desert. The rolling landscape opened and stretched into forever. It was beautiful but frightening because towns on the map grew further apart. The pain in my knee was a constant, but manageable, presence as I pedaled forward.

In the early evening hours, the sun broke through the clouds. The desert, though markedly different from my home in the Gobi or my short stay in Tucson so long ago, held a certain familiarity to me. My mood improved.

My ease was soon disrupted. A car sped by me and stopped abruptly on the side of the road. I was used to taking selfies with people by now, but the moment the four men got out of the car I could tell they'd been drinking.

One of them told me in broken English that he was a police detective.

What's your point? I wanted to say.

Instead I smiled.

The other men kept silent, in apparent deference to their de facto leader.

We posed for the obligatory selfies, and I took one as well to be polite. I was relieved when they piled back into the car and sped off, leaving me surveying south, east, and west for somewhere out of sight where I could camp. Prospects were slim.

An hour later, I was still pedaling and still fascinated by the landscape, a blend of short shrubbery dotting the rocky and sandy soil, the horizon a constant eternity away.

I heard another vehicle approach behind me and could tell it was slowing down.

Not again.

A white police car pulled in front of me and stopped. I paused next to it, in the middle of the highway. An older policeman had his hands on the wheel. He glared at me. A younger deputy sat in the passenger seat. The younger man got out, walked behind the patrol car, and stood next to me. He motioned south, in the direction I was heading, asking me where I was going.

I pulled out my map, pointed to a small dot on it, and uttered, "*Gostinitsa?*"

He shrugged. I held the map up to the older one, who remained sitting in his car, and repeated my question.

He shrugged too, then asked his own question. "Trump?"

Is he really asking about Trump?

My heart skipped a beat. Seventy percent of Kazakhs are Muslim. On the other hand, the government is secular, and the country has generated a considerable fortune from oil revenue. I didn't know whether this guy wanted a thumbs-up or a thumbs-down.

I replied with a shrug.

The old man scowled.

I thought our conversation was over.

Instead, the younger policeman asked, "American souvenir?"

What!

'I think he wants a bribe.'

No way.

'Agreed.'

Both officers stared at me. I shrugged again.

They continued to look at me, not satisfied with my reply this time. I reached into my handlebar bag and pulled out a pack of Extra gum. I held it out to the older one.

His stare became a glare, but he took it and muttered something to the deputy, who walked back to the passenger seat. Without another word, they drove off, leaving me dumbfounded and ill at ease.

There better be a hotel at that little dot on the map.

I surveyed the landscape. I was in the eastern Kazakh desert with no trees, no ditches, and no shelter from the road. I would be visible for ten miles in any direction if I set up camp.

I continued to the small town and walked into the only store right as they were closing. I bought four large bottles of water, packed them on my bike, and grimaced at the weight. Between the new bottles and my existing reserves, I had over twelve liters of water scattered among my panniers.

Ten miles past the village, I came to a bridge that passed over a wash. Because this stretch of highway was two lanes in each direction, the bridge was wide and offered full cover from the road. It was the perfect—and only—place to camp.

I followed a jeep trail down the embankment and under the bridge. A concrete wall held up enormous cement slabs that supported the highway. The sandy ground was covered with hoof prints. I kicked aside scattered dry animal droppings, stirring up a momentary scent of dung. Once the dust settled, I set up my tent.

I looped my long cable lock through a pole, then locked it into my u-lock, which I had secured around the bicycle frame and front wheel. If anyone tried carrying my bike away in the night, they would take the tent and me with it.

After hanging my sweaty jersey over the top of the tent and my socks over my handlebars, I used a water bottle to give myself a splash bath. I was impressed with my ability to bathe with a liter of water. I air-dried my cycling shorts, cringing at the thought of putting them on in the morning.

My solar charger lay in a patch of scrubby grass, absorbing the last rays of the sun to recharge my MP3 player and cell phone. When I was situated, I sat on my rain jacket, set some food on my Pearl Izumi coat, and ate, my shoulders relaxing as I looked around. From the dry riverbed, I had a stunning view of the desert to the west.

I watched the sun fall to the horizon. The clouds of the previous few days and the tensions of the past few hours dissipated with the diminishing daylight.

After dinner, I blared the album *Simple Forms*, by The Naked and Famous, from my phone and wandered around the wash, gazing at the stars slowly dancing their way into the evening sky, peeking out from behind white, puffy clouds. I was careful to stay hidden from the road.

Around two in the morning, I awoke to a bright, full moon as fabulous as the sunset. I drifted back to sleep before I could properly enjoy it. A few hours later I crawled out of my tent and observed the dawn paint the sky in brilliant shades of red and yellow.

Temperatures were in the mid-seventies, a marked change from the previous week. I packed up my things and was soon on the road again, smelly and disgusting, but also somehow refreshed after my meltdowns of the past several days.

CHAPTER 15

The Aral Sea was once the fourth-largest lake in the world. In the 1960s, the Soviet Union began systematically diverting the rivers that fed the lake to cotton fields as far away as Uzbekistan. By the mid-nineties, it had split into four separate bodies of water that together constituted only one-tenth the area of the original lake.

Aralsk was a fishing community on the shores of the Aral Sea, but as the water disappeared so too did the livelihood of its residents. Rolling into the small town under a blistering sun, all I saw was a sad, dusty shell of what was once a prosperous city.

I found a hotel near the train station and wasted no time showering and washing my clothes. Afterward I went for a walk. The only evidence of Aralsk's fishing industry was a small, dry harbor filled with desert scrub, dormant loading cranes, and four derelict boats sitting in a run-down park.

The city was dominated by concrete and sand with little in between. I inhaled dust with every breath. Unlike Aktobe, this city was predominantly Kazakh, with only the occasional white face meandering by.

The pain in my right knee was ever-present, but nowhere near the intensity it had been several days earlier. Walking around worked wonders.

Back in my room, I talked to Kendra, straightened up my things, looked at my maps, and edited photos. I also checked my email, an exercise in patience with the exceedingly slow internet connection. My friend had replied with only conjectures about the mystery of the black cars. I responded that they were Soviet limousines, proud my detective work had revealed the answer.

My hope to upload photos disappeared along with the bars of the Network icon on my computer. I passed the remainder of the evening in isolated, air-conditioned silence, thankful for a few hours to relax and recuperate.

*****

The previous spring, I read a book called *The Day Lasts More Than a Hundred Years* by Kyrgyz author Chinghiz Aitmatov. Set in an isolated community at a railroad junction in rural Kazakhstan, it traces the life of a rail worker who is questioning his choices and desires, a theme that resonated sharply with me.

The cover of the novel features a depiction of a Soviet rocket shooting into space, a reference to a secondary plot involving cosmonauts. Today, I was on my way to Baikonur, the real-life home of the Soviet space program. The romanticized image from the book danced in my head all day.

By early evening, I could make out the skyline of the mythical place. Innumerable satellite stations lay scattered on the steppe, backdropped by the Russian cityscape.

Reality encroached as I approached the city, which was divided into a Russian side, accessible only with a Russian visa, and a Kazakh side, officially known as Toretam. The dusty, bustling main street of the Kazakh city was lined with small shops and the sounds of honking car horns and rushed conversations.

I found an overpriced hotel room, washed up, and left to run errands. I got cash from an ATM in the train station, taking a moment to examine the massive Soviet workers mural adorning the inside of the building. I walked down the street to stock up on food and water. Goods in hand, I scurried back to my hotel for the evening, plotting my getaway for the next day, my glamorized visions of Baikonur squashed.

I spent most of the next morning gazing at the line of solitary train tracks mirroring the highway. Every time a train passed, its Eastern European design evoked memories of trips I took to Hungary, Poland, and the Czech Republic in my England days. The desolate desert backdrop enhanced their sad mystique.

Around ten, I dragged my bike off the highway so I could peaceably eat breakfast and drink the cold instant coffee I kept in a reused water bottle. Across the roadway, I watched another train rumble past, content with my food and the view. I took a sip of coffee and thought about my dented black thermos, which sat safely in a cupboard in Colorado.

You should have brought your thermos this summer.

'It weighs too much,' I replied with a tinge of regret.

I took another sip of coffee from the plastic bottle. As I screwed the cap back on, a construction vehicle pulled to the side of the road and three workers lumbered out.

Here we go.

The men shuffled toward me, their orange vests bright against the brown earth and shrubs. They waved, immense grins lighting up their faces.

My own lips involuntarily curved upward.

'Be nice. They just want a picture.'

The three men held cell phones in their hands. They beamed smiles, and my mood changed in kind. I reached out to shake their hands.

One camera at a time, we took photos. The men gave me a hearty thank-you wave and walked back to their truck. It seemed so random, yet so normal. Apart from the grouchy police officer a few days ago, the Kazaks were, I recognized, some of the friendliest people I'd met in all my travels.

'How many Facebook pages have our image posted to them?'

They will have a story to tell tonight.

'So will we.'

I finished my breakfast, smiling as I chewed.

*****

How much longer?

It was a valid question.

The landscape had changed to scrubland, a nasty, brown, in-between kind of place with no redeeming qualities. The train tracks, which kept my mind semi-occupied, would come within sight before disappearing for miles.

It was menacingly hot and I couldn't pause to eat because I needed shade if I stopped, and virtually every tree next to the highway was also a public restroom.

Worst of all, a slight headwind from the east made the unbearable lack of anything pleasant drag out even more. The distances I had yet to travel overwhelmed my thoughts.

You'll never get anywhere at this pace. And why is it so ugly?

'At least our knee is doing OK.'

I longed for the desert to return. Instead, the landscape was nothing but tall prickly bushes, brown and lifeless. The monotony continued for two days, and all I could do was pedal and think about the long distances ahead.

Nothing of any interest happened until I threw my back out.

Back troubles were nothing new to me. Once or twice a year, I would stand or twist the wrong way and my back would give out. The pain ranged from mild to severe and lasted a few days to a few weeks.

When I twisted the wrong way on the mattress in a random highway motel in the early morning hours, I wasn't surprised, only a little worried.

You don't have time to wait this out.

'We'll be fine.'

I could hear a slight panic in my imaginary voices.

I hobbled around my room, trying to pick up the scattered innards of my panniers and place them in the correct bag, a tediously slow process since I couldn't stand straight. I popped four Advil, instead of my usual three, hoping the pills could work their magic in both my knee and back.

An hour passed between the moment I got out of bed and the moment I pushed my hulking Soma to the highway, leaving behind an otherwise pleasant *gostinitsa*. I lowered the bike and threw my right leg over the top tube, a spear of pain shooting through my entire right side. I settled my feet evenly on both sides and pulled my bicycle upright.

'Now all we need to do is pedal.'

I wheezed in discomfort and cast a final glance toward my accommodations, set in a solitary building with a glassed-in patio entrance.

'Hmm. This one is named *Konak Ui*. Isn't that what the last one was called?'

I gave no further thought to the matter. I clenched my teeth, clipped into one pedal, and pushed forward, waiting for screams of pain from my back.

Instead, the moment I settled into my hunched-over riding position, my back pain disappeared. I propelled myself back into the headwind and back into the scrublands. In the distance I could hear the rumble of a train, taking passengers to some new phase of their lives.

My mood brightened as the desert landscape returned, the shoulder-high brown shrubs receding in size until they were no taller than my ankles, revealing sand and gravel. Around two, I heard a car approach from behind and recognized the changing pitch of gears downshifting.

More selfies.

I hoped the car would keep going, but when it pulled to the side of the road, I knew I had to be polite. I planted both feet on the pavement next to the driver's window, ignoring the screams of pain from my back as I tried to stand straight.

I peered into the car from behind my dark sunglasses, trying not to appear agitated.

The driver looked at me and then glanced toward the passenger, who started to speak in a soft tone of German-accented English. "Sorry to bother you. Our guide wanted to meet you."

It took me a moment to register that someone was speaking English to me, and slightly longer to decipher what he'd said. I looked deeper into the car. In the driver's seat was a Kazakh man. In the seat next to him was a young white man.

He told me he was from Germany. He motioned to the elderly couple in the backseat. "Those are my parents," he said.

I waved and offered my best, "Guten tag."

"We're on a tour of Kazakhstan's Silk Road sights," the man continued. "There's an ancient fortress off the highway a few kilometers ahead. It was conquered by the Mongols in the fourteenth century. You should visit it."

I considered his words. "Where is it, exactly?"

"Just ahead. You can see the road to the fort in the distance."

I squinted my eyes. I could make out the turnoff and the fortress itself.

You would have ridden right past it, you idiot!

"That looks interesting. I'll check it out. Thanks!" I was elated at the idea of seeing something touristy. "Where are you going after that?" I asked.

"We're returning to Turkistan," replied the German, "We are staying there. It has many Silk Road artifacts too."

I tried to take in everything the young man had told me. Turkistan wasn't far away, and it sounded like a major tourist destination with plenty of hotels. I could sleep in comfort.

"Thank you for the information," I said again.

"Sorry again for interrupting your ride," the young man said.

"No problem at all. Thank you!"

I gave a small wave to the man's parents and to the driver. As their car pulled away, I realized how good it felt to speak to someone in English.

If you'd bothered to read your Lonely Planet *guidebook you'd have known about the fortress.*

'It's hard to do any research when we're pedaling all day.'

I found the paved road that veered south off the highway and followed it to the ruins. Part of me wanted to visit the fort, but most of me wanted to talk to the German man again.

I locked my bike to a fence near the entrance of the fortress and entered the remains of the once proud city. According to *Lonely Planet*, the residents had surrendered to the Mongols after the town to the east was massacred for resisting the hordes.

I hobbled up the walkway to the fortress, my back aching horribly. I could see the three Germans walking several hundred yards ahead, but with my back muscles preventing me from standing upright, I literally couldn't catch up to them.

Look at the lonely American wearing tights hobbling to reach a trio of Germans in the ruins of an old Kazakh fortress that was overrun by the Mongols seven hundred years ago.

My back muscles spasmed.

Pathetic!

I laughed at myself despite my disappointment. The whole scene truly was pathetic, and ironic. I accepted defeat, enjoyed seeing the fortress in spite of myself, and headed back to my bike.

I turned onto the highway and snapped several photos of camels on the roadside. They started to run, and I quickly pulled ahead of them, sensing a better photo opportunity.

I scanned the shoulder of the highway until I spotted a small stake sticking out of the ground. I got to the stake and hopped off my bike, an agile move that made me question whether my back pain was real.

I leaned the bike on the stake, glanced in each direction for cars, then stepped back a few feet. I waited until one camel was near my Soma and snapped a photo. I knew it would make an iconic image.

I proceeded to Turkistan, a large city by Kazakh standards, with no shortage of hotels. It was a Silk Road highlight, with a towering mausoleum from the fourteenth century and plenty of other historical sites nearby.

You need to go to the mausoleum!

The distances ahead weighed heavily.

Look at all the hotels! You'd have your pick if you stayed here!

'It's not even four. We can't stop now.'

You do have a long way to go.

As the confused, self-contradicting arguments raged in my mind, I kept pedaling through the city, shaking my head in regretful acceptance.

Instead of seeing any Silk Road artifacts, I bought some Russian-made sunscreen at a pharmacy because I had only brought one bottle of sunblock from home. I also found an ATM and got more cash before finding a grocery store. Then I left town, bypassing countless hotels on my way out.

Twenty miles from Turkistan, I got my first flat tire of the season. I changed the tube and kept going east, where the landscape morphed into stretches of irrigated farmland. I pedaled another two hours before finding a pocket of trees and shrubs tucked between a homestead and a cement plant. It looked secluded enough to spend the next ten hours.

I pushed my bicycle into the vegetation until I found a small clearing to set up camp. An open concrete irrigation canal ran along the edge of the campground. About two feet at the top, it triangulated to a rounded base. Two inches of water flowed across the bottom.

After setting up my tent, I grabbed my camp soap and stepped gingerly into the culvert, careful not to twist my back. I proceeded to bathe, pondering where the water was coming from and what kinds of insidious diseases lurked inside.

My makeshift bathing facility was shielded by the trees, but a few feet past the leafy branches lay an open field. A group of cows meandered nearby, their incessant moos aimed straight at me.

Like I had done at the fortress, I envisioned the scene from above, the strange American cyclist bathing in an irrigation ditch while cows munched the leaves nearby. I found it ironic that a germaphobe like me, who uses hand sanitizer after touching anything a student has touched, would sink to such lows.

Yet here I was.

I smiled.

I felt alive.

This is not your typical Tuesday evening in Fort Collins.

'Shouldn't we all experience this at least once? Washing clothes and bathing in dubious water? Over a third of the people on this planet wouldn't find this to be much of an experience at all.'

I used water-bottle water to wash my hair and face and rinse the irrigation water off my skin. After changing into my civilian shorts and T-shirt, I had a tasty dinner of salty, braided Russian cheese, semidry bread, and a can of sardines.

I powered up my Acer laptop and focused my energy on editing my camel photos. I made multiple edits, including an elongated one that I would set as my Facebook cover photo as soon as I returned home.

Snug in my sleeping bag, I listened to the sounds of distant trucks on the highway, barking dogs at a nearby homestead, and the occasional cow nibbling on leaves. I slept well and awoke feeling rested. My back and my knee groaned as I got up, but I could tell they were on the mend.

I set out eager to ride another hundred miles and find a hotel at the end of it all. I needed a shower, and I desperately wanted to upload my camel photos in case all my worldly possessions were somehow lost.

*****

I uttered a hearty "Checkpoint!" the next day as I passed Shymkent, Kazakhstan's third-largest city, knowing that if I had any major issues, I could fly back the following summer and pick up where I left off.

As the day progressed, clouds encroached and the wind increased, propelling me forward for the first time in days. I passed a group of parked semitrucks. The drivers were milling around outside looking at the clouds. One of them flagged me down, so I squeezed my brake levers. The trucker wore an expansive grin as he handed me an unopened bottle of water. I smiled in return and thanked him in Russian. I hurried onward, appreciative of the kind gesture yet terrified of the wind and the weather.

The sky became darker, and the wind intensified. I ascended steep hills at fifteen miles per hour, with gusts of wind pushing me faster. It felt like someone's hand was on my back, nudging me forward.

It began to rain, or so I thought, but I wasn't getting wet. It came down harder, but there were no raindrops.

'Maybe it's not raining?'

It is raining.

'No, it's not.'

Then what is it?

'It's sand.'

I glanced behind me. The sky had turned brown, not black, and what I thought was rain were tiny granules of sand.

'We're riding through a dust storm!'

Cool.

I crested the top of a long climb and my pace increased to twenty miles per hour, then twenty-five, then thirty miles per hour. The sand dissipated as I approached a steep three-mile descent into a valley. I pictured my pannier flying off my bike on the hill outside of Tangiers and squeezed the brakes all the way down.

I settled into a cruising speed of twenty-seven miles per hour. The clouds and sand disappeared into the evening as subtly as they had arrived. I thought about stopping to camp but couldn't give up the tailwind.

The city of Taraz, which I'd considered out of reach that morning, was now an inevitable destination. I rolled into the sprawling urban area after eight, and entered the first dingy hotel I found, eager for a shower and eager to upload my photos.

My odometer read 159 miles, my longest ride ever. Any other day, I would have rounded it out to 160 miles, but tonight I was too frazzled to care.

I uploaded my precious camel photos to Shutterfly, a seemingly endless process with the painfully slow internet speeds. I emailed one of the photos to my school secretary, Kari. She always asked me about my cycling trips and had even given my name to the *Loveland Reporter Herald* the previous fall, convincing them to run a story about my daily bicycle commute to school. The email took half an hour to send.

I fell into a contented sleep, too tired to worry about anything else.

CHAPTER 16

I woke up on June 15th and looked at my map. I had ridden fourteen hundred miles across Kazakhstan. China lay seven hundred miles to the east. My knee was doing OK.

'We're going to make it to China!'

Maybe—but there's no way you'll get in. Not at some random border crossing.

'We'll worry about that when we get there.'

But I was plenty worried now. I shut down my computer and gathered my things for another long day of riding.

I passed through uneventful rolling hills, brown and hot, with nothing but my music to keep me company. I kept playing Chromatics's remake of "Girls Just Wanna Have Fun" to jolt myself out of the monotony.

The heat became oppressive and ominous clouds appeared in the east. Ten miles from the city of Merki, I rode into the weather system. Rain poured and lightning blazed across the sky.

Are you more likely to be killed if you stay in one spot or move around?

I visualized an expansive square on the ground with a little dot inside of it.

'Statistically speaking, wouldn't the odds of getting hit be the same at any given point in that box?'

I thought hard about the idea as another bolt flashed and dissipated in front of me, accompanied by a near-simultaneous crash of thunder.

The only way to improve your chances is to get out of this storm.

I put my head down and pedaled faster. My toes squished inside my cycling shoes. I barely noticed because I was fixated on being a dot.

The storm let up as I entered Merki. I crossed a small bridge above a creek that was covered with green vegetation, a marked and calming contrast from the hundreds of miles of desert steppe and scrubland I'd ridden across.

I found a hotel on the eastern side of town, a well-maintained structure three stories tall. On one side were the words *Konak Ui*. I wondered why so many hotels had that name.

The expansive lobby was sparkling clean, and I felt out of place walking inside with wet clothes. I paid a modest price for a room with a balcony where I could look down on my bicycle, locked in the courtyard.

I walked around town, meandering through an outdoor market before stocking up on food in a real grocery store with shopping carts. White Russian faces again equaled the Kazakh ones.

I took my spoils back to my room and ate dinner on the balcony before calling Kendra.

"Hello," she said, a hint of exasperation in her voice.

"Hi," I said. "What's wrong?"

"I'm so tired. Gracie got her second heartworm injection today. She keeps pacing and whining."

"I'm sorry. Is she on pain medication?" I knew full well she was, but I needed to say something.

"Yes, tramadol."

"Oh."

"But it isn't helping," said Kendra. "It's frustrating to see her in so much pain."

I frowned. "I wish I could help."

So why aren't you home?

"There's nothing you could do here," said Kendra, though we both knew I could relieve her of dog duty for a while.

"How are you?" Kendra asked after an awkward pause.

"I'm alive," I said, making a lame attempt at humor. "I rode through a major lightning storm. That was fun."

Kendra didn't reply.

"I'm in the town of Merki, not far from Almaty."

"You've made a lot of progress."

"Little by little."

Our conversation faded from there. After I hung up, I sat down on my bed, the mattress more board than cushion, and put my head in my hands.

'What exactly are we doing here?'

What's the point of any of this?

'We should be home.'

Yes, you should.

I pictured Gracie walking around, laying down, standing up, whining in pain, and Kendra sitting there watching her and not being able to help.

I walked out to the balcony and watched distant thunderstorms dance across the evening sky.

'What exactly do we want to achieve?' I asked again.

I had no answer.

The storms reached Merki that night. I listened to the rain and thunder from the safe confines of my room, hoping they would move away by morning. The spartan bed did not help my back, which still ached, but I realized I hadn't taken ibuprofen for several days.

'At least we have that going for us.'

I sighed and waited for sleep to arrive.

*****

From Merki, the highway followed a border fence with Kyrgyzstan. A headwind battered me for most of the day, and I passed the hours looking south in awe at the mountains of a country I knew nothing about. I passed distant *gers*, or yurts, the round white dwellings evoking memories of all those moons in Mongolia.

'How long ago was that?' I mused, thinking not in terms of years but lifetimes. 'How many of those homes did we visit, how many random people did we meet?'

No time to stop and chat now.

I thought back to my twenties, when everything I did centered on meeting people and doing things with friends and figuring out where I fit into other people's lives.

Now, everything seemed to be about me, and my journey, trying to figure out where I fit into my own life.

'When did that happen?'

Your social life deteriorated the moment you decided to lose so much weight, the moment you chose to start counting every calorie you consumed and ceased going out with anyone.

I found it more than a little ironic that my diet from so long ago had led me to this moment on this day, watching the tiny border fence between Kazakhstan and Kyrgyzstan stretch over myriad green hills, the silhouette of the Kyrgyz Ala-Too mountain range barely visible through the hazy atmosphere.

I was achieving something remarkable even as my social life and happiness deteriorated around me. The opportunity cost of the whole endeavor was not lost on me.

Is it worth it?

I looked south again at the fence, the mountains, and the haze. I visualized myself on a map, in the center of the Asian continent, alone, so out of my element.

I wondered how I'd be passing the time if I weren't here.

'What would we be doing all summer? Would we be volunteering somewhere, doing something useful for someone or something?'

I doubt you'd be helping at an animal shelter.

I thought back to the lonely dog in western Kazakhstan.

'No doubt we'd be training for some local bike race, trying to find meaning by pedaling in circles.'

I thought about all the possibilities of my life, all the things I could have and should have done.

Is this all worth it?

I passed a pair of beekeepers, selling honey on the side of the road. Their wooden oxcart was painted in vibrant colors.

'This trip has been amazing.'

But is it worth it?

I looked at the distant mountains of Kyrgyzstan. Its capital, Bishkek, lay a stone's throw to the south. I grinned.

'Yeah, it's worth it. But the price tag is pretty damned steep.'

I camped that evening in a wide valley that led to Almaty. Between the road and fields of wheat, small groves of trees afforded exceptional cover. Drivers were unlikely to notice any cyclists camping among the leaves when they were cruising on a narrow highway at sixty miles per hour.

Past the wheat fields, mountains rose up on either side of the valley, scarred by washes. It reminded me of my Peace Corps home in Ömnögovi, except here crops graced the foreground rather than the scattered brown plants struggling to exist.

I entered the trees, a world all its own, inhabited by a million crows talking in the most angstful way. I set up my tent, laid out my clothes and ate my dinner, listening to the perplexing bird drama play itself out in squawks and squalls.

After eating, I walked to the acres of wheat. Aside from the motorists stuck in their steel cubicles, I was the only soul for miles in any direction. Walking waist-high through the grain on a hot Kazakh evening, soaking in my present reality, only reinforced the notion that my little endeavor was worth the price.

My phone blared "Laid Low," by The Naked and Famous, and I moved my lips in unison with their ethereal lyrics.

The mountains, with their distant washes cutting tracks down the sides, were bathed in the subtle evening hues that I love so much, and in the moment, everything felt OK.

'No one anywhere could understand this euphoria.'

You almost seem confident.

'Things are going to be different when we return home.'

You might be right.

The music continued, waxing poetic about haunting memories.

I surveyed the mountains, the wheat, the trees, and the highway as I stood there, a solitary figure in an unparalleled landscape.

I soaked it all in, and when I had fully absorbed the enormity of it all, I went back to my campsite and prepared for bed, content for the first time in ages.

When I woke up, my tent was covered in crow poop.

*****

'Checkpoint!'

I was in Almaty. The air pollution was apparent from fifteen miles out. As I moved closer to the city center, traffic became heavy and pedestrians rushed along the congested sidewalks.

While dodging buses, cars, and people, and absorbing noxious fumes, I glimpsed a young kid under a tree. He was playing with a fidget spinner, the bane of every teacher in America the previous school year. The little plastic toy spun in his hand as he stared at it in fascination.

My God, the plague has jumped continents!

I laughed before returning my attention to the street, my hands tightly affixed to both brake levers.

I found an eight-story hotel that cost sixty dollars for the night. The room left a little to be desired for that price, but it did have a balcony overlooking Almaty's famous Ascension Orthodox Cathedral. Its ornate and colorful spires provided a remarkable contrast to the gray Tien Shan mountains hovering in the distance.

With the aid of the hotel Wi-Fi, I located a nearby bicycle shop. I needed to find a new handlebar bag because the zipper on my current one was broken. When I entered the shop, I felt like I was back in the States. High-end bicycles and expensive gear lined the walls.

There's no way you'll find a bag here.

I'd searched for a new handlebar bag in Fort Collins and across the internet before leaving, with no success.

'And yet …'

I noticed a handlebar bag hanging on a hook. I flipped over the price tag and examined the rest of it.

'This will make a functional souvenir!'

Before checking out, I asked a salesman for two tubes to replenish my stockpile of spares. He brought out a handful, asking me if I wanted more.

I waved the others away. "I only need two," I said, holding up two fingers.

I left with my new bag and my two spare tubes. I stocked up on groceries and returned to my hotel. I slept poorly that night, stressed as I was about the final push to China, which appeared more remote than anything I'd ridden across yet.

*****

The influx of new money for highways in Kazakhstan comes from all directions: the European Union, the United States, Russia, and China. China's Belt and Road Initiative, in particular, promotes extensive highway and railway development along the ancient Silk Route trade routes. The project goes straight through the border city of Khorgos, which was my planned entryway into China.

Because roads in Kazakhstan were being built at breakneck speed, I often found myself on divided four-lane highways that appeared as small backroads on my paper maps. Google Maps, when I could access it, was not always accurate either, sometimes showing roads that hadn't been constructed yet.

Leaving Almaty was like any other day. I got a flat tire thirty miles from the city, replaced it, and didn't think much about it. The day was blisteringly hot. As I rode farther east, the landscape became rockier and sandier, eventually turning to desert again.

I found a massive tree in a random town that afforded some shade. After eating a snack, I called my dad to wish him a happy Father's Day. I explained as best as I could where I was, but between his "oh's" and "uh-huhs," I wasn't sure he understood me very well.

After hanging up, I examined my paper map again.

You need to stock up on water.

I looked north, across the divided asphalt with its waist-high metal barriers. I could make out a store on the other side, but there was nowhere for me to cross.

'There are plenty of towns along the way.'

I noted the many black dots that lined the road.

'We'll stock up later.'

On the edge of town, I came to a construction area where the old road, a shoulder-less mess of bumps and potholes, veered right. A brand new, four-lane freeway stretched straight ahead. It was blocked off by huge piles of dirt and was clearly in the process of being built.

I considered my options.

'Look! Those two cars drove over the dirt. If they can do it …'

This is a bad idea.

I glanced one more time at the old road and considered how many more bumps my wheels could absorb. I walked my bike over the mound of earth.

An aggressive tailwind pushed me down the brand-new pavement. On either side of the highway, distant mountains grew upward, creating an immense, rocky valley. In no time, I was ten, then twenty, then thirty miles down the flat, smooth pavement.

I kept a close eye on my water, which was diminishing in the late afternoon sun.

Where are those towns on that map of yours?

A sinking truth crept into my mind.

I pulled up Google Maps, which I knew wouldn't be much help, but perhaps it would at least give me a vague sense of where I was. Though the detail was pathetic, the little blue dot made one thing clear: I was in the middle of nowhere.

The original highway goes through the towns, not this one.

This unfinished superhighway did what all superhighways do: it went in the most direct line possible, bypassing every town in its wake. I had three liters of water left and was surrounded by a nameless desert.

The only saving grace was my tailwind. A few miles later, as I was effortlessly pedaling at twenty-three miles per hour, an invisible dust devil enveloped me. Within moments, it spit me out into a tyrannical headwind, reducing me to ten miles per hour.

'What ... how ...?'

This is bad.

I was in a state of disbelief. Wind doesn't normally change direction so abruptly. But today it did, and it was a devastating turn of events, especially as the flat valley turned into a string of long, slow climbs.

I crawled forward, calculating how much water I had left and wondering where the next town lay. I was next to the railroad, and that glimmer of civilization gave me some small comfort. I thought there might be a building near the line that would have a water source.

I thought of characters in *The Day Lasts More Than a Hundred Years.* Images from the book flooded my mind, matching the landscape.

After a miserable hour clawing my way forward, a collection of four new houses materialized next to the railroad. As I approached, I saw they had air-conditioning and little yards. I wasn't sure who occupied them, but I felt a wave of hope.

Closer to the tracks were two basic, rectangular buildings with signals and other railroad fixtures. I pulled off the highway and walked my bike down the dirt road toward the structures. A young man came out of the nearest one and greeted me.

I held up an empty water bottle. The man nodded and motioned for me to follow him.

Inside the building, computer screens illuminated the entire room. They displayed sections of rail line, a technological juxtaposition to the emptiness outside. A stream of cold air emanated from hidden vents, a secret luxury that contradicted the evening heat.

The man's official collared shirt was draped over his chair, as was his hat. Another worker sat at the terminal, wearing his full uniform.

In a back room was a waist-high, cylindrical tin tub, much like I had in Mongolia, full of clear, cold water. The worker scooped some water and handed me the ladle. As thirsty as I was, I gave only a cursory sip, unwilling to consume untreated water. I filled several bottles and thanked the men profusely.

Outside, I took a selfie with the man, this one initiated by me. I waved one last time, then pushed my bike to the highway.

Out of view, I opened all my water bottles and dropped iodine tablets into them to treat the water.

Thirty minutes until we can drink it.

'At least we're not going to die out here.'

But where is here?

I looked around. I had no answer. I hopped on my bike and pedaled, slowly, into a heartache of a headwind. The sky grew darker and clouds formed over distant mountaintops, which illuminated frequently with lightning. A van driven by a man and full of children pulled next to me.

The driver motioned for me to climb into the vehicle, pointing to the sky and saying something about the storms.

I held up my hand, gently gesturing, "No."

I wasn't willing to call it quits. I could see the concern in his eyes, and knew I needed to find a safe place to camp. The ominous clouds were fast approaching.

I thanked the man several times.

He shrugged, waved, and sped away.

More lightning lit up the sky.

I checked my cell phone, hoping for bars, anxious because I wanted to text Kendra and let her know I'd be camping, but had no luck. I kept riding, uphill, for an hour. As I crested the top, I looked at the phone once more. I had one bar. I rattled off a text and waited until the app said "Delivered." A moment later, the bars disappeared. A wave of relief washed over me.

Um, you may have solved one problem, but …

I considered the situation. It was eight o'clock, the temperature was eighty degrees, and the storms appeared increasingly menacing as the sky darkened.

Several miles later, I found the shelter I needed. Construction crews had built a livestock tunnel under the highway. It was brand new and free of animal droppings. If storms moved my way, I could retreat further into the creepy darkness.

I ate and took a few final evening photos of Kazakhstan before trying to sleep. With the temperatures hovering in the mid-seventies all night, and no breeze to speak of, I barely slept.

Around four thirty in the morning, sunlight began to illuminate the land. I tried to keep sleeping, but it was futile. China was close, and I wanted to find out if my visa would get me into the communist state.

I started my last day in Kazakhstan, and my first day in China, tired, agitated, and anxious, and that was no way to start such an important day.

The beautiful landscape from the previous evening became monotonous. Worst of all, the headwind from yesterday continued to punish me. Headwinds are the most disheartening aspect of cycling, far worse than climbs. Hills are hills, and though going uphill will slow you down, it's simply how things are.

Wind is different. It doesn't have to blow at you—it could blow from the other direction. Headwinds are unfair.

With little sleep the night before, and the stress of China in front of me, it didn't take long before I succumbed to a tear-ridden meltdown.

Why are you out here?

'If only we had slept more last night.'

There's no way they're going to let you ride into China!

'Why *are* we out here?'

You could turn around.

I thought back to the painful stretch into Aktobe when my knee screamed at me.

'We got through that day.'

That was different.

'Why?'

Because back then you wanted to keep going. Your knee got in the way.

The wind pushed me backward as I pressed forward. I could feel tears welling.

This time it isn't about your knee.

This time it was about my desire to continue at all.

'This isn't fun,' I admitted. 'This isn't the way people are supposed to spend their free time. This isn't how people go on vacation.'

So why are you doing this?

'I don't know.'

Then stop riding already! This is ridiculous.

Tears poured down my face, clinging to my dirty sunglasses.

'I don't want to do this anymore!'

I kept pedaling.

The wind kept blowing.

The tears kept coming.

My legs kept turning.

My thoughts kept sinking, deeper and deeper.

"You're in trouble," I said aloud to myself. "You're in a fundamentally bad place. Keep moving."

I wiped the salt water from my eyes. The heat enveloped me. I felt more mentally fatigued with each passing moment.

'It's not important anymore. I don't know why we're here.'

"Keep pedaling," I said out loud again. "You will not turn around."

I did as I was told. I had nothing else to do. I was in the far reaches of eastern Kazakhstan, hardly a good place to pack up my things and go home. The nearest city was ahead of me, in China.

Toward late afternoon, the new divided highway ended. A construction crew directed me to an older stretch of road that wound its way toward China.

After churning my pedals past new, vacant, prefabricated homes, I found a gas station, some ninety-five miles after I'd gotten water from the rail workers. I stocked up on food and water and headed for the border.

I walked my bike through multiple checkpoints, becoming utterly confused about who was checking what. At one desk I was sure I was approaching a Chinese checkpoint, only to encounter guards with name tags and badges written in Cyrillic.

I was led outside, where I was allowed to jump a long queue of semitrucks, their Russian, Latvian, and Kazakh license plates a familiar disruption from the disorientation of the past thirty minutes. A uniformed guard opened a broad metal gate barely wide enough for me to squeeze through.

I realized then that the previous passport checks were to leave Kazakhstan. China was beyond the multiple fences stretching on for what appeared to be a mile. On the other side I could see Korgas, China, not to be confused with Khorgos, Kazakhstan. A few high-rise buildings reached into the sky. I followed the road, which looped and snaked through a tunnel of fences typically lined with trucks.

When I arrived at the Chinese border, I was ushered into a building, bike and all, by a young guard with a machine gun. I was sweaty and stinky, and my face was streaked with tears.

I took a deep breath.

This will never work.

'It has to.'

I walked inside and approached a counter. Holding my bike with one hand, I reached out with the other and gave the agent my passport, a fake smile plastered across my face.

CHAPTER 17

Border control counters in China have large buttons with three different faces on them: Sad Face, Straight Face and Happy Face. As you check in, the question, "How was your service today?" pops up on a little screen in your selected language.

Who'd honestly answer that?

I tried to balance the Soma while I stood in front of the stone-faced border agent. Panic crept in each time he returned to the beginning of my document and thumbed through it again. I wondered if I could get back into Kazakhstan if I couldn't get into China.

I was hot, sticky, tired, cranky, and had been crying all day.

I selected Happy Face.

Unexpectedly, the man gave a cursory shrug and stamped my passport. He handed it back to me.

I gave a small "Xie xie," the only Chinese I knew, and hurried away from the counter, toward the outer doors, where sunlight crept into the massive atrium of the cold building.

Before I reached the exit, two uniformed women waved me toward a hulking X-ray machine and pointed to my bike.

I nodded at their directions and leaned the Soma against a square cement post. I removed my bags and handed them to the women. They loaded each one into the X-ray machine.

The bags passed slowly through, but the woman didn't once glance at the screen.

I walked my naked bicycle to the other side of the apparatus and spent ten more minutes reattaching the panniers. Then I walked toward the light, a lone American cyclist free to wander across Xinjiang province, China's largest and westernmost state.

I passed a group of money changers outside the border control building. Even though I needed Chinese yuan, I had learned that exchanging cash with random people on the street was a bad idea.

'We'll find a hotel first,' I thought, 'and then find a bank to exchange our Kazakh currency.'

It seemed like a simple plan.

I started riding down the spacious, four-lane road through the city, noticing it was bereft of any traffic. Less than a mile away, I approached a six-story building with the words "Hotel" and "*Gostinitsa*" plastered across the bottom. Huge Chinese characters vertically descended from the roof to the second floor.

As usual, I went inside wearing my cycling clothes, looking filthy and smelling worse. I had translated some phrases into Chinese the previous spring and downloaded them onto my phone. When I got to the front desk, I opened the document and showed the phrase "Do you have a room for one person?" to the receptionist.

She responded rapidly in Chinese. I stared at her. Behind me, a small crowd of guests peered in my direction.

I held up my credit card. The woman blinked in exasperation and took it. She swiped it through a card reader multiple times, but it kept getting rejected.

The people who had been staring from the lobby formed an uninhibited semicircle around me, watching the excitement.

The woman swiped my card again, to no avail.

I could smell my jersey, sweat continuing to surface even with the air-conditioning blowing from overhead vents.

You should have exchanged some money back there.

The woman pulled out her phone, typed something, and held up the small screen. "Do you have cash?" she asked.

I shook my head and frowned. I opened my wallet and held up my Kazakh tenge. The woman reached across the counter, counted off some bills, and put them in a drawer. She handed me a key and a slip of paper with "¥150" written on it.

'I think you owe her 150 yuan.'

What about that other money she took?

I had no idea how much she had taken.

'Let's worry about that later.'

I took the key and uttered, "Xie xie."

The crowd dissipated, the eventful exchange over.

I walked outside, grabbed my front panniers, and went back into the building. I was directed to put my bags through an X-ray machine I hadn't noticed before. I panicked when I remembered I had a sizable jackknife in one pannier and another in my handlebar bag, but the elderly guard scarcely glanced at the screen as the conveyor belt carried my bags through.

I walked upstairs. With each step, a familiar knot gnawed at my stomach.

My room, huge, clean, and modern, was a pleasant surprise. It even had a hot water kettle.

I tossed my panniers on the floor, turned up the AC, and headed straight for the shower, eager to wipe the salt off my face.

An hour later, I opened a nondescript glass door and entered the Chinese Construction Bank, down the block from my hotel. A security guard motioned for me to put my Kazakh handlebar bag, which cleverly doubled as a shoulder bag, through another X-ray machine while I walked through a metal detector.

Crap! Your knife is in there!

I couldn't believe I had forgotten it, again. And I was walking into a bank.

Once more, the guard didn't give the screen much notice and my belongings passed right through. I walked straight to a cash machine and inserted my Visa card, punching in the numbers I had carefully memorized prior to my trip. The familiar sound of money spinning was comforting on so many levels.

I gave a small smile and waved to the guard as I left, three hundred dollars in Chinese yuan stuffed into my wallet. A sense of urgency, momentarily forgotten inside the bank, returned as I walked into the summer heat.

I entered the first store I saw. The scent of stale cardboard mingled with clove hit my nostrils. I walked down an aisle and stared at the assortment of vacuum-sealed foodstuffs, from chicken legs to hot-chili-covered tofu sticks to eggs of various sizes and colors. I stocked up on a bit of everything and hoped some of it would be edible. Ham, sausage, cheese, and loaves of bread, my staples since Lisbon, were conspicuously absent. I also noted that the beer and liquor selection was exclusively Chinese, a marked contrast to every other country I'd pedaled through.

I took my spoils to the hotel, pausing for a moment to sort my things. An unsettled feeling crept through my nerves, so I ventured outside again. As I wandered around the streets near my hotel, I was struck by the infrastructure. Huge concrete canals channeled roaring water through the city, drowning out sounds of traffic and people milling in front of shops. Small parks, wide streets, sidewalks, trees, and buildings rising six, seven, even ten stories high, all mesmerized me.

Interestingly, Korgas was a small dot on my Chinese map. On my Kazakh map, a dot was a town of, at most, two thousand people.

'What will a big dot be?'

A wave of anxiety overwhelmed me as I thought about the unknowns ahead. I picked up my pace, my breathing faster.

'We need to eat,' I told myself.

I opened the door to a small, empty restaurant and sat down. A man brought me a menu, written in Chinese, and I pretended to read through it before randomly pointing at something. A few minutes later a heaping noodle bowl arrived. I shoveled it down, relaxing as my belly filled. As the food disappeared, however, the nagging unease increased.

'We need to come up with a game plan. Let's look at Google Maps.'

I finished my meal and walked back to my hotel at an unnecessary speed.

Inside my room, I turned on my computer and opened Google Maps, waiting for the comforting shades of gray and green, and white roads. The page wouldn't load.

I logged into my phone and again opened Google Maps. The familiar shade of green was there, and I could see the blue dot showing I was in Xinjiang province. But aside from the outline of China, there were no other markings. It was useless, even with Wi-Fi.

I clicked on my Gmail bookmark. I got another blank screen. I entered "Google in China" into my search bar, but nothing happened.

The knot cinched tighter.

I tried Google Maps again. Nothing.

My breathing increased. I felt ill.

I clicked again and again.

Nothing.

I don't know why you're so surprised. It's not like you haven't read about this. Isn't that why you gave people your Yahoo email before leaving?

'I knew it but didn't believe it. How can we find our way anywhere without Google Maps?'

I stared at my screen, dumbstruck. It was as though circumstance had pulled the final straw from a day of uncertainty.

Tears welled again. I took deep breaths. I stood and walked to the window. I went back to my computer and clicked on Google Maps and Gmail again. Nothing.

Tired and terrified, I pulled out a card Kendra had given me before I left. The words "Open in the Event of an Emergency" were written in her neat, fluid handwriting across the front. When I saw it at the beginning of the summer, I smirked, thinking there was no way I'd need it. I was a seasoned bicycle tourist.

Now, I tore it open, eager for the sage advice Kendra had left for me. I read her words, written as they were in an open-ended, nonspecific way. While not exactly the motivational boost I was hoping for, the fact that she had prepared the card for me made me miss her all the more.

I missed Gracie too.

I sat on the bed, put my face in my hands, and let the tears flow.

Slowly, I regained my composure.

"Tom," I whispered to myself. "You woke up this morning under a highway in western Kazakhstan. You didn't sleep much."

My shoulders dropped; the sound of my own voice was oddly soothing.

"Two hours ago, you didn't have a place to stay, you were stinky and sweaty and uncomfortable, you didn't have any local currency, and you were hungry."

I considered the words.

"Now, you're in a comfortable hotel room, showered and shaved. Your laundry is hanging out to dry. You have a wallet full of cash and you just had a good Chinese meal. In China."

I sighed.

"Deal with tomorrow, tomorrow."

A last wave of tears flushed from my eyes. I stood, walked to the sink, and rinsed my face. Then I sat on my bed, pulled out my paper map, and looked at my next destination.

'There's only one road to Urumqi. Easy enough.'

I wasn't convinced.

I went back to my computer and changed my search engine and default map to Bing.

I don't want to use Bing Maps!

211

'We're going to have to,' I said in my gravest tone. 'It's that or MapQuest.'

Ugh. No.

'Well, here we are.'

Later, I opened my Yahoo email account and saw that Kendra had recommended a song for me to listen to. I clicked on my YouTube bookmark, but it was blocked too.

'Try Amazon Music,' I thought.

The little wheel of despair spun in circles on my screen. I was past frustrated. I popped a sleeping pill and waited for its magic to take effect.

"Worry about tomorrow, tomorrow," I repeated as I drifted off to sleep.

*****

All the road signs are in CHINESE!

'We are in China.'

I hoped a little sarcasm would stave off the rising panic.

Everywhere else the road signs have been in the local language and the Latin alphabet. Here it's only …

'Chinese. But look. They're in Arabic too.'

My mouth gaped open.

That doesn't help.

'Interesting how small the Arabic letters are.'

I thought about the letters for a moment. Forty-six percent of the people in Xinjiang province were Uighurs, a Turkic people whose primary religion is Islam. The Chinese characters stood prominently above the diminutive Arabic writing.

How are you supposed to know which way to go?

Reality jolted me from my moment of curiosity.

'Crap. This is bad.'

Roads diverged in more directions than I'd expected.

I pulled my bike to the edge of the pavement and opened my paper map. I zeroed in on Urumqi.

"Look," I said out loud to myself, as though talking to a small child. "Urumqi is written in both English and Chinese."

How does that help?

"If the road signs are in Chinese," I continued, "then we need to learn Chinese."

I took a hard look at the symbols representing Urumqi: 乌鲁木齐.

"The first one looks like someone sitting down," I said. "The third one is like a cross with two diagonal lines coming out of it. And the last one appears like someone who has to pee."

'What about the second one?'

"I have no idea. But look at the sign up ahead."

I squinted at the gray and white board, discerning one by one the characters I had memorized. An arrow pointed straight ahead.

"Urumqi is that way!"

I pedaled through Korgas, wondering when the city would end. Midsize Chinese cars bustled by, following the rules of the road. Mopeds and three-wheeled tuk-tuks maneuvered in all directions, spewing black clouds of exhaust that singed my nostrils. An occasional bicyclist would pedal by, oblivious to any traffic norms. Pedestrians streamed on the sidewalks past countless shopfronts.

In their brightly colored cotton clothes and round skullcaps, the Uighur people were unmistakable. Their Turkic facial features contrasted with the Asian eyes and high cheekbones of the newly transplanted Han Chinese inhabitants of the city.

As I pedaled, I noticed something odd. At gas stations across the city, tall bands of barbed wire surrounded each facility, and security guards checked drivers' IDs as they pulled up to a pump. The state of affairs in this westerly province was far from serene.

As in other ethnic regions like Tibet and Inner Mongolia, Han Chinese have inundated the Uighur homeland. Religious suppression and forced assimilation had, in recent years, driven Uighur separatist groups to commit terrorist attacks in both Xinjiang province and elsewhere in China, including a knife attack at a Xinjiang gas station the previous February. The Chinese government responded by increasing security in the region, thereby heightening tensions all around.

'That explains all the X-ray machines and metal detectors,' I thought as I surreptitiously pulled out my camera and snapped photos of several random gas stations.

An expressway paralleled my route for the first thirty miles of my ride. The on-ramps had signs with bicycles, tractors, and pedestrians covered over by an *X*, a clear indication that these paved arteries across China were solely for automobiles.

At the base of a small mountain range, all the roads converged. From there, the freeway appeared to be the only way forward, snaking its way through a narrow canyon. Several toll booths stood guard. With no other options, I proceeded straight ahead.

An attendant poked his head out of a booth and waved me through with a smile.

'It appears that bicycles are allowed in this stretch.'

I waved back.

'Here we go.'

I proceeded up my first real climb of the season, passing through green meadows and rugged mountainsides. Yurts sat humbly under clear blue skies and goats dotted the landscape.

Any worries I had about being on the massive four-lane freeway were soon alleviated by the presence of herders marching their livestock down entire lanes while semis lumbered past. My knee and back gave me no trouble as I ground my way up the steep climb.

I had grown accustomed to the expansive valleys of Kazakhstan and Azerbaijan, but now I was riding straight into the mountains. The highway climbed through narrow canyons, eventually completing a loop through a tunnel before emerging at the foot of an enormous bridge spanning two valleys. I snapped a photo of the imposing concrete pylons reaching into the sky.

'We're not in Kazakhstan anymore.' I smiled, my eyes wide behind my sunglasses. 'This is amazing.'

You should keep moving.

I sighed and pedaled along. Two police cars passed me, but the occupants didn't glance my way.

On the other side of the bridge, I took another picture, this one of the elevated highway framed by mountains, the colors of concrete contrasting with the shades of light green grass and dark green pines, an image topped by snow-capped peaks and blue sky. A pleasant breeze cooled the ambient temperature to a comfortable eighty degrees.

At the top of the twenty-mile climb, Sayram Lake greeted me. It was situated on a plain surrounded by distant mountains. I was not the only one impressed by the wide, lonely body of water. Numerous motorists were parked next to the lake, taking photographs of the water and of camels strolling across the mountain slopes.

'China isn't so bad!'

It is beautiful. But where are you going to stay tonight?

I had been so busy gazing at the visual splendor of my surroundings, and enjoying the uphill grind, that I hadn't thought about my evening plans. I looked at my paper map, where I saw nothing but vast expanses of open highway in my foreseeable future.

I checked my water supply and, satisfied I could pass the night comfortably, shrugged and kept going. Several hours later, as the sun made its exit over the distant mountains, I found myself with a vaguely familiar problem. I was in an open valley with absolutely no cover.

I'm pretty sure the Chinese authorities would frown on you camping wherever.

'Agreed.'

I descended a long, slow drop out of the mountains, surveying the landscape. I spotted a livestock underpass on a downhill stretch of highway where motorists couldn't possibly stop. It was accessible only via a steep concrete embankment.

I pulled the bags off my bicycle, checked to make sure no vehicles were within sight, and made my way through the barbed-wire fence that lined the Chinese expressway. Once through, I carried my panniers down the embankment one by one, maintaining a controlled slide as the metal cleats of my cycling shoes contacted the steep concrete. I pulled my Soma through last, carefully making my final descent to the narrow underpass.

I kicked aside dried animal dung to make way for my tent before proceeding to unpack my gear. I blared "Only God Knows," by Young Fathers, off the *Trainspotting II* soundtrack, while I set up camp.

I had seen the original *Trainspotting* when I lived in England, twenty years prior. I wanted to learn what became of the characters who, like me, were in the throes of middle age.

For the moment, I had to settle for the soundtrack.

"Well," I stated aloud, "it's your second day in the People's Republic of China and you've ridden 120 miles."

I looked proudly at my tent, surrounded by livestock droppings.

All of me smiled.

'Urumqi is less than three hundred miles away,' I pointed out, smiling even more. 'And we have over two weeks until we fly home.'

So what's your goal now?

'Let's worry about getting to Urumqi for now,' I responded.

But I knew Urumqi was no longer good enough. A slight wave of anxiousness overcame me as I considered how far away Lanzhou was.

A moment passed before the excitement hit me.

'Lanzhou isn't good enough either.'

Lanzhou is plenty.

"No," I said out loud. "Lanzhou won't do."

I gazed east at the broad expanse of brown.
"Anything less than Xi'an is unacceptable."

CHAPTER 18

The toll booths shimmered in the early morning haze, starting out as a faint flicker of worry before materializing into my worst fears.

Someone is going to kick you off the freeway.

I didn't see an alternative route.

'We just need to keep a low profile.'

I laughed at the thought.

When I reached the kiosks, the attendant looked at me and waved me through, an expression of utter indifference on his face. A patrol car nearby filled me with more worry, but it was empty.

I passed the rest of the day in relative boredom, the flat, desolate landscape an unwavering shade of gray. In the early evening hours, construction signs materialized with increasing frequency. The sun sinking behind me illuminated each successive one with an intensified glare. Ahead, I saw a string of cars and semis leaving the freeway.

I had no choice but to follow the line of vehicles down a secondary road, hoping I was heading in the right direction and toward a hotel. Bathing with a liter of water the night before left me longing for a shower.

The diversion led me to the junction of the G30 expressway and another highway. A small town, whose name I never learned, had grown up around the intersection. The place was little more than a strip mall, dusty, dirty, and devoid of character.

Using the translation on my phone, I asked a man for directions to a hotel. The man squinted at the screen and pointed to a building behind me. Multiple AC units stuck out of the windows on the upper floors.

I walked to the front door and peeked inside where a poster with images of hotel rooms greeted me. To the right, a spartan staircase ascended. I pulled my bike into the stairwell, locked it to the railing, and went upstairs.

"Nihao," I said as I approached the counter.

A young woman looked at me in surprise.

"Nihao," she replied.

I held up my phone to ask if a room was available. It seemed like a straightforward question.

The woman smiled, held up her index finger to say, "Wait a moment," and made a phone call. She talked for some time, uttering a lot of phrases I could only infer meant "uh-huh," before motioning for me to sit down on a couch. I nodded but remained standing, not wanting to impart a layer of sweat and sticky Russian sunscreen all over the furniture.

I knew from the little research I did before leaving home that in China a hotel needs a special license to accommodate foreigners. I wasn't sure how it worked in practice, and I had forgotten about that minor detail until now.

I stood and waited, growing worried I'd be camping again, when three police officers ascended the stairs.

"Hello," said the lead officer in English. He reached out to shake my hand.

"Hi," I said with a slight smile.

"Where are you going?" he asked.

"I started in Kazakhstan," I said. "I'm going to Urumqi."

I wanted to keep things simple. I didn't mention my grandiose plans to get to Lanzhou, much less Xi'an.

"How long will you stay here?" His tone was polite, professional, and somewhat friendly.

"Only tonight."

219

"I see," he said. "And you are riding your bicycle."

"Yes."

"OK," he replied. He gave a nod to the receptionist, thanked me and shook my hand before turning to leave. The other officers gave me a smile as they followed him out.

The woman wrote down the price for the room, which amounted to thirty dollars. I paid in cash and walked downstairs to retrieve my things.

Once again, I put my bags on a small conveyor belt that carried them through an X-ray machine an older guard ignored. I left my bicycle locked in the stairwell, a u-lock around the frame and a cable lock through both wheels, all attached to the sturdy metal banister.

Like my room in Korgas, this one was modern, clean, and had a water kettle. I savored the shower and spent a few extra minutes stomping on my clothes to remove the grime. I rinsed and re-rinsed and wrung them so hard my wrists ached.

Clean and refreshed, I sprawled on the bed and started editing and uploading my recent photos.

'At least the government doesn't have a problem with Shutterfly.'

I watched the images upload at a lightning pace.

'And the internet here is a far cry from Kazakhstan.'

I called Kendra and told her about my experience with the police.

"Well, things here aren't nearly as exciting," she said. "But Gracie is doing a lot better after her shots."

I was relieved to hear it. I desperately wanted Gracie to be home when I returned.

Our conversation was brief, and afterward I walked to an outdoor market across the highway, amazed at the indifferent reaction I received from people in the small town. I inspected the variety of hanging meats and produce for sale, unsure what much of it was.

I bought a few apples and went back across the street. I sat down at an open-air restaurant with only one other patron. I pointed to something on the menu and waited for my food, which turned out to be a huge bowl of soup with two steamed dumplings on the side. The owner seemed excited to watch me eat it, even offering advice on how to dip the dumplings into the broth.

I smiled and gave a thumbs-up. I wished I could tell him in words how good it was.

The next morning, I approached the hotel counter. The receptionist got up from a small cot and greeted me with a half-asleep smile. She counted out several bills and handed them to me. I took them, confused, and placed them in my wallet.

I gave a final thank you and walked down the stairs.

'Why did she give us money back?'

You got your Kazakh money back when you left the other hotel.

'Oh, yeah.'

You paid a deposit, genius.

'Oh.'

Maybe you should have done a little more research before trying to ride your bike across China.

'What fun would that be?'

*****

The city of Hutubi, a place I had never heard of until I read its name on my map next to a speck of black, was characterized by countless high-rises protruding from the sandy ground. From the highway, I stared at the thousands of AC units attached to the windows of the towering structures.

Who lives there? Who are all these people? What are they like?

The notion of so many people, crammed into so many anonymous apartment blocks, was overwhelming.

They have personalities and souls and wishes and desires.

'Who are they?'

My brows furled under my sunglasses and my head swam under the immensity of it all. I cranked up "Last Forever," by

The Naked and Famous, and listened to them sing about all the souls we'll never meet.

I exited the highway as the first hints of evening fell, hoping to find another hotel room. The boulevard leading to the city center was six lanes wide, yet devoid of traffic. It appeared the city was built in anticipation of an impending population explosion. At the moment, it was quiet. A nuclear power plant loomed in the distance, dark against the evening sky.

A small strip mall stood next to a barbed-wire-encased gas station on the outskirts of the city. I noticed the hotel because of the AC units dotting the windows and the telltale revolving front door. I locked my bike at the bottom of the steps leading to the entrance and walked up. It was late and I was tired, dirty, and wanted a shower.

I stepped in and the two staff members gaped at the sight of a foreigner. I showed them my translation of "Can foreigners stay here?"

One man, who I assumed was the manager, started rambling at me as though I could understand him. Then he pulled out his Chinese ID card and pointed at it, asking, "Where is yours?"

I held up my US passport, but he waved it away. I tapped on the translation on my phone again.

The manager started making calls. The conversations continued in circles. Ten minutes later, as I was about to walk out and set up camp somewhere, the manager pulled out a key card and wrote the fee on a slip of paper.

I held up my phone. I had added "Deposit?" to my list of Chinese phrases.

The man wrote something else and showed it to me. The total was now written as an equation: "¥100 + ¥30 = ¥130."

'So the deposit is thirty yuan.'

Look at Tom, getting smarter!

I smiled at my own cleverness.

"Xie xie," I said to the man.

Another employee led me to my clean and modern room. I followed my usual routine, annoyed that I had to lock my bicycle outside.

I was solidly asleep when the manager knocked on my door with two young police officers in tow. I don't remember the conversation, but it was more than a little unnerving.

The next morning, before leaving town, I decided to withdraw more cash. I rode into the city center, a dreary place of decrepit high-rise buildings and light traffic.

I inserted my card into the first ATM I found and was denied access. I went to the next one, and the next one, getting rejected each time.

Um ...

'Try another.'

I waited in line at a busy cash machine down the block. I was denied again.

I suppressed the panic rising in my abdomen.

At the seventh cash machine, I noticed an American Express icon in the upper corner. I pulled out my Amex card and inserted it. The beautiful sound of money being sorted permeated my ears and three hundred dollars in yuan spit into my hand. I tried my Visa cards next. Two transactions later I had a thousand dollars' worth of yuan in my pocket.

'Ha! I told you it would work out!'

Until it's all stolen.

I considered the possibility. I stashed the money in several places and hoped for the best. I found a sign pointing to Urumqi and followed it out of town, along the old highway rather than the expressway, proud that I was now fluent in reading a Chinese name.

The day was gray, hot, and dusty, and only my music kept my mind at ease. Thirty miles west of Urumqi I came to a police checkpoint. The policemen carried machine guns and bore grim expressions. They motioned for me to enter a building with a group of bus passengers, bike and all.

I handed an officer my passport and waited patiently while holding my helmet, bandana, and sunglasses. No one was smiling, not the police, not the other people inside, and not me.

This level of security on a secondary road is excessive, don't you think?

I nodded without nodding, questioning why the Chinese government imposed so many controls in this distant province.

The officer holding my passport examined it thoroughly, then handed it back to me. I uttered a faint "Xie xie," and got out of there as fast as I could.

*****

'Checkpoint!'

Even as a minor dust storm sprang up around me, and I was reduced to a crawl on the outskirts of Urumqi, I couldn't help but feel elated as I passed the entrance to Urumqi International Airport. Nine months ago, this moment was an absurd dream that I thought about on those dark rides between Fort Collins and Loveland. But here I was, with time to spare. I kept going, deeper into the city, pausing only to fix another flat tire.

A few miles later, I pulled into the parking lot of the Snow Lotus Boutique Hotel, housed in a high-rise building. I balked when I was told it cost the equivalent of sixty dollars, but when they told me they accepted credit cards, I had a change of heart. The view from the twentieth floor was worth the price.

With over two million inhabitants, Urumqi felt like so many other Asian cities I'd seen in movies and photographs, with tall neon lights and huge electronic marquees scrolling banners of Chinese characters, people walking everywhere, heavy traffic, and mopeds scurrying in every direction. This was my first time in a proper Chinese city since visiting Beijing sixteen years earlier. I cleaned up and headed outside to soak in my new surroundings.

My neck soon hurt from craning to stare at all the tall buildings. A certain energy emanated from the scene as people scurried from place to place under a darkening sky. I meandered down back streets and into an expansive, upscale mall. I laughed with joy when I found a grocery store with shopping carts and produce wrapped in cellophane.

One small thought nagged at me as I walked.

You should find a bicycle shop and buy more bike tubes. You flatted outside Almaty. Remember?

I considered the idea.

'We've got plenty of tubes left. Besides, we've made it three thousand miles with only three flats. We'll be fine.'

Your tires were looking pretty worn too. They're your backup pair.

'Stop worrying.'

I didn't want to deal with finding a bike shop; I wanted to wander around. I pushed the idea out of my head.

Lying in bed that night, I pictured a map of western China. A thousand miles of desert stood between me and Lanzhou. Unable to sleep, I walked to my window and stared at the city lights, dots of yellow, red, and blue. A thousand possibilities illuminated the darkness of the atmosphere.

I pulled out a compass I had brought with me, a souvenir from a brief road trip I took with my father in Scotland so many lifetimes ago. On the back, I had taped a quote from the writings of Chuang Tzu that said, in essence, if we walk in search of happiness and run from the fear of sorrow, we'll always remain trapped in the in-between places, unable to reach any state of calm, lost in the delusions of our mind.

I'd read the words many times in the past year, connecting them to the angst and discontent that had plagued me for so long.

'No one cares if we succeed on this trip or not.'

Except you. You care. A lot.

'But why? Four years ago we never even considered doing it. Now it seems like our entire happiness hinges on completing it. It shouldn't matter.'

But it does matter.

'Why?'

Far below me, on the streets, vehicles and people moved about in an orderly frenzy. I could hear cars accelerating and honking, doors slamming shut, and faint voices even from my perch in the sky. The wind felt cool on my face.

'Six months ago, we kept saying we needed to get to Urumqi.'

And here we are, leaving the city in record time.

'Now we have to get to Lanzhou.'

Don't you mean Xi'an?

Staring out the window, I acknowledged that even before I had achieved my first goal, I had already set a new one. Happiness, or contentment, or whatever it's called, was proving as elusive as ever. I kept putting it out of reach. The irony wasn't lost on me.

'We should try to be content with just riding.'

Great idea. There's only one problem.

'What?'

You know what it is.

Some revelation lingered in my mind, but I couldn't figure it out.

The lights outside became brighter as the sky got darker. The energetic hum of the Central Asian city continued, unabated, even as the clock ticked forward.

I climbed into bed, the vastness of the Taklimakan Desert looming heavy on my mind. I did not sleep well.

CHAPTER 19

Past Urumqi, new land formations greeted me every hour. Wide-open valleys with sleek modern windmills gave way to dusty yellow hillsides covered with rocks and boulders that left me feeling like I was on Mars.

Moments later, I'd rocket down a canyon at thirty-five miles per hour, savoring the adrenaline rush as the wind hit my face. On one speedy descent I flatted, the familiar squish in my front wheel tying my stomach in knots. I moved my bicycle as far to the shoulder as possible and did my best to ignore the semis and cars whizzing a few feet away from me. As I pulled the tire from the rim, the flat rubber surface caught my eye.

See! You should have replaced your tires in Urumqi.

'These are fine. And we have plenty more tubes mixed in with our camping gear.' I tried to sound convincing.

I changed the tube and reinserted the wheel into the frame, which sat sideways on the pavement held up by the two right-side panniers. I heaved the Soma back to its feet and resumed riding.

For most of the day, I had been watching signs for the city of Turpan, the characters 吐鲁番 ingrained in my head. All I knew about the place was that it was a Silk Road highlight, home to several historic ruins and temples.

The flat left me in a bad mood, as did my lack of sleep. A persistent headwind pummeled me all day.

Toll booths emerged on the highway with little rhyme or reason, and each time I approached them my upper body tensed. I passed through them with my head down, sometimes lurking behind a large truck, hoping I wouldn't be noticed.

My thoughts drifted and changed with the landscape.

We have a lot of miles left to go.

'I know.'

Do we really need to be doing this?

'I don't know.'

Have you heard from anyone lately?

I made a mental inventory.

'Kendra keeps in touch every day.'

What about your dad?

'We talked to him on Father's Day.'

Does he even know where you are?

I wasn't sure my dad knew who I was anymore, much less where I was.

Who else have you heard from?

'It's been a while.'

My shoulders slumped.

So you haven't heard from anyone.

'That's not exactly true.'

But in the hinterlands of western China, alone, it was starting to feel true.

'People have their own lives. For most of them, this is like any other summer.'

People respond to your emails maybe once, and that's it. No one wants to have a conversation anymore.

'There may be some truth to that,' I acknowledged.

My shoulders slumped further.

You're chasing windmills.

It was an apt metaphor. In the distance another wind farm sparkled with white towers, each spinning in unison, pointing east, savoring the gales that were destroying me.

And all for what?

I considered the question.

228

You have an interesting set of priorities. It's not like you had a lot of friends to begin with.

I thought about college and the Peace Corps.

You left those places with a poor reputation. No one likes you.

'We've made some bad choices,' I admitted.

I frowned behind my sunglasses, sweat dripping down my face. I watched a car fly past, its modern contours matching the brand-new pavement of the freeway.

'At least we got AmeriCorps right. And grad school, mostly. And people at Sarah Milner think highly of us.'

That was something. I'd built a solid reputation at work, and for all my flaws in my twenties, I had turned things around, if only a little.

I turned up the volume on my headphones to drown out the circular arguments that followed me from one day and one summer to the next.

*****

Turpan is home to the National Center of Inspection of Grapes and Grape Products, a curious fact I learned as I wandered around the Silk Road relic, now a modern, nondescript city. I passed groups of people loading trucks full of freshly harvested vegetables, wondering where the mounds of spinach and heads of broccoli grew.

'The Chinese are masters of irrigation,' I thought, reflecting on the many patches of green dotting the desert in the most unlikely places.

I ducked into a little store searching for food and beer. Instead, I walked out with several bags of locally produced raisins, biting down on a handful the moment I hit the sidewalk. My rear molar cracked down on a sizable rock. I winced.

It would be fitting if you broke a tooth and had to go home.

I shook off the near mishap and recoiled instead at the heat, which held firm at seven in the evening. A glowing haze enveloped the city. I scoped out several restaurants before settling on one that looked inviting. I opened the door, glanced around, and sat down at a table. A news channel resounded from the television and a few patrons ate by themselves, indifferent to my presence.

A waiter approached and I pointed to a stream of Chinese characters on the menu, once again hoping for the best. A few minutes later a lackluster noodle bowl was set in front of me, not what I'd expected, but it was hot and it was food, and I enjoyed every bite.

I finished my meal but lingered for a few minutes before setting out in the muggy evening, back to the hotel I'd found on the edge of town. By the time I reached the entrance, my clean clothes were drenched in sweat. I gave a quick nod and smile to the receptionist and walked up the stairs to my room, hoping I wouldn't have any visits from the local police.

I went straight to my computer and turned it on, clicking my Yahoo Mail bookmark.

Nothing.

I stared at the static screen.

'Everyone's lives are going on like normal back home,' I told myself again.

I knew it was true, but it didn't make me feel better.

Why do you care anyway? You don't even like being around people.

That was also true.

'Solitude and isolation are very different things, even if the line between them isn't always obvious.'

I'd say you crossed that imaginary line a thousand miles ago.

'More like a few years ago.'

I visualized a map of my route again to take my mind off my empty inbox, zooming out in my head to view the entire globe. I was getting close to Ömnögovi province in Mongolia. I imagined the desolation of my former Peace Corps site, situated a hundred miles north of the Chinese-Mongolian border.

Sitting in my little hotel room, staring at my empty inbox, I felt the same way I had in my early twenties: anxious, self-conscious, and in need of some kind of calm.

I focused my energy on figuring out the remote for the AC unit. All the labels were in Chinese. After fifteen minutes, I acquiesced to a warm night. Between the heat and the rock-hard mattress, sleep was futile.

I woke up fatigued. A wave of sadness crept over me the moment I opened my eyes. It wasn't even seven o'clock.

Why are you in this random little hotel?

I had no clever answer. Tears pooled in my eyes as I stepped out of the shower.

'Why are we feeling this way?'

I couldn't understand what was wrong with me. Stone-faced, I got dressed and started packing up my things. I couldn't bear to be in my room any longer.

I had to move.

I packed my final pannier when, unexpectedly, my phone rang. I glanced at the caller ID and saw it was my brother. I swiped up.

"Hello," I said, trying to keep my voice from shaking.

"Hey, Tom," Kevin said. "How are you? Where are you at?"

"I'm in Turpan, China. In the middle of nowhere. I'm fine, I guess."

"It's been a while. I was just calling to see how you were doing."

I almost burst into tears.

"Things have been going all right. But I'm so …"—I struggled to find the right word—"tired."

"Well," Kevin said, "we're not in our twenties anymore."

That's not what I mean! I wanted to shout. *I'm in way better shape than I was in my fat twenties.*

But I understood what my brother meant. He was thinking in physical terms. I was coming apart in existential ways.

"I suppose not," I conceded. "I've been riding over a hundred miles a day for almost four weeks." Saying it out loud made me think that maybe my brother had a point.

We talked a bit more before I told him I needed to go.

"Thanks for calling," I added.

"Sure," he said, as if it were any other weekend phone call. "Have a good ride today."

"Thanks," I said. "Talk to you soon."

"Bye."

I hung up and teardrops streaked down my face.

That was good timing.

I finished packing, took a final look around the room, and walked downstairs.

The entire lobby was dark. The security guard was asleep on his cot, next to my bicycle, and I wondered if he had purposefully slept there to keep an eye on it.

Quietly, I pulled my Soma out from behind the small bed, affixed my panniers, and walked it outside, into the sweltering desert heat.

On the eastern outskirts of Turpan, the road flattened and I gazed at the muggy sunrise. I was not doing any better and had to accept a simple fact: The dormant feelings of malcontent and longing that had erupted over the school year were still there. Absconding to the other side of the globe had not helped me elude them.

I opened my map and noted that the train tracks followed the highway all the way across the desert.

You can quit anytime you want.

I hated to admit it, but quitting was an option.

'We could stop in one of these towns, buy a train ticket, and fast-track it to Lanzhou or Xi'an and fly home.'

I peered at the elevated tracks, set in a dead-straight line. The engineering was nothing short of miraculous. I pictured the inside of an air-conditioned carriage filled with plush, comfortable chairs.

You could see China through a pane of glass, a nice drink in your hand.

I pedaled. I looked at the dusty haze. I detected every ounce of sleep I didn't get. A million visions of my life raced through my head, a hundred thousand regrets. The flat pavement in front of me disappeared into an opaque abyss.

With each pedal stroke, I was met with quiet resistance. The headwind had returned.

You have another reason to give up.

The highway had other plans. It bent left, ever so subtly, and up. The landscape changed, with rounded lunar hills rising from the veiled horizon.

I climbed, pushing back in my saddle as I spun my cranks, shifting into a lower gear. My heart pounded. Endorphins surged through my veins.

As the sun rose behind a mountain in the foreground, I stopped to take a photo. Photos in those conditions, when the atmosphere is little better than foggy dust, are difficult at best. I took one anyway.

As I put my camera into my handlebar bag, I noticed a protected area southeast of the highway. Little caves, too many to count, dotted the base of the sandstone mountain, the former homes of Buddhist satvis who inhabited the region a millennia ago.

'People in search of enlightenment.'

Or something like that.

I wasn't sure if I was using the correct word to describe the inhabitants of the caves, but it didn't matter. Grinding my gears and fixating on something other than the headwind left me energized. There was an aura about the place that reinvigorated me.

I looked around and said, in a calm, decisive voice, "Tom, here's the deal. If you want to quit, then quit."

I couldn't believe my ears.

"But ..."

I thought back to my Peace Corps service when I considered quitting every waking moment. There was one piece of logic that kept me going. Back then, I'd say to myself, "You'll never regret sticking it out. But you'll regret quitting forever."

It was true then, and it was true now. My mind came back to the present.

"Tom," I said, using my own name again so my statement would sound important. "You can quit if you want."

I paused.

"You just have to wait seven days."

I let that sink in and then got more specific.

"You have to ride seven more days and do a hundred miles every day. At the end of the week, you can quit."

'Wait a second.'

You. Are. So. Clever.

'Seven hundred miles from now there's no way we'll give up.'

"Of course not." I smiled. "All I'm asking for is one more week of full dedication. One hundred percent, even at your darkest."

I gave a nod. I knew what I was getting at. In a week, I'd be so close to somewhere that the idea of quitting would seem ludicrous. I'd be too motivated to keep going to stop.

"You're not going to quit. Not today."

I examined the holes dotting the cliffs.

Well played!

'Yes, well played.'

I took a deep breath and soaked in my surroundings, feeling the heat and eyeing the grey pavement. I thought of the little caves filled with mystical men seeking something more. I wondered if any of them had found it.

I stood on my right pedal and the Soma lurched forward. I resumed climbing, feeling something that resembled, however faintly, hope.

A few hours later, the winds picked up, gaining momentum with each passing minute, ruthlessly pounding me. Riding in open stretches of desert with long straight hills extending upward for miles past countless wind farms, I didn't feel much of anything at all. I put my head down and kept pushing forward, watching windmill blades spin in the distance.

'Where could we possibly camp tonight?'

I imagined my tent blowing away the moment I set it up, picturing myself chasing after it across the desert. I was jolted out of the daydream by a highway sign showing a rest area ten kilometers up the road.

'Let's get there, stock up on supplies, and then worry about camping.'

For the next six miles, I put my head down and carried on, amazed at how calm I was pressing into the headwind. An hour later, I rolled into the parking lot.

Chinese tollway rest areas were usually two-story buildings painted an off-white color. Typically, they had bathrooms, a small store, and a restaurant. During the day, they were bustling with people.

This one, situated at the top of a climb surrounded by sweeping vistas, was sleepy this evening. The few semitrucks parked outside appeared lonely. Several windmills were so close to the building that I could hear the sweep of their blades.

I walked into the shop and perused the sparse shelves, picking out a few things to eat. The older man and woman who ran the shop looked at me and gave friendly nods.

'Sometimes these places have hotel rooms that aren't advertised.'

Or at least obvious to someone who can't read Chinese.

'It might be worth asking …'

I walked to the woman and showed her the Chinese character for "hotel" on my phone. She smiled and pointed upstairs.

I smiled back.

No sleeping outside!

I paid for my food and was directed to wheel my bike around back. The woman handed me a key and motioned toward the staircase. I hefted my two front panniers to my room, a large, airy space with eight beds, more dorm than hotel room.

I hope no one else checks in.

I wasn't sure if I'd paid for the whole room or only a bed. A shared bathroom was down the hall, not ideal, but as the winds howled outside, I was in no position to complain.

My window opened to the rooftop, and I had a view to the north that included the rest area, the highway past that, and rugged desert mountains sitting in the distance.

'Mongolia is over there!'

I'd gazed south from my front doorstep in Mongolia many times during my two-year stay, imagining what lay beyond my village.

'Now we know.'

You weren't missing much.

I grinned.

I dressed in my civilian garb and went for a walk around the grounds. The wind continued to rage, but the evening colors, as bland as they were, bounced off the nondescript features of the rest area and calmed me.

I took photos of the building, the most random of places to pass the night, before returning inside to the restaurant. I pointed at something on the menu and soon had a hot meal in front of me and warm walls on all sides of me, tucked away in a freeway rest area in central Xinjiang province.

The window frame banged all night in the relentless wind. I tried closing it a few times, but the room became too hot. I had to leave it open and listen to it knock, simultaneously cooled by the breeze and kept awake by the noise. I thought about the endless nights in my apartment in Mongolia when the winds howled and the roof tiles clattered mercilessly. I didn't sleep much.

The winds pummeled me the next day. They started as a headwind, but as the road climbed into the mountains, they hit me from the side, slamming me into the freeway guardrail as I crawled uphill at four miles per hour.

A motorcyclist stopped to take a picture of me as I made my clumsy ascent. His audacity would have been annoying, but he made up for his gawking when he pulled out an energy drink, put it into my hand as I pedaled by, and gave me a quick push uphill. He hopped back on his high-speed motorcycle and sped away, issuing a thumbs-up as he passed me.

I thought of the old man who encouraged me on the seven-mile climb outside of Tangiers. The image left me thinking about Morocco, Spain, France, Turkey, and everywhere else I'd been leading up to this windy morning.

*****

Liushuquan was five miles off the expressway, but it was the only town for fifty miles in any direction. I followed a tree-lined canal where I considered camping, but the trees didn't offer enough cover from the road. Besides, the evening air was pleasant, the smells of fresh vegetation a rejuvenating reprieve from the desert landscape. I continued toward town.

When I arrived at a police checkpoint, I expected the worst, but the officers were more than friendly. Two of them spoke English and directed me to a hotel where I checked in with no hassle.

After settling in, I went out for a stroll, looking for food. The buildings, primarily new townhomes, evoked images of ski resort villages. Many of them were vacant.

I found a store and stocked up on my favorite packages of spicy tofu on sticks, vacuum-sealed eggs, compressed date biscuits, and a plethora of other items I hadn't tried before. I also bought a bottle of Xinjiang red wine that paired well with my ramen dinner.

Later, I checked my email and realized I could access my Gmail account via the hotel Wi-Fi.

'They must use a VPN to bypass the Chinese firewalls,' I thought. 'Brilliant!'

I sorted through my emails, deleting some and filing others, feeling increasingly elated as I cleaned out my inbox. A wave of excitement rushed through me when I paid my utility bills.

I called Kendra and made an exciting announcement.

"It's time to rebook my flight home."

I was scheduled to fly home from Hong Kong in mid-July. I had planned to fly to Hong Kong from whichever Chinese city I was closest to when I ran out of time.

Now I was aiming for Xi'an.

"I've been looking at tickets," Kendra replied. "Did you know there are direct flights from Xi'an to San Francisco?"

I did not.

"That sounds perfect!"

Goodbye, Hong Kong, I muttered. While I had been excited about going to Hong Kong, I was more enamored by the idea of a direct flight to the United States. Even if I only made it to Lanzhou, I could take the bullet train straight to Xi'an.

"Thanks for taking care of everything."

We talked a bit more before I returned to the silence of my room. I pulled up Booking.com.

'Time to decide where to stay in Xi'an.'

After much deliberation, I settled on the Xi'an Sheraton North. At four stars and seventy dollars per night, I now had a proper destination. However this trip sorted itself out, my last several days in China would be spent in comfort.

In the morning, as I was standing in front of the hotel sorting my things, the receptionist came outside. With a sincere smile, she handed me a bottle of fruit juice. A young couple who had checked out ahead of me fetched two big tomatoes from their car. They came over and handed them to me.

All three of them stood on the hotel steps and waved goodbye as I rode off. I was overwhelmed.

"Xie xie" wasn't enough, but between that and a humble smile, it was all I had.

I made it back to the highway without incident and continued east, not a toll booth in sight. I wiped off the tomatoes with a wet wipe, rinsed them, and ate them both, all while riding my bicycle.

Soon after, I came to a mileage marker sign. Several distances were listed, but my eyes fixated on one in particular:

兰州 1223 km.

Lanzhou, 759 miles.

'We can do that!'

A wave of confidence overcame me.

'And we won't have a long train ride when we quit two hundred miles west of there.'

I laughed at the thought.

CHAPTER 20

When I saw the gully, I knew it would be the perfect place to camp. It was close to the freeway, yet out of sight from passing motorists.

There was a gate through the ubiquitous barbed-wire fence that lined the expressway. A long concrete staircase led from the edge of the road into the gully. I carried my panniers down, two at a time, before returning for the Soma.

I reassembled everything and pushed my gear deeper into the gully, away from the highway. I unpacked and set up my tent, gazing in awe at my surroundings, the sandy wash meandering through rocky hills cut by eons of erosion. The evening sun cast everything in a yellow tint.

You should check your spare tubes if you're getting your camping gear out.

'Good idea.'

I fished out my camping supplies, then my extra water bladders, then some backup food, then my tool kits, then my original set of tires, then … nothing. My fingers grasped in all directions. The bottom of the bag was empty.

Um …

'Don't panic.'

I felt around the other rear pannier. My hand emerged, clutching air.

Are you serious?

My jaw gaped.

How many tubes do you have left in your saddle bag?

I opened the little bag and counted the tubes.

'Four.'

A kaleidoscope of butterflies flapped their wings in my stomach.

'We have a few patched tubes as well.'

Patched road tubes? With their little seams? You know those won't hold.

'They might.'

I knew they wouldn't hold for long.

I returned to my tent and finished setting it up. There was nothing more to be done.

I walked around, barefoot, feeling the sand between my toes, pushing my present circumstances to the back of my mind and soaking in the spectacular scene. The desert dust accentuated the round orange orb hanging motionless in the western sky.

I put on my running shoes and hiked up the opposite side of the gully, amazed at how small my tent looked with the expressway snaking by in the distance, a random semi or two rumbling to distant locales. I ate dinner next to my nylon quarters and went to bed, sleeping well despite the troubling revelations of the evening.

The next morning, I woke up to a rear flat tire. I gaped in horror at the wheel, part of it nestled in the sand. I hurriedly installed a patched tube and then packed my things.

I was not in a good mood as I ascended the concrete steps to the highway and resumed my journey.

I took a selfie with two Chinese cyclists on the eastern fringes of Xinjiang province. They were clad in long sleeve jerseys and wore tights down to their ankles, even in the raging heat. I assumed sunscreen wasn't widely used in China.

We took a few shots from different angles. I felt validated being on the freeway, knowing that Chinese cyclists were on it too. They waved goodbye and continued in the opposite direction.

The expressway pavement was new, and my tires rolled easily over the beautiful, smooth blacktop until my rear tire hissed. I merged to the far edge of the highway and inspected the damage. I pulled out a small sliver of metal and examined its razor-sharp tip.

'That's from a truck tire.'

How many more of those are scattered over the pavement?

The thought weighed heavily as I changed the tube, glad that it was a patched tube I had ruined. I examined the pavement in front of me, spotting small, black remnants of semi tires everywhere.

'Those we can see.'

I looked at the piece of metal in my hand.

Those you can't.

I spent the rest of the day with my eyes fixated on the concrete.

My only joy that day came when I crossed the border into Gansu province and the signs changed from a mix of Chinese and Arabic to a mix of Chinese and English.

At mile ninety, I exited the freeway, hoping to find accommodations in the small town of Liuyuan. I hadn't ridden my hundred miles for the day, but the next city, Jiayuguan, was over two hundred miles away. I had a sliver of hope that I might find tubes at a hardware store.

As I approached the exit booths, my front and rear tires simultaneously hissed. Within moments, both were flat. I panicked on multiple levels. Not only was I using up my precious tubes, but I was now lingering far longer than I cared to at a toll booth.

Two employees came out to see what I was doing. I pointed at my tires and shrugged. Both of them, a man and a woman, dressed in matching slacks and white collared shirts, gave me a sympathetic frown and walked back into their respective booths.

I put one patched tube into the front tire and a new one into the rear and continued toward town. I checked three hotels before I found one to accommodate me for the night. When I returned to my bicycle to grab my things, the front tire was flat again.

'Let's deal with it later.'

You have two new tubes left.

I unpacked and showered quickly, then left to search for tubes. It was a fruitless endeavor. I gave up, entered a restaurant, and pointed to the translation on my phone for "What do you recommend?"

The server smiled and brought me a steaming bowl of meat and veggies. I savored every bite, taking time to sit and relax, putting off returning to my room and the reality of my situation.

Later, I patched four tubes in my room, gluing the small patches over barely visible holes in the rubber. I put a patched tube in the front tire before bed. It was flat the next morning. I inserted another patched tube, and it appeared to hold.

Back on the freeway, I kept my eyes glued to the pavement, but the metal fragments were impossible to see. I was cycling across a minefield and wasn't sure how I could ride two hundred miles to the next city without getting more flats than I could repair.

Within ten miles I had another flat, this time in the rear wheel. Thoughts raced through my head.

'Don't panic. Calm down. We can't panic. Just fix the flat. Ignore the semis ...'

I was in a construction zone and the left lane was closed, forcing every vehicle within feet of me. The draft from semis flying by at seventy miles per hour blew my tire levers, my extra tubes, and everything else scattered on the ground in every direction.

How many tubes do you have left?

That question gripped me as another semi flew by.

'Don't panic ...'

A car, going faster than the semis, passed uncomfortably close. I crouched near my wheel and replaced the punctured tube with a patched one, the movements a reflexive act by this point. My Soma lay on its side in a crippled heap. Another vehicle passed.

'Ignore it. Fix the flat.'

Another semi swept by me. The draft knocked me sideways.

'What's the worst that will happen if we run out of tubes?'

I seated the tire.

You'll hitch a ride to the next city and the trip will be done.

Another semi sped past, blowing my tools everywhere again.

'We'll go home and no one will think less of us for it.'

No one? You will, you idiot! Why didn't you buy more tubes in Urumqi? Or Almaty? We can't go home without having made it anywhere.

Another car went by, and another whirl of wind pushed more tools across the pavement.

'Keep calm.'

I took steady, measured breaths.

'Focus. Don't look at the cars.'

I seated the tire and pumped it up. Within minutes, I had the wheel secured into the frame. I heaved the mass upright.

'Don't panic.'

You're the only one who cares if your trip ends here.

For the next seven hours, I stared at the pavement, waiting for another flat. None came.

As evening descended, I set my tent up between two trees, hidden from the highway to the north but visible to the farmed plots of vegetables to the south.

I had seen people working the fields all day, noticing that the desert of Xinjiang was slowly being replaced by arable land. At this hour, the place was empty and calm. I perceived a slight humidity in the air as well, something I hadn't felt for weeks as I made my way across the deserts of Kazakhstan and China.

'This place is pretty, at least.'

I surveyed the scene, feeling peculiarly calm about everything.

Crawling through that barbed-wire fence wasn't easy.

'A small price to pay for being hidden from the freeway.'

You could have put another hole in your tires shoving your bike through.

'But we didn't.'

You have two new tubes left and a hundred miles to Jiayuguan.

'We have two patched tubes too. Those might hold.'

But …

'We're done talking.'

I looked again at my surroundings. Flowers dotted the corners of the field. The evening air grew heavier and the setting sun cast a summer-evening glow over the acres of green. I examined the tall grasses surrounding the vegetable plot as they danced in the wind.

I ate a dinner of canned fish, spicy vacuum-sealed tofu, and peanuts, washing them down with a can of hot Chinese beer.

I awoke at six the next morning, surprisingly well rested. I crawled back through the barbed-wire fence and reassembled my bike, my heart pulsing with anxiety and hope.

There's no way you're going to make it.

'We'll make it.'

I set out. My eyes scanned furiously for pieces of semi tire. I kept waiting for the inevitable.

Ten miles into the ride I heard the familiar hiss. I pulled out the incapacitated tube and replaced it with a patched one. I pumped it up and put the wheel back into the rear dropouts of my bicycle frame.

Another ten miles down the road I sensed the familiar wobble and softness of a flat tire. The patched tube wasn't holding.

I replaced it with another patched tube. I made it forty miles before that, too, gave out. I pumped it up, hoping to get another forty miles.

I made it ten.

I put in one of the new tubes, leaving me with only one new tube.

You're down to one spare tube. One spare tube. Do you hear me!

I ignored myself. I passed a highway mileage sign.

245

嘉峪关 50 km.

'Jiayuguan. Thirty miles.'

Hope welled.

You have one spare tube! You don't actually think this random city in western China is going to have 700 x 28c road tubes, do you?

I didn't respond. Deep down, I knew it would. It had to.

My breathing was shallow. My eyes scanned the pavement and I waited for another insidious piece of semi tire to slice through my paper-thin cycling tires. My shoulders tensed.

I passed another road sign.

嘉峪关 30 km.

My shoulders relaxed.

嘉峪关 10 km.

I smiled.

'Six miles? We can walk that. This isn't over.'

*****

Gansu province comprises a long and narrow valley tucked between two mountain ranges. On my map I saw multiple sections of China's Great Wall.

Five miles from the city, the freeway dipped below an underpass. On the top was a brown, earthy structure about ten feet high.

'Is that the Great Wall?' I asked with awe.

Of course not! They don't just build a highway under the Great Wall of China.

A short distance to the north, I saw a line of train tracks. They went straight through the same wall of dirt.

See! Who would do that? Who would put train tracks right through the Great Wall?

Even as I ridiculed myself, I emerged from the underpass. The road curved left and I reached the exit for Jiayuguan. As I passed by the toll booths, I received several unfriendly glares from the attendants.

That doesn't bode well.

'No,' I agreed, 'it doesn't.'

But I had more pressing matters. My goal was to find a hotel near the train station, because if I couldn't find a bike shop, I would have to take a train the next morning.

Like other new Chinese cities, Jiayuguan had grand boulevards which seemed unnecessary. The city was bigger than I had anticipated, and I had to ask directions twice before making my way to the station.

I was turned away by two hotels, because I was a foreigner, but the receptionist at the second one pointed me down the road to an eight-story, expensive-looking hotel. I checked in easily and took an elevator to my room on the sixth floor.

I immediately threw my panniers on the carpet and walked to the window of my room, still clad in my smelly cycling gear.

I peered outside. A small lake, complete with a pedestrian path around it, met my gaze. Trees and benches lined the route. It was peaceful and calm. I imagined walking around it and relaxing for a few days.

As I observed the scene, it occurred to me that the consequences of not making it to Xi'an, or wherever, were all in my mind. In the end, it didn't matter if I made it or not. It wasn't like I was going to lose my home, my wife, my job, or anything else if I didn't make it.

Yet it did matter.

'Humans are hardwired for conflict,' I thought. 'When there isn't any, we create it. Some people generate drama with those around them, some get fired up about sports, others pour their hearts into their jobs.'

What about you?

'We have to ride our bicycle around the world.'

That seems entirely self-inflicted.

'We're victims of our own undoing. Some of us are hardwired not to be content.'

Aren't you privileged?

I thought about all the people with real problems while I looked out the window of my fancy hotel room. The tranquil lake with the path held my attention.

'It would be kind of pleasant to stroll around the lake in defeat tomorrow, wouldn't it?'

You don't really want to find any tubes, do you?

I thought about the question for a moment.

'The train would be nice.'

Seriously?

'No.'

You're not past the seven-day rule, by the way.

'True.'

But if we can't find any tubes here …

'Then we have a respectable way to quit.'

I stared outside for a few more minutes. I organized my things, cleaned up, and otherwise procrastinated. I was doing everything I could not to go outside and find a bicycle shop. Part of me feared the outcome, whatever it may be.

"Tom," I finally said out loud, "get your crap together, go downstairs, and find a bike shop."

I hesitated.

"Now!"

I took a quick shower, dressed in my street clothes and walked to the front desk. I showed the receptionist the words for bike shop and taxi. She nodded, wrote something down on paper, and motioned for me to go outside to the grand roundabout near the hotel.

Within moments, I was in the backseat of an ordinary sedan, a magnetic Taxi sign on top the only thing differentiating it from other cars on the road. It smelled like cheap air freshener. The taxi driver glanced at the paper and took off. She drove by a large, modern mall, down huge boulevards, past new apartment blocks, and through countless roundabouts before dropping me off in front of a row of tiny shops. I paid her and stepped out of the car.

This doesn't seem hopeful.

I scanned for some sign of a bicycle shop.

Perhaps the receptionist wrote down the wrong thing.

I walked to the storefronts and made my way past one after the next, hope extinguishing with each step. Suddenly, a racing bike materialized, hanging in the window of a narrow store that was hidden in the shade of tall trees. I walked inside and gazed at the stands filled with road and mountain bikes.

The owner looked at me and smiled. He was about my age, mostly bald, and although he had the first hints of a belly, appeared fit. I held out an empty tube box to him.

The man opened a cupboard and retrieved a bin full of tubes. He pulled out several in my size and held them up as if to ask, "Is this enough?"

I held up my fingers. "Do you have ten?" I asked.

He started digging again, removing five more tubes. He handed them to me and shrugged. "This is all I have," he said without words.

I pointed to the phrase "How much?" on my phone.

He got a calculator and typed in some numbers. The total was 180 yuan.

I balked. *That's over five dollars a tube—almost what you'd pay in the States.*

'Those are our tickets out of town,' I countered.

I pulled cash out of my wallet and handed it to the man.

Before I left, the owner showed me a map on the wall with a route highlighted. He indicated that he had done a tour of China too. We went outside and posed for a selfie together. My smile was genuine.

Fifty feet down the sidewalk, I passed another bicycle shop. I walked in, repeated the same routine, and emerged with seven more tubes and an even broader grin on my face.

I hailed a cab and got into the backseat, where the driver's son was sitting. She made an apologetic gesture toward him, but I shrugged. I was too happy to worry about Chinese taxi etiquette.

As we moved down the road, the boy started typing something into his phone. "Can I take a—"

I nodded before he finished, and we posed for a few selfies.

I was happy again.

Back in my room, I threw the tubes on the bed and went to the window.

'We're in a different place than we were an hour ago.'

Despite my spoils, a certain melancholy hit me as I looked at the lake and the little path.

You wanted to go sit out there tomorrow and ponder things, didn't you?

'Relaxing for a change would be a rare delight. Now we have no excuses.'

I walked around town and stocked up on food. I found an ATM and replaced the cash I had spent, a simple transaction compared to the disastrous morning in Hutubi when my cards wouldn't work anywhere.

When I returned to the hotel, I entered a small tourist office and booked a tour for the following morning. Apparently, there was an ancient Silk Road fortress outside of town. The usual arguments raged in my head, but in the end, I decided it would be OK to leave at noon if it meant I could see something historical.

The Jiayuguan Fortress was built in 1372 during the Ming dynasty on the western frontier of imperial China, a vital outpost on the Silk Road. On the west side of the building is a huge, ominous door, called the Traveler's Gate, from which many a poor soul was exiled into the hinterlands of Asia, sent to their deaths through starvation, exposure in the vast desert, or execution by roaming Mongols. Camel rides and archery lessons were available for visitors, and echelons of soldiers, decked out in centuries-old gear, marched through the courtyard.

I squeezed past groups of Chinese tourists on the upper ramparts of the fortress, the wind howling out of the west. From the southern tip of the structure, the western fringe of the Great Wall stretched due south, past the railroad tracks, which cut right through it, and over the highway, which passed right under it.

'Ha! I was right. That was the Great Wall. I can't believe they put the freeway under it. Good for them!'

The wind knocked me around as I marveled at the view. I could see now that I was in a wide, treeless valley, with mountains to the north and south. The Great Wall went all the way from one mountain range to the other.

This wind ... you're wasting it.

Even though I was enjoying being a tourist, I knew I was right. A gale was roaring out of the west, a current of energy I had to harness.

I returned to the hotel at eleven. After packing, I headed to the freeway entrance where the toll booth operator tried to prevent me from entering my lifeline east. I acted confused, said something to her in English, smiled, and rode past.

It was an audacious move, but I couldn't give up a tailwind like that.

CHAPTER 21

The gusting winds propelled me forward with gleeful urgency over a rolling mix of desert and farmland. I passed dirt-poor rural peasant dwellings and skirted anonymous cities where the masses lived in cramped high-rise apartment buildings. All the while, brand-new cars zipped past me on the freeway, likely filled with people who worked posh jobs in eastern China, heading back from family vacations.

'This isn't Mao's China—not by a long shot.'

I didn't think communist China's founding father would have envisioned a wealthy middle class dashing past peasant fields on their way home from holiday.

Because I had left so late, I only planned on riding 60 miles. But the winds pushed me 136, despite two more flat tires, which I replaced with my new tubes.

I crossed a bridge that spanned a modest river flowing down from southern hills. Vehicle tracks covered the compacted dirt on either side of the river, but at this hour the place was deserted. At the east end of the overpass was a concrete stairway to the banks of the river. I stopped, glad there was no barbed wire to block my way, and lowered my panniers down two at a time.

I found a sandy spot close to the water that was shielded from the howling wind. The highway above me blocked out the sky, although there was a wide gap between the eastbound and westbound lanes where I saw gray clouds amassing.

A few construction trucks rumbled in the distance, but the workers didn't notice me. A man and woman walked past me under the bridge, but they gave me only cursory stares and went on their way. I set up my tent and unpacked my bags. I eyed the river as I worked.

You're not stepping foot in that nasty water.

'It's coming out of the mountains. We're not going to drink it.'

I compromised by wading waist-deep to wash off the most egregious parts of my body. I washed my clothes too, thankful I could give them a proper rinsing. I spent five minutes in the frigid water, surprised by how cold the ambient temperature had become. The clouds grew thicker.

I rinsed my head with bottled water, sending myself into shivers. I hastily dried and bundled up in my Pearl Izumi coat and long pants.

Before bed, I patched my two flat tubes for good measure. Then I crawled into my sleeping bag, grateful for the warmth. I woke during the night to the sound of rain. My tent was close to the gap between the freeway lanes and the steady downpour was getting everything wet.

How did you not see that coming with the excessive wind and drop in temperature?

I tried to ignore the patter of rain and go back to sleep. A few moments later, I forced myself out of my sleeping bag and into the cold. I dragged all my belongings ten feet away from the line of drizzle, oblivious to the holes I had cut in the floor of my tent. I fell back to sleep.

Peeking outside in the morning, I saw a fine mist sprinkling over my campsite. I looked at where my tent had been a few hours earlier. It was soaked.

'That was a good call.'

Everything is still wet.

I sighed and opened my tent zipper. Instantly, I could view my breath. I thought back to that day in England, when I left the small inn outside Winchester for a sixty-mile trek to Stroud in a frigid drizzle.

At least you knew where you'd be staying at the end of that ride.

I grimaced in response and packed my things, cramming my wet tent into a trash bag before stuffing it into its pannier. I lugged my gear to the highway and set out into the rain. A light headwind greeted me at once. Temperatures hovered in the high forties.

Crumbling stretches of the Great Wall, more mounds of dirt than the impressive structure shown in textbooks and brochures, marked my route. Fifty miles into my ride I began a long, steady climb. The effort kept me warm, and I welcomed the reprieve from the chilling misery even as I was reduced to six miles per hour. The ascent took over three hours. I retreated into my thoughts, my head shielded under the hood of my rain jacket.

The descent, conversely, was twenty miles of finger-numbing, body-shivering cold.

'Please don't get a flat, please don't get a flat,' I pleaded to no one in particular.

After reaching the bottom, the road went up a short, steep hill. My body warmed again. I started to feel alive again. And then my rear tire hissed.

I breathed on my hands as I changed the tube, glad that the flat happened on the toasty uphill. Minutes later, I was back on my bicycle.

I passed the evening in the city of Yongchang, where I found a comfortable hotel and two more bike shops where I purchased six more tubes. One shop only sold mountain bikes. The owner there gave me the sole road tube he had as a gift. I posed for a selfie with him and his wife in front of the store. The skies above were cloudy, but the rain had subsided.

*****

I had a bad feeling as I approached the toll booths that guarded the freeway entrance. I pulled up behind a car and watched as the driver paid the attendant. The gate lifted and the car accelerated onto the expressway. I moved forward.

A woman's head popped out of the booth. She started yelling at me, gesturing for me to go back, to retreat from the lane.

There's no talking your way past this one.

I gave an apologetic wave and turned my bicycle around.

'It's time to navigate the back roads.'

The secondary highway was wide and smooth at first, but the pavement soon narrowed and became bumpy. I felt like I was navigating a heavily loaded tugboat on rough seas, except my tugboat had spokes.

I glimpsed the expressway through a line of trees, the familiar barbed wire protecting it from livestock and random cyclists. Innumerous pieces of sharp metal lay hidden everywhere, but the pavement was first-rate. I could replace tubes much easier than I could replace spokes. It was also the most direct route to anywhere.

I eyed the barbed wire for miles until I found a man-made hole in the fence. I pulled my panniers off the Soma, tossed them through the small opening and lifted my bicycle over the precarious barbs.

I reassembled everything on the shoulder of the freeway and kept pedaling, happy with my decision and wary of every car that passed, assuming it was the police who would tell me to exit my lifeline, or worse.

Around midday, under sunny and warm skies, I passed Wuwei, a place I'd never heard of before. On my paper map it was only a dot. In reality, it was a city of over half a million people, bigger than Denver, with high-rises touching the smoggy sky.

How many dots are on your map?

'Countless.'

I absorbed that reality as the skyline of Wuwei came closer and faded away. The expressway veered south and up, into the mountains. I glimpsed the first tunnel from two miles away.

I hated going through tunnels because the shoulders always disappeared, exposing me to the whims of drivers who may or may not see me. Going through them uphill was more terrifying because it took me that much longer to pass through them.

I pedaled through the first tunnel without incident. As I exited into a vista of sunny green hillsides, I heard a voice.

I think he's shouting at you to leave the expressway.

I turned my head and glimpsed a figure to the west, waving his arms.

You're done for.

I pretended not to hear the man and kept pedaling.

'He's only some worker. He can't do anything.'

I passed through five more tunnels that afternoon, with lengths ranging from one to four miles. Each time I entered another sodium-lit passageway, I was convinced I was going to die. But cars and semis zoomed by me in the left lane, giving me plenty of room, and the cave-like setting offered a cool respite from the blazing sunlight and heavy hot air outside.

Upon exiting what turned out to be the final tunnel, mountainsides of green grass greeted me. I stopped to take in the view and pull out some food when I heard the unmistakable sound of a car slowing behind me.

It's the police. This is it.

When I turned to look, I saw a random motorist sticking his head out the window, giving me a smile and enthusiastic wave.

I smiled and waved back.

Relieved, I kept climbing and the views kept getting better, with jagged distant peaks materializing the higher I went. White-graveled roads traversed the meadows, leading to remote villages.

When I reached the top of the climb, after riding 115 miles, the highway curved left into a valley marked by small-scale vegetable farms and rural homes.

'China is a beautiful country,' I thought as I pulled into a rest area.

I leaned the Soma against a wall and entered the store. I grabbed a large bottle of water, only to realize it was windshield wiper fluid. I set it back on the shelf, thankful I caught my error, and checked the next bottle I picked up more carefully before taking it to the cashier.

Outside, I reexamined my map and saw that I was twenty miles from the city of Tianzhu. As I loaded my things on my bike, I saw a footpath that led from the rest area to the secondary highway.

You should head over to that road. It follows the valley to Tianzhu. Think about the guy yelling at you.

I thought about it.

Think about the toll booth clerk who wouldn't let you onto the freeway this morning.

I thought about that, too.

You've been pushing your luck.

Everything I said made sense. I was close to Tianzhu, and it wouldn't be difficult to cruise down the old highway into the city.

'Expressway's faster,' I said.

I turned up my music and happily pedaled away.

Twelve downhill miles from the exit to Tianzhu, a police pickup truck passed me. My stomach sank even as I hoped it would continue on like all the other patrol cars had before it.

Instead, this one slowed to a stop on the shoulder ahead of me. Four police officers stepped out of the vehicle. The words Gansu Expressway were written in Chinese and English across the front and back of their black uniforms. One of them motioned for me to pull over.

They were all smiling.

The driver was a middle-aged man, slightly younger than me. Two officers from the backseat were in their early twenties. The other officer was somewhere in between. The driver came up to me first and pointed at the highway, and then to my bicycle.

Apparently, I was not supposed to be riding on the freeway.

I wanted to blurt out that I had been riding on the freeway for over sixteen hundred miles and no one had said anything yet. Instead, I feigned surprise. I was a tourist and didn't understand such things.

I pointed to the secondary road and motioned with my hands, trying to ask, "Can I head over there?" But there weren't any dirt paths like the one at the rest area. Here, it was all barbed-wire fence.

The officer pulled out his phone and typed something. He held it up to me. "We are taking you to the next exit."

That means there will be a twelve-mile stretch you didn't pedal!

'How does that work? Can we count it?'

Those thoughts raced through my head as I pulled off my panniers and handed them to the officers, who carefully loaded each one into the back of the pickup.

In the morning you'll have to go back to the rest area on the secondary road.

'That will probably work.'

I handed over my last bag and then reluctantly gave my Soma to an officer. He gently set it into the bed of the truck and tied it down with bungee cords.

Throughout the whole process, the youngest policeman took a video on his cell phone. I wondered if it was for the official records or simply to show his friends later. After all, no one had asked for any identification.

My belongings in place, the officers opened the doors. I headed to the back seat, but the man who had been sitting up front motioned for me to take his place, giving a slight bow as I stepped forward. I felt more like a guest than a detainee.

After being on my bicycle so long, the transition to sitting in a truck was surreal. A video cam showed the road ahead of us, the pavement so much closer to the lens than what we could see out of the windshield.

The lead officer smiled broadly as he put the truck into gear and proceeded forward. As the outline of the city approached, I thought again about the small section I should have been riding.

'You know,' I considered, 'being detained by the Chinese highway patrol is an OK excuse to drive twelve miles.'

But only because it's twelve downhill miles.

I relaxed.

'Let's enjoy the view.'

The driver turned up the volume on the radio. An Adele song started. He looked at me, grinned, and began lip-synching the song. He knew all the words; I knew none of them. I laughed and considered what a great story this would make when I got home.

Tianzhu appeared, and we drove through the roundabout exit. Our driver stopped near the tollway entrance where a tall, angry-looking officer came out and glared at me, clearly not as amused by the American cyclist as her colleagues. Despite her presence, I asked the other officers to take a selfie with me. They happily obliged.

I checked into the first hotel I found with no problems. As I unpacked my things, the exhilaration of being detained in China subsided and within moments I developed a sinking feeling about what I was going to do tomorrow.

According to my map, the highway descended through a canyon. Although I could discern a secondary road, I didn't know how I would find it. It seemed logical to assume all the roads funneled into the canyon, but I was overwhelmed.

Can't you get a break!

The secondary roads continually splintered in multiple directions, and the road signs on them were written exclusively in Chinese.

There's no way you'll find your way to Xi'an.

I took a short sip of Chinese rice wine, my face cringing at the semisweet fire on my tongue, before heading out to find dinner. I despondently wandered around the city, noticing that every sign on every storefront was written in Tibetan and Chinese. It was strange because I was nowhere near Tibet.

Meandering through narrow, smoky alleyways where street vendors hawked everything from towels to plastic toys offered only a momentary distraction from my worries. I was fatigued beyond comprehension and couldn't make sense of anything.

I walked past one restaurant after the next, oblivious to the delicious aromas of cardamom and clove, past countless shops filled with all manner of wares, weaving around people on the sidewalk. Rather than sit down and think, I kept walking. I passed a planter filled with generic green shrubs and instinctively reached out to pick some leaves. I rubbed them between my index finger and thumb, watching both digits turn a faded shade of green.

'It's been a long time since we've stopped to look at something so mundane. And so amazing.'

My legs ceased moving. My shoulders sulked downward. I let out a sigh and sensed the tears behind my eyes. I thought back to the bad roads in Kazakhstan, my right knee giving out, the miles of pedaling through empty no man's land, the constant flat tires. I thought about the cold, rainy climb. I visualized the myriad tunnels and the man yelling at me and the police loading the Soma into their truck.

I mentally turned my hands upward. I was done. I didn't care anymore. I couldn't care anymore.

'We've given everything we have.'

You can't control everything.

'It doesn't matter how this ends.'

You give up?

Tears hovered at my eyelids.

"I think," I said aloud, "that you have to be OK with how things turn out."

My shoulders dropped in somber acceptance.

I hadn't given up. There's a cosmic difference between giving up and just letting go. I was done fretting about whether or not I'd get to Xi'an. More importantly, I was also done berating myself for not stopping to smell the roses. I knew in the morning, I'd rush out of town without stopping to see anything, including the intriguing Tibetan stupa on the hillside overlooking the city. I wouldn't pause and think and contemplate the moment like I'm supposed to. Instead, I'd rush onward, to my next destination.

I let go of worrying about that too.

I realized that just because my idea of a "vacation" was out of synch with everyone else's vision didn't mean I should apologize to them or to me. It was OK to keep going, as quickly as I could, without feeling guilty. I also let myself accept that it was OK if this trip didn't end the way I wanted.

Back in my fifteenth-floor hotel room, I watched the sun cast a final glow over the rolling hills and mountains in the distance. The city stretched west for miles, the dancing lights fading into night-blackened hillsides.

'Why are we doing this?' I asked myself one last time.

"I think you're beginning to understand," I said out loud.

I stepped away from the window, trying to figure out my own enigmatic comment, contemplating how even the slightest emotions can create tidal waves of change in our lives.

I woke up the next morning pondering the forces that shape our existence, as well as the difference between giving up and letting go.

'We'll keep riding,' I told myself. 'It'll turn out how it turns out.'

You're fine with that?

I gave a muted smile.

'We have to be.'

It was Tuesday, July 4th, and my flight home was scheduled for July 13th. I had five hundred miles left to Xi'an and fifteen spare tubes scattered across my panniers.

Of course, there's no way you're going to make it. Something bad will happen. Something …

"There's no way you won't," my decisive self interjected. "You'll find a way. You always do."

I located the entrance to the secondary highway two blocks away. The pavement sloped downward, alongside the freeway, into a deep canyon.

I grinned as gravity took hold of my bicycle and pulled me forward.

CHAPTER 22

I navigated my way to Lanzhou through one dusty little village after the next, dodging the pedestrians and vehicles that moved in every direction. I changed several more flats, one in the pouring rain. I rode alongside the bullet train for days, fascinated by the perfectly straight tracks that punched through misty green mountainsides while my route twisted and turned through the rocky slopes of the landscape.

Despite the arduous hills and giant trucks, the secondary roads held their charm. Clouds wrapped mountaintops cut with man-made terraces and the sun cast an array of tones and shadows across valley floors. Even when I lost another pannier to an unseen bump in the road, and later when a tree branch got caught up in my rear wheel, a near disaster I refused to acknowledge, I couldn't get over the impression I was cycling through a Chinese painting.

After I passed the city of Baoji, home to four million people, I entered an open plain. The pavement was bright gray under the glaring afternoon sun. I stared at it for miles, my thoughts silent for once.

Abruptly, my negative self announced something unexpected.

You're going to make it to Xi'an, aren't you?

I smiled.

'Success is inevitable.'

I pictured the November campfire with Kendra and considered how my journey had started with a ridiculous, impossible dream.

On my last day of riding, I was too tired to feel anything. My body was slowing down. Normally, when I eat something on a ride my heart rate will spike and gradually subside as the calories burn off. Today, my body was done, and no amount of food could curb the continuing atrophy.

I trudged forward, making my way into Xi'an, a metropolis of fourteen million people, hoping to find a "Welcome to Xi'an" sign. Instead, I passed through one ring road after the next, gradually approaching the city center where dense gray skyscrapers lifted into hazy clouds. Fatigued and lost, I dragged the Soma onto a sidewalk next to a random trash bin and unwrapped a granola bar.

'I'm pretty sure we're in Xi'an.'

Yup. This is it.

'Yup.'

Cars hummed nearby along the divided two-lane ring road as I had this epiphany. I called Kendra, hoping to share my victory with her, but she didn't answer, adding more anticlimactic anti-drama to my finish. I threw my wrapper into the bin and continued deeper into the city.

I pulled into the parking lot of my hotel dirty, dusty, tired, and still in need of a picture. I leaned my bike against a wall next to the Xi'an Sheraton North sign and snapped one of the most awful, uneventful photos of the entire journey.

I was in Xi'an. I had ridden there from Tbilisi, Georgia, covering 4,400 miles in thirty-nine days of riding.

And I was too tired to care.

*****

I read somewhere that British colonial troops stationed in India were adamant about shaving every day and sticking to a schedule to maintain morale away from home. I took the creed to heart when I was in the Peace Corps for two years, and I practiced it on these trips, particularly when I crossed the finish line.

It started with shaving. If not my face, then at least my legs. And that was the first thing I did after settling into my spacious room. Next, I made a to-do list, and the first thing on it was to ride the next day. I couldn't stop riding entirely because I still had to burn my calories. That didn't stop because I'd ridden a lot in the past six weeks.

That never stopped.

I got into a routine of watching BBC news, stretching, and drinking coffee each morning before my ride. In the afternoons, I went sightseeing. I toured the imposing medieval city walls that surrounded the center of ancient Xi'an and the city's famous Bell Tower. I wandered through the old Muslim district. I visited the Great Mosque, constructed in traditional Chinese style, as well as a Taoist temple tucked on a side street strewn with loose power lines.

I also went to see the Terracotta Warriors, navigating the bus system to get there. I met Yuchén, a twenty-five-year-old graduate student, while trying to find the entrance to the site. We toured the facilities together. He would study something for as long as I would and get bored, like me, and move on.

I had dinner with Yuchén and a friend of his in a shopping center with a seven-story waterfall gracing the atrium. We ordered one item after the next, a fabulous seven-course meal that left me stuffed. It was the highlight of my stay in Xi'an, though I didn't see Yuchén or his friend again.

I found a bicycle shop and used a Chinese translation on my phone to ask for a box so I could bring my Soma home. I purchased a new suitcase in an outdoor market to carry everything else.

I watched *Step Brothers* one afternoon, experiencing a moment of normalcy. I spent lots of time staring at the city from my massive sixteenth-story windowsill, mesmerized by the multitudes of high rises, stretching on forever, air-conditioning units affixed to every single window.

Mostly, I walked, for miles and miles, so much that I was sore from the effort. I discovered the most random places the city had to offer. Through it all, I tried to digest the magnitude of my journey, but I couldn't wrap my head around it.

On July 13th, I took a hotel shuttle to Xi'an International Airport. My thirteen-hour flight to San Francisco passed without incident, as did my connection to Denver.

Kendra met me at the airport. I was too dazed to fully appreciate our reunion. She drove me back to Fort Collins, an hour-long drive during which I readjusted to being back on the Front Range. I tried hopelessly to feel something, to celebrate my victory, but my mind was flat.

Kendra got off the freeway at the Harmony Road exit and drove west. Six miles later we reached Shields Street and turned north, driving another mile before hitting Horsetooth Road. With each passing block, emotions built up inside of me.

Some invisible force pressed on my shoulders. My breathing increased. The chords of "Silk," by Wolf Alice, played in my head as we approached our neighborhood, slowly at first, then pouring over into a crescendo of anxiety.

A few turns later we pulled into our driveway. I stared at our house for a moment before getting out of Kendra's silver Corolla. I went to the trunk and pulled out my suitcase. Kendra grabbed my backpack. My bike box remained lifeless in the car, waiting for my return.

We walked toward our front gate.

In my mind, I kept thinking, 'We did it! We're back and we made it to Xi'an!'

But something was wrong. The victory was drowned out. It was practically nonexistent. Because when I walked through that gate, everything I'd run away from was there, waiting for me. Every bit of angst, every insecurity, every bit of sadness, surged through me with crushing force.

Nothing has changed! I cried out. *It's like you never left.*

I felt weak and disillusioned by my own disappointment. I wanted to scream at the unfairness of it all, right there on my front step.

But I didn't want Kendra to think I wasn't happy to see her.

Tom Sweeney

With my dad and brother, Lansing, Michigan

Waterfront, Baku, Azerbaijan

Jeep trails that replaced the highway, eastern Kazakhstan

Campsite under a bridge, western Kazakhstan

Lonely stretch of highway, Kazakhstan

Campsite, east of Turkistan, Kazakhstan

Entering the mountains of western Xinjiang province, China

Rest area in the middle of Xinjiang Province, China

Lanzhou, only 1223 kilometers

Another flat, Gansu province, China

The Great Wall of China, Gansu province, China

Postcard-worthy scenery west of Xi'an

PART IV: 2017-2018

We thought of life by analogy with a journey,
with a pilgrimage, which had a serious purpose at the end,
and the thing was to get to that end.
Success or whatever it is, or maybe Heaven after you're dead.
But, we missed the point the whole way along.
It was a musical thing, and you were supposed to sing, or to dance,
while the music was being played.

-Alan Watts

CHAPTER 23

The Leelanau Peninsula is situated on the northwestern corner of the Michigan mitten and extends to form a barrier between Lake Michigan to the west and Grand Traverse Bay to the east. It is marked by vineyards, breweries, hiking trails, and beautiful back roads for cycling. It was the ideal place to reunite with my wife and reintegrate myself into the real world.

Except that it wasn't. While Kendra and I enjoyed our time together, my six days at home in Colorado had left me emotionally spent. That my epic ride across Central Asia had done nothing to help my mood only compounded the despondency.

After four days in the Leelanau Peninsula, Kendra and I dropped south to my brother's house. One afternoon, I found myself at his kitchen table. Two of my nieces sat across from me, perusing something on their phones. My brother sat to my right, sending a text on his work phone. I was scrolling through Facebook on my Motorola.

Good to see you're reconnecting with everyone.

To my left, my dad was rambling about his days in the seminary. It was the only thing he talked about with any comprehensibility. Occasionally one of us would chime in with an "Uh-huh," but mostly our eyes stayed glued to our phones.

Finding no end to my Facebook feed, I turned to Kevin and whispered, "Does he ever talk about Mom?"

"No. He only talks about the seminary."

"That was such a distant part of his life. What about his family?"

"I think it's his memory," said Kevin. "He doesn't remember much about Mom."

He spent over half his life with her and now he doesn't recall any of it?

I listened to my father talk. He barely paused for a breath. *What's the point of anything?*

I let out a long exhale, pondering the notion of identity, speculating on who I was and what I'd eventually become. My distinction as a cyclist in a foreign land had ended for another season.

You'll be a teacher again, soon enough.

I cringed.

Ready for those long, lonely weekends?

I returned to Facebook, a welcome distraction from my thoughts. My dad continued talking to no one in particular.

A few weeks later, I was back in Loveland, in my classroom, sitting across a table from Rachel.

"How many do you have?" I asked.

"Thirty-two. You?"

"Thirty-two."

We both stared at our rosters, an unfortunate result of budget cuts in districts across Colorado.

"This is ridiculous," I said, breaking the silence.

"I still think this year will be better," Rachel said.

"It couldn't be any worse," I replied.

Way to sound supportive.

"With so many kids, success is going to look different," I added.

"I suppose it will," said Rachel, still examining her list of students.

"Let's figure it all out after lunch," I said with hopeful irony. "I need to go to the office."

"Sounds good."

I walked down the hallway, running my fingers along the blue pushpin wall like the kids always did. I could smell the carpet cleaner the custodians had recently applied and knew that within a month the musty odor of feet would overtake any attempts to clean the building. I turned a familiar left and descended the ramp into the central foyer where the main office sat.

Kari, our school secretary, was hard at work juggling piles of paper. She looked at me and asked, "How's the planning coming?"

"Oh, the usual. We have thirty-two kids in our classes."

Kari's eyes widened with sympathy. "I'm sorry. I saw the lists. There was no good way to divide them."

I shook my head. "Too many. We'll manage, I suppose."

A small image behind Kari caught my eye. It was my Soma and the camel. I grinned. "My photo! I can't believe you printed it. And hung it on the wall!"

"Of course! It's not every day I receive an email from Kazakhstan."

"I'm honored!"

I walked past Kari to inspect the image. I remembered how badly my back hurt when I took the photo. Seeing the image gave me a boost of confidence.

"Rachel and I can handle thirty-two kids," I told Kari.

She smiled, and for a moment I believed what I was saying.

But teaching thirty-two fifth graders proved every bit as difficult as I thought it would. To be clear, they were a nice group of kids, and the arguing from the previous year was absent. But with so many in one room, I found it impossible to connect with individual students, many of whom needed that personal relationship with their teacher.

Often, asking the class to pull out a folder or book from their desk was a time-consuming affair that required repeated, personalized directions. When the students walked down the hall, the line extended past the corner where lines from previous years ended.

Compared to two years earlier, I had ten more of everything: papers to grade, parents to call, desks to move around. The additional hours didn't come out of the school day; they came out of my evenings and weekends.

The sad part was that I welcomed the extra work on Saturday and Sunday. If I had a nagging feeling of loneliness last year, now it was head-on. Every Friday, I created a list of things I needed to do for work so I wouldn't have to face my empty weekends.

Once again, I let my cycling and my job consume me. I was on my rollers before I was even awake, and after working on my computer, I would pedal into school, exercising at least two hours before reaching my classroom.

Kendra and I repeated our conversations from last year, talking about the friends we didn't have while making no effort to fix the problem. Kendra continued to suggest I look for a job in Poudre School District, in Fort Collins.

I brushed those suggestions aside, even after a chance encounter in October with an assistant principal at a school in Fort Collins. He said he'd be happy to offer advice if I ever wanted to switch districts. I thanked him and told him I might be in touch, although the idea of giving up a tenured position at a place I loved made little sense to me.

*****

In mid-October, right after conferences ended, I decided to go camping. I drove an hour west of Fort Collins, into the mountains, and parked my Camry.

I heaved my Gregory backpack over my shoulder, the same pack I had taken to Mongolia, and lamented that I only pulled it out once every few years. I followed a creekside trail through a narrow valley, breathing in the cold fresh air, scented with ponderosa pine. Snow covered the ground in patches, but even at that elevation snowshoes weren't yet necessary.

The valley opened into a vast bowl with mountains on three sides. I set up camp at the top of a small hill that offered views of distant peaks, the Never Summer Wilderness gracing the horizon.

I stared at the scene, waiting.

Where's your moment of epiphany?

Rather than feeling enraptured by the evening sky, I got bored sitting there. I thought about the REI ads where well-dressed people stand on mountaintops experiencing a penultimate moment of realization. All I got was detached silence. I watched the first stars materialize before retiring to my tent where I waited for sleep to take hold.

The next morning, I crammed my belongings into my rucksack and stuck it under a tree. I hoisted my day pack over my shoulders and set out, the early morning frost chilling my bones. I headed straight up the mountain, warming as I moved. Winds beat at me as I worked my way westward, along the barren ridgeline.

I snapped one photo after the next, each image better than the last. I became more interested in them than the surrounding scenery, visualizing how they would appear on Facebook and wondering how many "likes" I would get.

The thought of all that dopamine running through my system made me want to hurry home and post my pictures. I kept checking my heart rate monitor too, happy with how many calories I was burning at eleven thousand feet.

That evening, I posted my photos and waited for the "likes" to roll in. A few came initially. I checked back every few minutes, the familiar blue banner and endless feed staring back at me.

By bedtime, I had twelve "likes."

In the morning, I had eighteen.

I stared at the screen, anger and dismay bubbling up from somewhere deep. I reloaded the page. Nothing.

I exited the tab. Moments later, I checked it again.

I walked through my Saturday evening with my shoulders slumped. I told Kendra about my trip with the same enthusiasm I'd use relating an outing to Safeway.

By Monday morning, my post was dead to the world. The knot in my stomach cinched tighter. I stewed all day, especially on my ride home from work.

If you only got a few more "likes," this whole problem would go away.

'Getting a few more "likes" wouldn't make the problem go away. It would only hide the fact that we have one.'

How can you be so upset about this? You're forty-one years old.

I couldn't answer. I felt ridiculous. The bantering raged, and I considered my options: stop using Facebook altogether, because I couldn't handle it, or learn to deal with it.

Option two seemed better. I had caught up with a lot of friends and relatives on Facebook. But I had no idea how to turn off the consternation that social media can bring. I thought about all the kids and teenagers out there in similar situations and a newfound empathy for them surged through me.

After extensive internal arguing, I made a decision.

"Tom," I said out loud, "you need to stay off Facebook, at least through the holidays."

I glanced at a passing car, hoping the driver hadn't seen me talking to myself.

This won't solve anything.

'But it will alleviate the symptoms for a while.'

I cruised along in silence under clear blue skies. The city of Loveland faded from view as tracts of homes in Fort Collins materialized. I turned up "I Wanna Get Better," by Bleachers, and let my mind drift into the lyrics.

*****

At school, I felt more ineffective than ever. I couldn't seem to manage my classroom or teach anyone anything.

'Maybe,' I thought, 'we've become complacent after nine years in the same job.'

Maybe your students would be better off with a different teacher.

Both arguments were valid.

Even worse, I wondered if Rachel would return the following year. She was struggling as much as I was. I decided to ask her after winter break about her future plans.

Until then, I had plenty of other things to worry about, starting with another snowy drive to Michigan. This year, I dropped Kendra off in Omaha and continued east by myself. I abandoned the idea of following our family Christmas Eve traditions from years past, instead reconciling myself to a store-bought sandwich while my father ate a frozen dinner.

On Christmas Day, I sorted through the many gifts from my brother and his family but grew disheartened when I realized my dad hadn't remembered to get something for me. It wasn't that I wanted anything in particular, other than for him to remember.

I spent a few quiet, lonely nights in the basement of his condo, looking at old photographs, before returning to Omaha to see Kendra and her family. At her parent's home, I had a proper Christmas with adults who remembered what month it was. I actually relaxed for a few days.

In January, Kendra and I watched a movie called *Things to Come*, a French film about an aging professor facing difficult changes in her life. At the end of the film, the main character reads a quote to her students by Jean-Jacques Rousseau from his novel *Julie, or the New Heloise*. In my interpretation, Rousseau says hoping for happiness is better than achieving it, and that the anxiety inherent in the search is, in itself, enjoyable.

Leave it to an Enlightenment philosopher to reveal the truths you can't seem to figure out.

'He has a point, though, doesn't he?'

What? People are supposedly happy only before they're happy? What does that even mean?

'It means people are always going to be striving for something more, and the moment they get what they want …'

They want something else.

'We're only happy before we're happy.'

I let that sink in. I wondered if part of me enjoyed feeling unhappy, because it left me hoping for something better.

'Maybe life is really about looking for that thing around the corner, rather than actually finding it.'

Does this constant anxiety feel like hope to you?

I considered the question.

This perpetual knot isn't normal.

That much was true. I couldn't fathom that Rousseau had this in mind when he wrote his words. Every waking moment, I had the sensation I get after relatives or friends stayed with me for a few days before returning home, leaving behind vacant rooms where dust floated softly through muted rays of sunlight.

Those kinds of moments filled me with pangs that left me reeling, but they would eventually subside. Now, I was feeling like that all the time and I couldn't escape it. It was a piercing ache that made me think I'd never find peace again and never be happy again.

And yet, part of me liked being unfurled. I liked to feel a modicum of discontent, because it made me feel more alive than I had in a long while. It was, in many ways, better than floating from one day or month or year to the next, feeling nothing at all.

My taste in music reflected my melancholy. I loved songs that would leave me unraveled, like "No Way," by The Naked and Famous, or "All My Friends," by LCD Soundsystem. But I also liked to change the track and calm down when I wanted. For the past year and a half, I didn't seem to have access to the "off" button.

That frightened me.

Yet, I still had hope. I still believed one day I'd have an epiphany and return to normal. Or, at least, normal for me, and stable enough to appreciate my home, my wife, and my job.

My melancholy was apparent to Kendra.

"You should apply to schools in Fort Collins," she told me yet again. "The change would be good for you. You'd meet new people."

I shrugged. "I love my school. And besides, leaving would be like admitting defeat."

"You know it's not about your classroom management."

"I know," I responded, looking at the floor.

"It's about us," continued Kendra. "It's about giving Fort Collins a chance, again."

Kendra's comments made crystal clear sense. I had given up on my hometown.

"And if you were closer to home, we might be able to get a dog."

Gracie had been adopted in September. I was happy for her, but the house was quiet without her.

"I don't want to leave Sarah Milner."

"I know. But things won't change if you stay there."

I knew Kendra was right. Things might not improve if I left, but they definitely wouldn't get better if I stayed.

'There's a monumental difference between quitting and letting go,' I reminded myself.

"I'll think about it," I said.

We finished our meal in silence.

*****

On February 15th, Rachel and I had a training at Winona Elementary, on the opposite side of town from Sarah Milner. At lunch, we went for a walk, eager to enjoy the unseasonably warm sunshine. The metal cleats of my cycling shoes clicked with every step.

"Where are you going for spring break?" I asked.

"We're heading to California with a couple of friends."

"What are you doing out there?"

"I know this might sound silly, but we're going to Harry Potter World at Universal Studios."

"Sounds like fun," I said. The notion that she and her boyfriend were going on a trip with friends struck a nerve.

"I finished *The Deathly Hallows*," continued Rachel. "I can't wait to see Hogwarts up close."

"That would be cool," I said. "I'd like to visit Diagon Alley." I pictured the fabled London street for a moment.

Ask her what she's planning for next year!

I hesitated. A moment of silence passed.

"See that old, rusted truck over there?" I pointed to a tarnished pickup, which dated to a bygone era. "The one with the tree growing out of it?"

"Yes."

"I pass it frequently, on my morning rides. I always find it so fascinating."

"Oh, huh."

Really interesting. Just ask her!

The road curved to the right, to the north, but we stepped onto a bicycle path that veered south, toward the Big Thompson River. Out of the shade of the tree-lined street, the sun intensified, hitting us from above and below, the white concrete reflecting its glare.

Neither of us said anything for several paces. Suddenly, Rachel turned to me.

"So, I don't think I'm coming back to fifth grade next year. I'm going to find a job closer to home or move to a different grade level if something else at Sarah Milner opens up."

Without hesitating, I gave a rehearsed reply. "You know I'll support whatever decision you make."

We walked in silence for a few somber moments.

"I'm sorry these two years have been so rough," I said. "Teaching isn't always like this."

The conversation became a blur after that. We continued down the path where it met the Big Thompson River and then veered west. Rather than follow it, we sat down on the riverbank and pulled out our lunches.

"To be honest," I said, "I've considered looking for a job in Fort Collins. Kendra and I don't know anyone there anymore."

"Jay and I hardly know anyone in Boulder either," Rachel admitted.

Her statement surprised me, but it made sense. Commuting an hour each way, whether by bike or car, wasn't conducive to meeting people.

"Sarah Milner is a great place to work," I said, "and it feels like home. But sometimes I wonder how other schools do things."

"It is a good school," Rachel said. "But I'm not sure it's for me."

"I definitely think you'll be happier teaching primary somewhere. I'll get a recommendation letter drafted for you."

"Thanks. Let me know if you need one too."

I smiled. "We'll see."

We finished our lunch and walked back to our training.

On my ride home, the gravity of the conversation slowly registered. I was so focused on what it meant for Rachel that I hadn't thought about what it meant for me.

Another teaching partner is leaving. Like clockwork. It's been two years.

'Time to start interviewing again.'

My brows furrowed behind my sunglasses. I examined the familiar roads, the familiar houses, and the familiar storefronts. Loveland was such a part of me, but it wasn't my home at all.

As I rode north, my future, my dissatisfactions, and my angst all unfurled with every turn of the cranks.

I mechanically pushed forward, a new reality sinking in moment by moment. When "Sober Up," by AJR, started flowing out of my MP3 player, I increased the volume as loud as I could handle and stomped on the pedals.

I got home and pulled my bicycle into the garage. I unpacked my things and piled them on the entry table. I showered and changed. I ate dinner with Kendra, a quiet meal where I only mentioned in passing the conversation I'd had with Rachel.

Afterward, I sat on the couch and digested my food and the day's turn of events. I turned on my laptop and navigated to my resume folder. I double-clicked the file called Resume 2014 and waited as Microsoft Word leisurely opened it. I stared at the document and then began to update it.

As I typed, my head turned, back and forth, a subtle subconscious "no" emanating from my psyche.

"No," I announced to my screen. "I'm not doing this again."

I wasn't going to wait around for another teaching partner at Sarah Milner. My life had gone too far in one direction. Kendra and I had found ourselves in a friendless void. We weren't happy. I was miserable. And chasing nebulous dreams halfway around the world obviously hadn't solved anything.

It was time to make a change in my real life, a change that dealt with my real problems, here in Fort Collins. If I was going to sit through another interview, I was going to sit on the other side of the table, as the interviewee.

It was time to move my real life forward, again.

Before bed, I told Kendra that I was going to get in touch with the assistant principal I'd met in October, to ask him more pointed questions about working in Poudre School District.

Kendra smiled. "It's about time."

I lay in bed replaying the day's events, fascinated that my life had somehow completely shifted direction over the course of an afternoon. It didn't matter that I hadn't put anything into motion yet. If I'd learned anything in recent years, it's that when I make a decision, I stick it out to the end.

Jobs in Poudre School District posted in mid-April. I applied to a multitude of third-, fourth- and fifth-grade positions and landed two interviews, neither of which panned out. I was growing anxious. My principal was supportive when I told him I was looking for a new job, but if I didn't find something by May, I wasn't going to leave him interviewing potential fifth-grade teachers the last week of school.

Even as I perused postings, my upcoming ride from Xi'an to Shanghai nagged at me. Although it was only a thousand miles, it was a thousand miles across China, and success was not guaranteed.

At eight in the morning, on the last Monday in April, I walked into Bennett Elementary for an interview. The school was a block away from Colorado State University, less than a mile from Kendra's office and only three miles from our house. I considered the latter distance with mixed feelings, wondering if I'd ride as much working so close to home.

An even bigger problem loomed. The job was posted as a one-year contract. That meant I would have to reapply the following year, and the position might not even be there.

The interview went well, and when I asked whether the position would be there next year, the principal's answer was promising.

But not certain.

That final point followed me the next day.

You can't leave a tenured assignment for a one-year contract. Are you crazy?

I had spent years building a reputation at Sarah Milner. I thought about how things were going in my classroom.

'Maybe it's time to leave with our reputation intact.'

Do you know how stressed you'll be next April? What if you don't get rehired?

I grimaced. It did seem irresponsible to take a risk of such magnitude.

I stared at the floor, unsure what to think.

My resolute side spoke up. "Consider this. Last summer you rode your bicycle, solo, from Tbilisi, Georgia, to Xi'an, China."

'And …?'

Your point being?

I gave an annoyed sigh, as if my point should be obvious. "If anyone can pull this off, you can."

The principal from Bennett called me Wednesday evening. I took the call in my living room, the same place I'd received a call from the principal at Sarah Milner nine years earlier. Now, like then, the principal offered me a fifth-grade teaching position.

I accepted the offer, again.

A week later, Rachel took a second-grade position at Sarah Milner, meaning a whole new team would replace us in fifth grade. It pained me to think there might be someone who could do my job better than I could, but it was time to let them try, whoever they might be.

A few weeks later, I said goodbye to the Sarah Milner staff, one by one. I made my way down the fifth-grade hallway, past the cabinets I had spent years trying to clean out, past the familiar walls where I had hung up so many random pieces of student work.

I went into Rachel's room to say a final farewell before returning to my classroom to gather my things. I studied the familiar walls, desks, and cabinets, my second home for so many years, before wheeling the Soma through the outside door.

I'd walked out that door over a thousand times, bicycle in hand, riding home in every condition imaginable. Today, the weather was beautiful.

I pushed away from Sarah Milner's playground before turning west to Wilson Avenue. From there, I turned north, toward Fort Collins, completing the circuit of my horizontal hamster wheel one last time. I cranked up Arcade Fire's "Everything Now" as I pedaled home under the glorious blue skies of Colorado.

THE ROUTE: 2018

Daily Log

June	Miles	Description
2018		
Thurs 7		Walk around Vancouver airport for one hour
8		Walk around Beijing airport one hour, frantically
9	109	Ride Xi'an to Danfeng. Tailwind helped.
10	115	Danfeng to Tuandongzhen, roads really bad after crossing into Henan province.
Mon 11	101	Tuandongzjem to within 20 miles of Tongbai, where I camped; broken spoke today
12	95	Campsite from above to Luoshan. Sluggish, horrible slab pavement that felt like riding on waves
13	136	Luoshan to Liu'an. Good ride
14	108	Liuan to about a mile east of Liuzhenzhen, halfway between Hefei and Nanjing, camped
15	65	Campsite above to Nanjing; had to take a cab under the Yangtze River
16	121	Nanjing to Shuofangzhen, halfway between Wuxi and Souzhou. 80 miles from the Bund
17	85	Shuofangzhen to Shanghai. I pulled it off! And feel nothing
Mon 18	54	Downtown Shanghai to Xinchengzhen, on the East China Sea
19		Easy ride along coast of the East China Sea to get groceries. That's all.
20	60	Xinchengzhen to central Shanghai, in pouring rain
21		Power walk 2 hours with five 5-minute jogs, then two more solid hours of walking.
22		Ride 10 laps around Century Park, Shanghai; 3 mile loops, 10 laps
23		Power walk to Confucian temple; jogged total of 8 minutes. Rode around Shanghai pm
24		Ride 32ish total miles, bike path along river
Mon 25		Thirteen laps around Century Park; then jog 25 minutes; then walk two more solid hour
26		Ride 14 laps Century Park, plus two hours walking.
27		Run 10 minutes on east riverfront, Shanghai, then walked, then ran again, before my flight home

CHAPTER 24

My arrival in Xi'an was not promising. The tarmac was wet and the sky gray. Riding into the city in one of the few taxis spacious enough to accommodate my bike box, I watched as the evening clouds cast the buildings and concrete in an ethereal glow.

The driver kept looking at his phone for directions to the Holiday Inn Express, which I'd reserved several weeks before leaving. I instinctively pulled out my own phone and tapped the Google Maps app. The familiar green and white map opened, the little blue dot moving toward the bottom of the page. I typed "Holiday Inn" and the hotel name appeared. I knew the driver was going in the right direction even if he didn't.

A few minutes later we pulled in front of the twenty-story building. I checked in and pulled my bike box and luggage to my room. Despite being exhausted and frazzled, I assembled my bicycle and sorted my gear before leaving to hunt for a grocery store.

I left my room early the next morning, the remains of my bike box and an old suitcase piled next to the trash bin. After returning my key, I walked into the morning sunshine and hopped on the Soma. Cranking up Van Halen's "Jump," I pushed forward onto Xi'an's familiar roads.

A few miles south, I snapped a photo of the Xi'an Sheraton North, my home from the previous summer. I passed under the North Gate of the Old City wall, continued forward another mile and then turned left, out the East Wall and out of the city.

My first day of riding took me a hundred miles over a small mountain range and through a long valley. I found a motel in the city of Danfeng with no hassle and promptly settled into my routine of showering, washing my clothes, recording my caloric intake and output, and editing photos. I went for a stroll and updated Kendra on my whereabouts.

I had planned to eat in my room, but as I passed a series of outdoor restaurants that sat on a plaza across from an open-air market, one of the owners smiled and motioned for me to sit down. I accepted the invitation and pointed to something on the menu. The owner returned a few minutes later with a large bowl of noodles. I devoured it.

'Three days ago,' I thought, 'we were home. Now we're on the other side of the world.'

Living the other side of your life.

I leaned back in my chair and savored the moment. Things were off to a good start.

The next morning, I stopped in front of a mileage marker.

'That can't be right,' I thought.

I double-checked the math in my head.

'The sign says 1,264 kilometers to Shanghai. That's less than eight hundred miles.'

Google said it was over a thousand.

'But that route was circuitous. This sign is for the G312.'

I'd been on the G312 for four hundred miles the previous summer. It was like an old friend.

We should stay on this.

'Settled.'

An hour later I reached the border with Henan province. The moment I crossed the provincial line, the road changed from smooth pavement into a mess of potholes and the shoulder disappeared. Dust, absent a mile ago, permeated my lungs, and the scenery turned into an industrial wasteland.

I weaved and maneuvered my bike as semis and other large trucks crawled by me, swaying with every bump in the road. My wheels were taking a beating worse than the jeep trails of eastern Kazakhstan. It continued most of the day, with temperatures nearing a hundred degrees. There was nothing redeeming to see and very little shade.

In the evening, I entered the lobby of a decrepit hotel covered in peeling paint and dust. Two women in the lobby greeted me and motioned for me to sit down on a cheap, vinyl-covered bench. They were friendly at first, but soon they started laughing in my direction.

'There's a real hotel nearby. I remember seeing it when we researched our route last month.'

The women glanced at me again and laughed.

I could visualize the dot on Google Maps. I glanced at the paper maps in my handlebar bag and fumed over their uselessness at this scale.

I pointed at the women's cell phones a few times, indicating that they should translate what they were waiting for, but they were oblivious to my cues. They smiled and motioned for me to stay seated in my disgusting cycling clothes.

In a fit of utter annoyance, I pulled out my cell phone. It was a reflex built on habit; I can typically solve all my problems with a few taps on my screen.

Today was no exception.

I pulled up Google Maps. Like the cab ride a few nights before, my favorite blue dot appeared, surrounded by street-level detail of everything around me.

'Are we connected to the Wi-Fi here?'

I checked my settings, but I was clearly not connected to anything.

'We can use Google Maps this year? How …?'

And why didn't you notice this in the cab, in Xi'an?

I looked at my phone again.

'I think we selected a different international plan than last year.'

Are you kidding me?

'Afraid not.'

We could have had this last summer!

I laughed, loudly, in the lobby. I had Google Maps again.

This is so typical of you.

I shut out my internal diatribe and typed "hotel" into the search bar. Instantly, I saw the international hotel I had googled before leaving home.

I stood, grabbed my bike, gave a quick wave to the two women, and walked out the door. Behind me, I could hear them shouting for me to stay, but it was too late.

After easily checking in at my new accommodations, I took a pleasant walk along a concrete path paralleling a small river. I talked to Kendra as I strolled, glad for the chance to recuperate after such a hot and unpleasant day. Despite the opportunity to unwind, however, I had trouble sleeping. I felt unsettled.

Leaving the comforts of my international hotel the next morning, descending a glass elevator that overlooked the riverfront, my thoughts were a blur of things past, present, and future.

I unlocked my Soma in the parking lot and suddenly remembered a postcard I received while living in Mongolia. It was from a Peace Corps colleague who had completed her service and was traveling through India.

On the cover of the card was an image of a Hindi sadhu, or holy man. On the back, my friend had written something to the effect of, "I hope you find whatever it is you're looking for in those Gobi Desert sunsets."

I thought hard about the statement as I packed my lock and hopped on my bicycle. Here I was twenty years later, still searching for something.

But do you really want to find it?

I considered the question as I accelerated onto the G312, cars easing by me, the early morning traffic surprisingly light.

What will you do after you get to the other side of that sunset?

I navigated busy intersections until the city faded behind me. Ahead, the highway maintained a dead flat and straight trajectory. The humid morning air was heavy. Moving through it was like pedaling through water.

'If we're so close to the end, shouldn't we feel some sort of closure? Shouldn't we feel better?'

Yes, you should. You're only six hundred miles from Shanghai.

'We start a new job in August,' I pointed out. 'We've made a huge step forward.'

I attempted a smile.

So why don't you feel any different?

I didn't have an answer. Sadness crept over me.

'Have we learned anything from this trip?'

I. Don't. Know.

'Surely we've discovered some new insight into the universe.'

I surveyed the scene. My urban surroundings had changed to farm fields. Small fruit trees stood stoically, devoid of anything edible. Tractor prints cut through the boundless greenspace in all directions.

'Surely we're a better person because of it. Otherwise ...'

What was the point?

I glanced at my Soma. It looked like I felt—beaten and weathered. The black frame was scratched and dented, revealing bare metal in places. The cranks, pedals, and luggage racks showed a decade of wear. It seemed that each mile I rode forward was a step toward failure, because my frame of mind had not changed from last year. It was as tattered as my Pearl Izumi coat.

Don't get to Shanghai too fast.

'The new job will change things.'

What about now?

I continued the back-and-forth in my head until I wore myself out and reached a state of capitulated calm.

Then a spoke popped. I heard the loud snap and detected harsh rubbing in the back brake.

"Don't panic," came my familiar phrase, even as my stomach sank, and I succumbed to momentary irrationality.

This is bad. How far are you from anywhere?

I did the math, figuring the last city was forty miles behind me. It would take a full day, or more, to hitch a ride, find a bike shop, and buy a new wheel.

I pulled off the road and walked my bike down a tractor trail. I removed the wheel from the frame and dug through my saddle bag. I removed a cassette tool and a mini-adjustable wrench I'd purchased at Mr. Bricolage's hardware store in Sofia, Bulgaria, so long ago.

I crammed the wheel halfway back into the bicycle because I didn't have a chain whip, necessary to hold the gear cluster in place while I unscrewed it. Instead, I placed a foot on the crank arm to brace the bicycle chain, and the gears, in place.

This better work.

I put pressure on the wrench and sighed with relief as the cassette lockring loosened. I pulled the cassette off the hub and set it on the ground. After removing the tire, I slid out the broken spoke.

I thought back to my days working as a mechanic at Lee's Cyclery, haunted by the advice I'd given so many customers over the years: "If one spoke breaks, that means they've all been under a lot of stress. It's only a matter of time before more follow."

How many people did you say that to?

I had a set of spokes taped to the rear rack. In over a decade, I had never removed a single one. Now, I tightened one of them into the rim and gave the wheel a cursory truing, or straightening, then installed the rim strip, tire, and tube.

I reassembled and repacked my bicycle, feeling a rush of relief when it was upright. I wheeled the bike to the road, put my foot on the pedal, and gingerly pushed forward.

Every moment, I imagined more spokes would pop. My eyes scanned the pavement for any kind of bump or deviation. Consumed with my new paranoia, I no longer worried about getting closer to Shanghai and closer to defeat.

At four in the afternoon, I pulled into a deserted park near a school and ate a snack in the shade of a pagoda. As I was packing up, I noticed two small faces staring at me. I looked behind me and several more children appeared out of nowhere, their eyes fixed on me with intense curiosity. Soon, I was surrounded. A sea of infectious smiles made me forget about my spokes, the miles ahead, the heat, and my impending victorious failure.

I surreptitiously snapped photos of the mob before two adults at the school building yelled for the kids to line up. As quickly as they came, they were gone.

The sun made its way across the sky. The landscape became hillier and more remote. I stopped at a small roadside store, its glass exterior covered in ads for an array of products. I leaned my bicycle against the transparent wall and walked inside.

It was another ninety-degree evening and my body odor followed me around. I pulled vacuum-sealed tofu, compressed-date biscuits, and anything else I could eat off the shelves.

The clerk tallied up my purchase with a calculator and showed the numbers to me. I smiled at the universal language of math and counted out my yuan.

Jamming my spoils into my panniers, I pedaled until I reached a sign that read, in Chinese and English, "MoGou Ecotourism Scenic Area," with arrows pointing south. I followed the markings and ascended into the hills. It took ten minutes to push my hundred-pound mass two miles to a hilltop where I could see several small reservoirs of water to my left.

The pools were situated down a twenty-foot embankment lined with trees. The base of the embankment was hidden from the road and offered an excellent place to camp.

I unloaded my bike and carried my gear down. Sweat oozed from my pores, my clothes stuck to my skin, and bugs hopped around my ankles as I set up camp. The faintly audible sound of running water, trickling from one pond to the next, provided a calming white noise.

Once situated, I eyed the reservoir closest to me.

Absolutely not! Do you know how many parasites live in the water?

'Do you know how well we'll sleep if we wipe this sweat off?'

I set my cycling clothes on a patch of grass and waded into the water, cringing at the thought of what lurked within. I thought of the concrete culvert in Kazakhstan.

'That didn't make us sick,' I reassured myself.

But don't get the water on your head.

That was reasonable. I used my environmentally-friendly camp soap and pond water to wash everything up to my neck. I opened a 1.5-liter bottle of distilled water to wash my head.

Afterward, I rinsed my cycling clothes in the reservoir. Once sufficiently sweat-free, I laid them out over my tent and my Soma to dry.

I ate dinner, organized my things, and looked around. I had three hours until bed.

'What now?' I wondered.

Mostly out of curiosity, I took a photo of my campsite with my phone. Then I opened my Instagram app and uploaded the image of my random campsite in central China. I checked the box to add the post to Facebook.

I labeled the post, "Nice spot to camp, despite all the bugs," and tagged the location as "China."

Instagram and Facebook from Central China?

'And it doesn't matter how many "likes" we get.'

I had succeeded, mostly, in overcoming my anxiety about posting things to social media.

I thought back to Mongolia, where I communicated with my friends and family through letters. If I needed to send something fast, I would go to the telegraph office to dispatch a telegram. My two years in the desert flashed through my head, the heat, the cold, the sunsets, my classroom. I couldn't have coped with social media in those days.

'There's something to be said for experiencing life in the age of telegrams.'

Agreed.

'But we're not giving up Google Maps anytime soon.'

*****

Are you kidding me! I wanted to scream.

It was ten o'clock at night. Two staff members were holding up their phones. The translations were clear: "Sorry, but you can't stay here."

I'd checked in several hours earlier. It was a sizable hotel and seemed like the kind of place that could accommodate foreigners.

I hid my disbelief and packed my belongings before heading to the lobby, bicycle in tow. At the front desk, the receptionist apologized several times, refunded my money, and made calls to other hotels. I stood impatiently, eyeing the brass fixtures and gaudy chandeliers.

An employee motioned for me to follow him. We went out into the muggy night. Huge glowing marquees with scrolling Chinese characters, affixed to high-rise buildings, contrasted with the dark sky. We walked a mile to the Milan Boutique Hotel, which had a facade that reminded me of Las Vegas.

Inside, my guide negotiated with the receptionist. Despite the exorbitant prices listed on the wall, the clerk charged me the same price I had paid for my previous room. While I was annoyed that the staff at my original hotel didn't understand the rules regarding foreign guests, or tried to circumvent them, I appreciated the effort they made to find another place for me.

On my way out of town the next morning, I came to a stoplight where the G312 crossed a broad boulevard. On the northeast side of the intersection, three new high rises protruded from the ground, covered in scaffolding. They seemed to grow out of the soil like some Tolkien fortress. I wondered who would inhabit them and imagined the army you could create with so many citizens.

I rode into Hefei, a city of eight million people and twenty-seven miles wide. Midway through, I lost my bearings and lost the G312. Examining Google Maps, I realized I could continue thirty miles east on a secondary route and rendezvous with it.

After the previous night's fiasco, I had no desire to stay in a hotel. I scoured Google Maps until I noted a spot where the road dipped under a set of railroad tracks and then banked sharply right to parallel the rail line on the north side.

As I went under the small train bridge and made the turn, a thick patch of woods emerged above me. I waited for a few cars to pass before carrying my belongings into the trees.

I found a small clearing where I set up camp, walking barefoot through the grasses and other plants. I bathed and washed my shorts using two liters of water. Trains flew by sporadically, too fast for anyone to see me. I sat on my rain jacket and spread out my food on my Pearl Izumi winter coat, which served no other purpose this summer.

I edited photos while lying on my sleeping pad in my tent. As it grew darker, I waited for another train to rocket by and illuminate my site, hoping to catch a photo. I was unsuccessful.

The next morning, my legs were covered in bug bites. I shrugged, put on my damp shorts and stinky shirt and jersey, and got back on the road.

*****

The city of Pukou sits across the Yangtze River from Nanjing. In my mind, the Yangtze River was a major turning point, the last notable landform to cross before entering the final lap to Shanghai. I envisioned myself crossing the frontier aboard a ferry, or riding across a spectacular bridge, taking in the view of the famous river, the air in my face as I triumphed over all kinds of adversity to reach the penultimate leg of my journey.

Unfortunately, ferries don't exist between the two cities, and the only bicycle-friendly bridge was shut down for construction. I found a subway line, but after making multiple trips with my bags down four flights of stairs, I was denied entry because I had my bike with me.

I rode six miles north through Pukou, searching for a way to cross the river. After wasting an hour, I decided the only way across was through a wide tunnel designed solely for automobiles.

You're going to get arrested, for real this time.

'There's no other way.'

I headed toward the cavernous opening that descended below the water. Cars streaked past me. I glanced back to assess traffic and saw a cab approaching. Without thinking, I flagged it down.

The driver pulled over, and we put my bags in the backseat. I removed the front wheel of my Soma, and he set the bicycle upright in the trunk and strapped it down tightly, the lid open to accentuate its humiliation.

The tunnel was three lanes in each direction. Dim, overhead lights cast the concrete in a familiar glow. The road emerged on the other side and ascended a small bridge that crossed a tiny tributary of the Yangtze, my only glimpse of the magnificent river.

The cab driver dropped me off at a street corner. I gathered my things, paid and thanked him, and set about looking for a hotel. It was only two, and I'd only ridden sixty miles, but after camping the night before, I needed a shower.

More importantly, I was getting close to Shanghai, but wasn't ready to finish my ride.

CHAPTER 25

With nearly nine million inhabitants, Nanjing is China's eighth-largest city. Horrifically occupied by the Japanese during World War II, the Nanjing I visited was an entirely different place. The London plane trees that lined the streets and boulevards offered unparalleled shade and calming beauty. The remnants of an old fortress stood against the tranquil backdrop of Xuanwu Lake.

I meandered to the lakefront where an arched bridge led to a small island lined with trees, a quintessential picture of Chinese architecture and beauty. On the shore, couples and families wandered around the ruins of the ancient fortress or relaxed on shaded patches of grass. The scene should have been calming, but something was bothering me.

Two hundred miles to go, huh?

'A hundred and eighty at most.'

You're actually going to make it?

'Yes, we are.'

The thought of arriving in Shanghai filled me with despair. I left the lake and headed back to the city center, walking briskly.

I pictured the Bund, the most famous place in Shanghai, where the river bends to yield postcard-perfect views of Shanghai's skyline. It was my photo finish, the spot where I would take countless selfies of me and the Soma basking in the glow of a job well done.

But it won't be the finish you anticipated. Not on the level that matters.

I cringed. I was supposed to be feeling better.

'We at least have a backup finish line.'

The East China Sea lay fifty miles beyond central Shanghai. From there, I couldn't ride any further.

I reached an intersection and waited for the crosswalk light to turn green. I crossed the street and entered a canopy of trees.

'It can't end this way,' I thought.

You don't feel any better than you did a year ago.

'If we can't arrive in Shanghai with the right frame of mind ...'

What was the point?

'We've got two days to figure it all out.'

A successful failure awaits.

I increased my pace, gliding my hand over the trunk of each successive London plane tree. I walked urgently and aimlessly, like I used to on those lonely evenings in Mongolia when I was a million miles from anyone and needed to calm down. The unease followed me through the evening and into the night, until I finally drifted off to sleep.

Countless new skyscrapers greeted me the next day, and I pondered yet again the multitudes that inhabited them. I watched as a woman on a moped sped past me. Her son sat behind her, staring at me. Neither wore helmets. They disappeared into the traffic.

I crossed an unforgettable steel truss bridge, its angular framework held together by huge bolts. From the railing, I observed low-riding barges filled with coal and rocks lumbering down a wide, nameless river.

I ended the day in the city of Shuofangzhen, less than eighty miles from the Bund. I found a pricey hotel that took credit cards. The view from the window was spectacular in an industrial, sprawling, dusty Chinese kind of way. I didn't sleep well and woke up on my last day, the day that I would enter Shanghai, in a dour mood.

As I ate breakfast at the hotel, I learned on Facebook that a high school friend had gotten married. I didn't even know that he was dating anyone. It was another brutal reminder of how out of touch I had become with my friends over the past four or five or nine years, ever since my diet began and I started riding compulsively and didn't have time for anything else.

At seven in the morning, on Sunday, June 17th, 2018, I pushed my Soma out the front doors of the Reagan International Hotel and started my final leg to Shanghai. I was tired and cranky, and Chinese traffic was the last thing I needed.

While cars move in predictable ways in China, and follow basic traffic laws, mopeds and three-wheeled carts go every which way on every side of the road, running stop signs and red lights at will. It was an insanity I was used to, but today I wanted nothing to do with it. I replayed "Broken," by lovelytheband, over and over, the beats and melodies flowing with the chaos of the traffic.

The deeper I went into the world's biggest city, the worse it became. In places, the road was three levels high, with the busiest, bottom section reserved for the likes of me, the middle layer full of cars traveling within the metropolis, and the highest levels housing the freeway system for people looking to exit the mess. It continued for four hours.

I fantasized about passing a giant "Welcome to Shanghai" sign, but my experience in Xi'an last summer told me that was a dream. Like the previous year, there was simply a moment when I realized I was in the city.

In central Shanghai, mere miles from my photo finish, police officers materialized on every corner, directing mopeds and bicycles into orderly lines, suppressing the crazy maneuverings rampant a few blocks back. Signs that read "No Bikes" emerged and blocked my way forward.

The direct route I'd planned to the Bund was diverted by angry police whistles and one-way streets. With law enforcement cracking down on anyone disobeying the law, I had to obey the law too.

'Shanghai is the most bike-unfriendly city in the world!'

They've taken all the fun out of riding in China!

Little by little, I found my way to the Bund, which was marked by an elevated pedestrian area that follows the river and offers spectacular views of the Shanghai skyline.

I followed a long ramp to the top of the walkway, hopped off my bike, walked it to the railing, and peered down on the Huangpu River.

'We did it!'

My optimism was halfhearted.

The photo finish in my mind hadn't included crowds of people. I waited for countless selfie takers to move before I could snap an unimpressive photo of my bike with the Shanghai skyline behind it.

I looked for someone to take a picture of me and the Soma. Before I could catch anyone's attention, I heard a short whistle. I turned my head and saw a policeman walking toward me, pointing at my bike. He motioned with his hand for me to leave the pedestrian area.

Unbelievable.

Not one to give in to defeat, I smiled and held up my camera. The officer reluctantly took it and I stood next to my bike. He pointed the lens at me, but I could tell he was pointing at the most unimpressive stretch of skyline behind me.

He clicked the shutter.

"Xie xie," I said.

He motioned for me to leave.

Disheartened, I returned to the main road where I was yelled at by more police officers. I cut into the side streets that paralleled the Bund. I went to another pedestrian area but was ushered out. I squeezed my bike over a small bridge teeming with people and tried to get a shot on the other side, only to be turned away again.

One officer directed me to a bike path that followed the river north of the Bund. It passed through a small park that backed up to the river. I snuck through the trees to take a photo but was busted again.

I found an area that afforded a rather pathetic view of the city skyline and took another photo. It would have to do. I was too dismayed and frazzled to care anymore.

I leaned my bike on a bench in the shadow of a glass building and sat down. I called Kendra.

"Hi!" she said enthusiastically. "Are you there?"

Tears pooled in my eyes.

"Yes, I suppose." I related the day's events to her and then told her I needed to find a place to stay.

"OK," she replied, attempting to find some words to make me feel better.

"I'll call you again from the East China Sea," I added with a hint of optimism.

I sat for a few more minutes trying to figure out where everything had gone wrong. Then I got up, found a ferry station, and hopped on a small boat to the other side of the river where I figured there would be fewer tourists, fewer police officers, and less expensive hotel rooms.

On the other side, I pulled out my phone and clicked on my Booking.com app. My lips curved into a smile as I scrolled, finding it ironic that last year my apps didn't work without Wi-Fi. I settled on the Novotel Hotel, only a few blocks away.

From my nineteenth-floor room, the arc of the city skyline pressed against the waterfront, with Shanghai's iconic buildings illuminated against the night sky. Out of the bustle of traffic, I could enjoy a small taste of victory.

'And we have the final leg tomorrow. We're not quite finished.'

I ate a bowl of instant ramen, savoring the salty broth and freeze-dried carrots, while staring at the city lights. After dinner, I reserved a room for two nights in Xinchengzhen, a small town next to Dishui Lake, two miles from the coast of the East China Sea. I also booked a hostel for my remaining seven nights in Shanghai.

I went to bed hopeful I'd figure everything out the next day.

*****

Ten miles from central Shanghai, the city faded away and I found myself in an agricultural hinterland, the sultry morning sun baking the landscape. I rode by industrial parks where major US companies had established their Chinese headquarters. I passed signs pointing the way to Disneyland Shanghai and the Shanghai Zoo. I cycled through one dusty town after the next.

As I neared the coast, I imagined arriving in a place filled with posh hotels, troves of tourists, and elegant restaurants. Instead, the city of Xinchengzhen, which sits next to the man-made, perfectly circular Dishui Lake, turned out to be a quiet, deserted place built in anticipation of future crowds. Everything in the town was brand new, but empty.

A series of three ring roads encircled the lake, the closest of which was five miles in diameter. I followed Google Maps around the secondary ring road, looking closely at a small stretch of pavement that straddled the shoreline of the East China Sea. A mere mile away, the app took me through a construction zone that was walled off, creating a barricade between me and final victory.

I pushed my bicycle down a footpath and around the high concrete barrier, navigating a hundred yards of dirt, rebar, and rubble. As I emerged around a second wall, I recognized a vast emptiness that could only be projected by an expanse of water. I hopped on my bike and rode straight ahead.

'Finally ... finally ... finally ...'

The road curved left, paralleling a sidewalk and a small cement fence. I hoisted the Soma onto the sidewalk and looked over the wall. On the other side was a breaker that separated the land from the East China Sea.

I gazed out over the water.

After cycling 11,145 miles from Lisbon in 109 riding days, I had arrived.

I was there.

Even though I hadn't figured out anything about anything, I couldn't help but smile, a real, genuine smile.

I sat on the wall and stared at the East China Sea, feeling the breeze on my face. I removed my headphones and let the sounds of the waves fill my ears and the scents of the sea fill my nostrils.

I was content for about a minute before my usual chatter broke the silence.

It's not much to look at, is it?

'Not really.'

I wondered whether the brown hue was its natural color.

A concrete causeway to the south flowed into the horizon. I could make out semis and cars driving on top of it. I knew from the map that the expressway continued another fifteen miles to a small island.

Shouldn't you …

'It's freeway. We're not going to try.'

Are you truly done if there's still room to pedal?

I watched the brown water lap the concrete barriers of the Chinese coast. I cast another glance at the causeway, then turned my attention back to the water.

"It's not your battle anymore," I said out loud.

I had ridden my bicycle from Lisbon to Shanghai. That was enough.

I descended a set of cement stairs to the concrete breaker, balancing my hundred-pound bicycle in my right hand. I propped my camera on a washed-up wooden box and snapped a few proper selfies.

I looked at the water one more time, then walked up the steps and left to find my hotel.

The Dishui Lake Jinjiang Inn was inexpensive, and the staff were friendly, but my tiny, dark room faced the inner parking lot. Worse, I didn't know what I was going to do for two full nights. I couldn't simply leave the next day. I unpacked my things and went for a walk, pushing tomorrow out of my mind.

I wandered around the Dragon Boat festivities, an annual Chinese holiday I didn't know about until that evening. I ate a noodle bowl at a lonely strip mall restaurant and then meandered along a wooden pier next to Dishui Lake. A few solitary fishermen threw lines into the water.

As darkness descended, an uneasiness crept in. I walked faster, trying to outpace it. In my head I made a list of things I had to do the next day. I returned to the hotel and fell into an uneasy sleep.

I rode early the next morning. Unencumbered by gear, my Soma felt light and responsive, yet jittery too, as though it wasn't grounded anymore.

Pedaling along the shoreline road, which cut south and east for several miles, I arrived at a beach where families walked on the black sand, exposed by low tide. As disgusting as the water appeared, I took off my shoes and joined them, sensing the granules between my toes and jumping every time the nasty water washed over my excessively white feet. Little crabs popped out of invisible holes and disappeared again.

Back on my Soma, the road took me past a lonesome hotel standing near a curious stone monument. Upon closer inspection, I saw that the structure was a compass with arrows pointing to multiple cities.

I grinned when I saw the arrow pointing to Sydney. My line of vision followed the marker southeast, over the water. I was planning to ride across Australia the following summer and visualized the continent nation just beyond the horizon.

Back in town, I toured a maritime museum with a life-size replica of a Chinese junk, its sails towering over marble railings three floors above me. I sat in a bookstore café for over an hour, sending emails while sipping a watered-down Americano in air-conditioned bliss.

I watched as a quick rain passed my open hotel window. It started off as a sprinkle, turned into a drizzle, and left as quietly as it began. I savored the damp scent, so familiar even on the other side of the globe.

Evening was in its nascent stages and the grass was moist when I set out for another walk. The stillness of the town fell over me. I wandered aimlessly but rapidly. I thought back to my village in Mongolia, when I would try to escape the loneliness and anxiety every day, walking in minus twenty-five-degree winds simply to leave the confines of my apartment.

I walked faster.

'We've been here before,' I told myself.

The emptiness and angst of the past two years hovered outside my body.

We need to leave.

I looked at the walls of a concrete building. They were familiar and comforting in a cold way. I continued down a darkening sidewalk.

Disquietude circled me. My pace quickened and my heart raced.

'We've been here before. We can deal with twelve more hours.'

I returned to the pedestrian area on the Dishui Lake waterfront. The grass under the young trees was damp. Streetlights illuminated the concrete path, covered in a watery glaze. A few people strolled or stood on the dock, enjoying the humid night air. The water was calm.

The entire scene left me feeling oddly serene, a marked contrast to a few moments before. I paused to savor the post-rain dampness.

Are you ready for seven days in Shanghai?

'We'll make it.'

My shoulders relaxed. I gazed at the water.

Are you ever going to feel OK again?

I thought about where it all went wrong, wondering when the negative feelings had intruded, even though nothing had really changed in my life.

'Maybe, if we can feel OK for a few minutes here in this lonely little town, if we can grasp even a moment of calm, then sooner or later those moments are going to turn into longer moments.'

I examined the damp pavement of a sidewalk, curving through the grass and trees under pale lights.

'If we can find a moment of peace in this sad little place …'

Things might get better back home, too.

'They have before.'

I thought back to the compass. I thought of Australia.

Perth to Sydney has a nice ring to it.

'So does Bennett Elementary.'

"The journey isn't over," I declared softly. "You still have time to figure things out."

*****

On my final ride, back to Shanghai, the temperatures plummeted into the forties and a steady drizzle hampered my efforts to navigate to the center of the metropolis. Six hours after I set out, I arrived at my hostel, wet and miserable.

I managed to maintain some semblance of sanity during my seven days in Shanghai. I rode each morning, visited temples, museums, and parks in the afternoon, ran errands, and had dinner at a different restaurant promptly at six.

Each evening, I retired to the Hidden Garden Hostel where I sat in the outdoor garden with my Acer computer, the same computer that had accompanied me all the way from Lisbon. It was in that garden where I started writing about the journey, beginning for some reason with a synopsis of my short time in Bosnia.

On my last morning in Shanghai, I went for a jog along the waterfront. Looking west, across the river, I visualized the miles of pavement stretching all the way to Lisbon. I hit play on my MP3 player and "I Miss Those Days," by Bleachers, echoed through my ears. I smiled as a reel of images from the most remote locales on earth rushed through my head.

The cab ride to the Shanghai airport passed in silence. I was oddly calm. It seemed like I should feel something more, but at that moment I just wanted to go home.

'We'll process everything later,' I thought.

But I wondered how I could possibly process something as consequential as riding solo from Lisbon to Shanghai in four summers.

I peered out the window of the cab as the familiar Chinese countryside passed by.

That would take an entire book, was my only answer.

Walking out my classroom door on a rainy November day

Great spot to camp, despite all the bugs. -China

The only shade for miles

Crossing the Yangtze River in humiliation

Shanghai traffic

Arrival at the Bund

EPILOGUE

In August, I met with my new fifth-grade team at Bennett Elementary to plan for the coming school year. Sunlight poured through the classroom windows as we talked. I looked around the room, making note of the sparkling-clean desks and shampooed carpet.

I met other staff members in the following weeks. I decorated a new classroom for the first time in nine years. Every single day was full of novel moments, all so familiar yet so refreshing. As August turned to September, and September turned to October, the knot in my stomach began to loosen.

One sunny morning, as I rounded the curve on Bennett Road and my new school came into view under blue autumn skies, a broad grin lit up my face. I couldn't believe I'd successfully pulled off the move. For the first time in a long time, I was proud of something unrelated to cycling.

The irony wasn't lost on me. After all that pedaling and perseverance and devotion, what finally made me feel better was something as mundane as switching jobs, something anyone can do.

Soon, my weekends were no longer lonely. I went out with my new coworkers, remembering how easy it is to go out with people when they live in the same town, when the restaurants or bars they go to are within cycling distance. I started seeing parents and students in the parks and grocery stores near my house. I was part of my community again.

Sometimes, I wonder if I would have had the courage to make the leap into a one-year contract if I hadn't ridden across Kazakhstan and two-thirds of China. Talk about the ultimate confidence booster. I may not have figured out the secret to happiness on my journey, but I certainly developed more faith in my abilities than before.

Things weren't suddenly perfect, of course. I did my best to ride twelve miles each way on my daily commute, even though my house was only three miles from school. I didn't want to lose my edge, after all, and I was intent on keeping my caloric intake and expenditure at a 138-pound balance.

My graduate classes likewise consumed an inordinate amount of my time. I continued to compulsively check Facebook and Instagram every day, although I did let go of my need to get a certain number of "likes" on the rare occasion I posted something.

I sometimes declined invitations to go out with my new coworkers because I was, at heart, an introvert. Switching jobs didn't magically change who I am, a reality I had to accept. I also had to acknowledge that some problems don't have solutions. Back in Michigan, my dad's mental faculties continued to decline. I called him every week, and visited as often as I could, but otherwise could only watch events unfold from afar while my brother took care of him.

I was raised on TV shows like *Different Strokes, Little House on the Prairie,* and *Family Ties,* where every problem has a solution and people's lives move forward in happy bliss. I grew up reading books like *The Lion the Witch and the Wardrobe, A Wrinkle in Time,* and *The Lord of the Rings* trilogy, where good always conquers evil in a penultimate final scene. Growing up with these segmented episodes and convenient narrative arcs left me with a skewed view of reality.

Real life is more complicated than that.

Epiphanies, if they come to us at all, reach us in pieces. Rarely is there a single epic moment where it all comes together. Many problems are years in the making and fixing them doesn't just happen. Sometimes, when you fix one problem, you create others.

When I announced my intention to ride my bicycle around the world on that cold November evening, I was seeking something I assumed to be happiness. What I didn't understand as I trained hours a day, month after month, year after year, and spent my summers away from home, were the opportunity costs that came with those choices. I didn't see that chasing my dreams meant giving up so many other amazing facets of ordinary life.

Part of the problem was that I didn't train only to be in shape the following summer. I also trained to stay thin. I kept counting my calories, day after day, knowing I couldn't simply diet for six weeks and expect to keep the pounds off forever. Losing weight is a condition, not a onetime endeavor.

In hindsight, part of me wishes I'd simply accepted being overweight. It's difficult to wake up every morning and ride, not to mention time-consuming, and it's demoralizing to be incapable of eating at restaurants without experiencing a rush of anxiety when I look at the menu and silently count all the hidden calories.

In the summers, I kept moving, at great expense and great inconvenience, to faraway places that I moved through in the blink of an eye. I never got to know any of those exotic locales to any worthwhile extent, and in the process of visiting them became isolated from everyone and everything back home.

Colorado is one of the most beautiful states in the nation, yet in the past four years I've barely spent any time hiking or camping or enjoying anything the state has to offer. After a lifetime away, I realize Michigan is equally beautiful, in its own way, and sometimes I wish I'd stayed put, near my family.

Everything has a price, and for every incredible experience out there, I've paid for it with the time spent away from the people I care about. On the opposite side of that coin, if I never left the comforts of home, the amazing places and experiences that span the globe would remain hidden.

Even feeling content comes with a fee. The melancholy and malaise of the past two years may have been miserable, but in an odd way I've felt more alive than I have in a very long time.

Ages ago, when I lived in Leicester, I took a drive with a friend one morning across the English countryside. She told me it was strange how I would point out quaint stone houses, as we drove by them, and comment on how I'd love to settle down and live in one, and then in the same breath talk about where I'd like to travel to next and what I'd like to do next. It was like two opposing sides of me, one that wanted to settle, and one that wanted to keep going. In between lived a million layers of me with different thoughts and opinions and yearnings from one moment to the next.

If I could have selected my own desires when I was born, I would have chosen to play team sports that kept me close to home. I'd be content with the things most people enjoy, like relaxing in the morning, Sunday afternoon football, and backyard cookouts. I'd prefer the beach with friends and family over traveling to far-off, unpleasant places by myself. Most importantly, I'd derive satisfaction from volunteering at animal shelters and doing things that help others.

For as much effort as I put into things, it seems there's not much purpose in what I do, at least none that serves the greater good. My inner ridicule and scorn, fueled by the cacophony of voices on the news, in social media, permeating movies and shows, floating through our schools, and echoing through our friends and family, never lets me forget that.

Feel this, do that, eat this, avoid that, slow down, live in the moment, be more social, have more friends.

I wish I could think and feel everything I'm supposed to, and follow every sage piece of advice. But I can't force myself into anyone else's idea of how things should be. And if I've learned anything over the past four summers, it's that I need to stop berating myself for it.

Whatever it is that drives me, I wouldn't wish on anyone. Yet I wouldn't trade it for anything. My little neurosis has taken me to some amazing places.

I like to work. I like to feel dour and agitated. I like to wander in those in-between places and listen to music that unsettles me, because when I'm there, I'm the most me.

And perhaps that's what I've been looking for all along. Not happiness as used in the colloquial sense, but rather a new definition of the word that means feeling like the most authentic version of ourselves.

By that definition, we shouldn't have to chase after happiness, because if we're staying true to who we are, we're already living it. Be who we're going to be, do what we're going to do, love who we're going to love, and feel how we're going to feel. No one else can define that for us.

For me, I'm happiest when I'm seeking whatever it is around the bend in the road. I feel the most me when I'm pedaling my bike or when I hit the perfect stride on a long run, when my heart is pounding and I experience something I can't explain.

More than anything, I feel most like myself when I'm listening to some song that makes me want to rush off into the sunset searching for some crazy existential moment of enlightenment that I know I'll never find, simply because I like chasing after it.

I'm going to keep counting my calories, because it's fun, and it works. I'm going to continue pushing myself and thinking new thoughts and going to new places, because I hate to sit around. I'm going to keep feeling this angst, this desire for more, no matter how conflicted and confused it leaves me, because it's the one thing I can't not do.

Searching and seeking and pining for whatever I was looking for in those vivid Gobi sunsets defines me. And though chances are I'll never figure anything out, I'm fine with that, because I don't know what I'd do with myself if I found any answers.

Chasing fleeting dreams is my definition of hope.

Next summer, I'm going to continue this journey. I've already booked my flight to Australia. I'm going to pedal from Perth to Sydney as fast as I can. And in between those two cities, I'm hardly going to see anything at all.

I want to go, to ride, as fast as I can. There's not going to be an end to it, and it isn't because I'm racing toward some destination that I ought to arrive at.

This is just how I dance.

ABOUT THE AUTHOR

Tom Sweeney lives in Fort Collins, Colorado, with his wife, Kendra, and dog, Cooper. He has taught fifth grade for twelve years. His favorite thing about working in education is being around fifth graders. Their sense of humor, natural curiosity, and unique way of looking at the world are a refreshing break from the realities of adulthood.

Originally from Michigan, Sweeney has traveled to over forty countries, including a study abroad program in England, graduate research in Belize, volunteer work at a nature preserve in Guatemala, and a two-year service in Peace Corps Mongolia.

Sweeney has been an avid cyclist since he was old enough to pedal and started racing road bikes when he was fifteen. He completed his first extended bicycle tour around Colorado in 2012.

While he has written more academic papers than he can count, this is his first book.

MEDIA REFERENCES

- *A Wrinkle in Time*, by Madeline L'Engle. Ariel Books, 1962
- *Austin Powers,* written by Mike Myers, directed by Jay Roach. New Line Cinema, 1997
- *Chuang Tzu, Basic Writings*, translated by Burton Watson. Columbia University Press, 1996
- *Different Strokes*, written by Ben Starr, et al, directed by Herbert Kenwith, et al, 1978
- *Family Ties*, created by Gary David Goldberg, 1982
- *Little House on the Prairie*, developed by Blanche Hanalis, 1974
- *Pink Floyd: The Wall*, screenplay by Roger Waters, directed by Alan Parker. MGM, 1982
- *Things to Come*, written & directed by Mia Hansen-Løve. Arte France Cinéma, 2016
- *The Day Lasts More Than a Hundred Years* by Chinghiz Aitmatov. Indiana University Press, 1983
- *The Lion, the Witch and the Wardrobe*, by C.S. Lewis. HarperCollins, 1954
- *The Lord of the Rings*, by J.R.R. Tolkien. Allen & Unwin, 1954
- *Trainspotting,* novel by John Irvine, screenplay by John Hodge, directed by Danny Boyle. Channel Four Films, 1996
- *T2: Trainspotting,* written by John Hodge & Irvine Welsh, directed by Danny Boyle. Tristar Pictures, 2017
- "Why Your Life is Not a Journey," a video by David Lindberg
- Songs and albums in order of appearance: "Close Your Eyes" by The Chemical Brothers; "Chandelier" by Sia; "Anisina" by Pink Floyd; "Porcelain" by Moby; *The Wall* by Pink Floyd; *Animals*, by Pink Floyd; "Born Slippy" by Underworld; "Are You With Me?" by Lost Frequencies; "Do It, Try It" by M83; "Wide Open" by The Chemical Brothers; "Running to the Sea" by Röyksopp; "Russians" by Sting; "Are You Lost in the World Like Me?" by Moby; "Bang My Head" by Sia; "No Retreat, No Surrender" by Bruce Springsteen; "Born to Run" by Bruce Springsteen; "A Murder of One" by Counting Crows; "We Don't Know" by The Strumbellas; "Lust for Life" by Iggy Pop; *Simple Forms* by The Naked and Famous; "Girls Just Wanna Have Fun" by Chromatics; "Laid Low" by The Naked and Famous; "Last Forever" by The Naked and Famous; "Only God Knows" by Young Fathers; "Silk" by Wolf Alice; "I Wanna Get Better" by Bleachers; "No Way" by The Naked and Famous; "All My Friends" by LCD Soundsystem; "Sober Up" by AJR; "Everything Now" by Arcade Fire; "Jump" by Van Halen; "Broken" by lovelytheband